Longing for the Bomb

Longing for the Bomb

OAK RIDGE AND ATOMIC NOSTALGIA

LINDSEY A. FREEMAN

The University of North Carolina Press CHAPEL HILL

*This book was published with the assistance of the
Authors Fund of the University of North Carolina Press.*

An earlier version of chapter 6 appeared as "Happy Memories under the
Mushroom Cloud: Utopia and Memory in Oak Ridge, Tennessee," in *Memory
and the Future: Transnational Politics, Ethics and Society*, ed. Yifat Gutman,
Adam Brown, and Amy Sodaro (Palgrave Macmillan, 2010), 158–76. An earlier
version of chapter 7 appeared as "Manhattan Project Time Machine," in *Death
Tourism: Disaster Sites as Recreational Landscape*, ed. Brigitte Sion (Seagull
Books, 2014). Each is reprinted with permission of the publisher. "Atomic City
Boogie," by Willie "Little Red" Honeycutt, © 2014 Phyllis Honeycutt Simpson
and The Honeycutt Family. Reprinted with permission.

Cover illustration: Postcard of Jackson Square, Oak Ridge, Tennessee, published by
Werner News Agency, Knoxville, and seal of the city of Oak Ridge

Library of Congress Cataloging-in-Publication Data
Longing for the bomb : Oak Ridge and atomic nostalgia /
Lindsey A. Freeman. — First edition.
pages cm
Includes bibliographical references and index.
ISBN 978-1-4696-2237-8 (paperback : alkaline paper) —
ISBN 978-1-4696-2238-5 (e-book)
1. Oak Ridge (Tenn.)—History—20th century. 2. Oak Ridge (Tenn.)—
Social life and customs—20th century. 3. Oak Ridge National Laboratory—
History—20th century. 4. Official secrets—United States—History—20th century.
5. Atomic bomb—Social aspects—United States—History. 6. Manhattan Project (U.S.)—
History. 7. World War, 1939–1945—Tennessee—Oak Ridge. 8. Popular culture—
United States—History—20th century. I. Title.
F444.O3F74 2015
355.8'25119097309044—dc23
2014038124

THIS BOOK WAS PRINTED DIGITALLY

For Nan

Contents

Illustrations

Acknowledgments

One of the most beautiful gifts I have ever received was a vigorously annotated early draft that became this book. I remember when Vera Zolberg handed it over to me, full of seemingly endless, multi-colored post-it notes sticking out from every angle. The mass of text resembled a stegosaurus with a rare disease. Slowly and methodically I worked from these notes to try to cure the ills of my creaturely text. I cannot thank my professors at the New School for Social Research enough—Vera, Jeff Goldfarb, Elzbieta Matynia, and Oz Frankel. Without their close reading, support, and wrangling, this book would not have been possible. I'm also grateful to Oz for pointing out that doing academic work is not the same thing as joining the Navy.

I'm thankful for the intellectual community in and around the NSSR, where the ideas for this book emerged and gradually came to take shape. Special thanks to Monica Brannon, Linsey Ly, Aysel Madra, Ritchie Savage, Dan Sherwood, Sam Tobin, and Hector Vera for the years of camaraderie and support, intellectual and otherwise. Work on this project was also encouraged and enriched by the New School Memory Group, especially Naomi Angel (who left too soon), Adam Brown, Rachel Daniell, Yifat Gutman, Laliv Melamed, Benjamin Nienass, and Amy Sodaro. Long live the octopus of memory!

Throughout the years of work on this book, in between pushing around my own paragraphs, I taught in the sociology and social science departments of FIT, Pratt, Eugene Lang College, Rutgers-Newark University, and SUNY-Buffalo State. At Rutgers, I taught evening classes in social theory, reading drafts and pounding out notes for this manuscript on the most beautiful train route from New York City to Newark: marshes and rusting industrial ruins provided the backdrop for new insights and turns of phrase. In the first-year writing department at Eugene Lang College, I taught classes on utopia and memory, the two poles of this work. Special thanks are due to Sherri-Ann Butterfield and Kate Eichhorn, who led those departments, and to all my sharp students who pushed my thinking. I would also like to thank Jonathan Veitch, whose interest in utopias and nuclear spaces fortuitously lined up with my own.

The social geography department at the Université de Caen, where I presented earlier versions of this work, provided a space for thinking, spirited collegiality, and calvados. Thanks go to Pierre Bergel, Patrice Caro, Jean-Marc Fournier, Benoît Raoulx, and especially to Stéphane Valognes, who introduced me to nuclear Normandy. The folks at the Center for the United States and the Cold War at New York University offered valuable feedback and endured my non-linear approach to the nuclear past. I am also grateful to my new students and colleagues in the sociology department at SUNY-Buffalo State, where I was able to put the finishing touches on the manuscript. Special thanks go to Allen Shelton, who tolerated my long sentences and gave valuable advice to a greenhorn writer and professor.

I am forever indebted to Sara Jo Cohen, who picked me out of the wilds of the Association of American Geographers' program; to copyeditor Eric Schramm; and to all the hardworking and talented folks at UNC Press: Stephanie Wenzel, Alison Shay, and my wonderful and charming editor Joseph Parsons, whose support, smarts, and good humor constantly exceed expectation. I would also like to thank Karen Engle, Hugh Gusterson, and Bruce Hevly, who carefully read earlier drafts of this book and provided helpful critical insight. The book is much improved for your efforts. Additional thanks to Karen and Yoke-Sum Wong for their support of the secret telephone.

And much love and appreciation to Jessi Lee Jackson, who abided all the bees in my bonnet, encouraged me when I felt blue, read endless scraps of texts, and listened to so much talk about the atomic bomb, even allowing me to read pieces of the text to her at Rockaway Beach.

Finally, most of all I would like to thank all the Oak Ridgers who took the time to talk with me and to share their stories. Without you, of course, none of this work would have been possible. Special recognition goes to the late Bill Wilcox, D. Ray Smith, Jay Searcy, Earline Banic, Jim Comish at the AMSE, Phyllis Simpson and the Honeycutt family, reference librarian Teresa Fortney at the Oak Ridge Library, the folks at the Center for Oak Ridge Oral History, my mother, Bobbie Freeman, my uncle Frank McLemore, and my grandmother Nan McLemore. I would also like to thank my father, Dennis Freeman, who began his career as a clinical psychologist at the Oak Ridge Mental Health Center when he was a young PhD.

Prologue

"I'm from Oak Ridge. I glow in the dark." This was the luminescent phrase that graced my favorite T-shirt when I was seven. It was the mid-1980s and all kinds of neon and day-glow attire were popular, but this was different. The shirt meant "I'm radioactive and I have a sense of humor about it." During World War II, Oak Ridge, Tennessee, was one of the three top-secret locations created for the sole purpose of producing an atomic bomb as part of the Manhattan Project. I didn't quite understand the glowing then. It felt magic, like something a superhero could do. When you turned the lights out the letters actually glowed—illuminating the message—making me feel even more powerful than my Wonder Woman underoos did. Smart as I thought my T-shirt looked in all its 50 poly/50 cotton glory, it was not a good sartorial choice for hide-and-go-seek, as I learned the hard way.

My connection to the city of Oak Ridge—a place involved in an advanced geopolitical game of hide-and-go-seek of its own—began in the early 1940s, when my grandparents, Nan and Frank McLemore, moved to the secret Manhattan Project city after my grandfather was injured in the war. He had been stationed in France. Where? Nobody seems to know exactly. He didn't like to talk about it. He had "grown silent—not richer, but poorer in communicable experience," as Walter Benjamin writes of the soldiers returning from the First World War.[1] What we do know is that "over there" my grandfather was hit by an artillery shell fragment in the ankle and sent home purple-hearted, limping a bit. Quickly, he took a job he heard about near Clinton, Tennessee, not far from where his wife and two small children, my mother Bobbie and my uncle, also Frank, were living while he was away. My grandmother was from Cocke County, a wild knot of land in East Tennessee known for rooster fighting and moonshine; my grandfather hailed from just across the state border in North Carolina. The geographical distance from their birthplaces to this new place was not far, but socially and culturally it was a vast distance away.

The jobsite was called the Clinton Engineer Works, a code name for the place that would become Oak Ridge. At first they called it the Kingston Demolition Range, after a nearby town, but the alias proved too frightening to neighboring communities. Even though the name seemed nondescript, my grandfather was told that the work was of the highest importance and that it would help end the war. On top of this, good money and housing were promised. Even with the clatter of the battlefield still throbbing in his ears, he liked the sound of the job; it would feel like he was still fighting.

Overseas, my grandfather drove a tank for the U.S. Army. Stateside, he would drive again for the war effort, this time as an atomic courier. He manned the wheel, first for the Manhattan Project, and then kept driving through the Cold War for the Atomic Energy Commission. This sort of driving was an old occupation, but with new risks. The job consisted of crisscrossing the United States in an unmarked white truck with classified materials, including the yellowcake of fissionable uranium tucked inside, like the yolk of an atomic egg.

My grandfather died from a heart attack when I was nine, and, regrettably, I was never able to ask him about his job and his secret atomic missions. The stories I know, I know through my grandmother and others. I know that he would drive whatever, wherever they asked him to, carefully and methodically, and that he never drove above the speed limit, that he never had an accident, that he carried a gun, and that he could never tell my grandmother where he was going. Even though my grandfather passed away before I began my sociological research, my grandmother, now ninety, was able to share many of her stories with me. My grandparents' placement in time and space allowed for auspicious connections to their peers and community, giving me access to spaces and stories that might be denied other researchers.

From a very early age when I would hear folks talk about the former Manhattan Project city of Oak Ridge, I would believe that a secret life was slowly being revealed to me—and it was. I was obsessed with stories of this mysterious place, and from even the smallest scrap of information or hint of rumor I would feel a bit closer to the glory days of the Atomic City. When visiting my grandparents who lived there (and by there I mean both in the landscape and to my young mind in that other time), I would become hyper-aware of any clue to the atomic past or the precarious nuclear present. It was the freezing time of the Cold War, so one had to be vigilant. The Ruskies could be up to anything. My brother and I practiced our own duck and cover drills—the Russians are coming! We would shout in mock fear that slipped into the real thing and hurl ourselves under the kitchen table, our bony knees slamming hard into the linoleum that would yield to our slight frames. Then we would grow bored and run into the yard, our "I'm from Oak Ridge. I glow in the dark." shirts lit up like lighting bugs in the bosky postnuclear landscape of our grandparents' lawn.

I lived the first few months of my life as an Oak Ridger, until my father got a job in another, less interesting town and we moved seventy miles northeast to the far corner of our long skinny state. Like most other points in the world where I would go afterward, there had been no secret wartime atomic bomb project in this new place, and as I grew and traveled I saw this lack in other places as a stamp of dullness. This way of seeing marks my own atomic nostalgia for a community of which I am a part but in a tangential way—closer maybe for having written this book.

The following pages are about this place and the atomic culture it produced. Throughout my archival research, scribbled field notes, interviews, and tinkering with text, I have been driven by the great southern writer Eudora Welty's notion that "one place comprehended can make us understand other places better."[2] In Oak Ridge, there are so many mysteries to untangle. It is a city where history, memory, and myth compete and conspire to tell the story of America and the atom—and where every day a bit more of the atomic past slips away. In Welty's spirit, I rescue the atomic pasts I am able to and question the myths and stories that have been told. Here is an attempt to make sense of a community that witnessed the rise and fall of the Atomic Age from the very start and to show its trajectory from atomic utopianism to atomic nostalgia.

Longing for the Bomb

Introduction

The story of Oak Ridge, Tennessee, began in 1942, when the federal government of the United States erased five small communities in the northeast corner of the state in order to turn a bit of Appalachia atomic. In this freshly vacant space, a new secret city and several atomic factories emerged through an act of *magic geography*, a way of presenting, thinking, and creating a place as if it were already fully formed and merely lying in wait until the cartographer put the finishing touches on her map and set it in motion.[1] The mapping of Oak Ridge was further magical in that once the city was created, it needed to be disappeared. Now you see it, now you don't. This new, strange, busy city was one of the key sites of the massive scientific and industrial program known as the Manhattan Project—the ultra-secret atomic bomb project of World War II.

Along with Oak Ridge, two other key clandestine sites were constructed and positioned in strategic areas throughout the continental United States. Obscure codenames were given to the trio, remarkable only in their blandness: Site X (Oak Ridge, Tennessee); Site Y (Los Alamos, New Mexico); and Site W (Hanford, Washington). Within this top-secret network of invisible places, each location played a different role in the process. Oak Ridge pioneered the first large-scale plutonium reactor and then focused on separating isotopes of uranium to collect enough of the fissionable isotope uranium-235 from the more commonly occurring uranium-238; it was this product that powered the bomb that devastated Hiroshima, nicknamed Little Boy. Meanwhile, Hanford concentrated on producing the fissionable plutonium-239 that would eventually power both the gadget exploded at the Trinity Test and Fat Man, the bomb dropped on Nagasaki. Simultaneously in Los Alamos, J. Robert Oppenheimer and his crack team of scientists worked nonstop designing and assembling the bombs. From within and between these three atomic sites came new methods for the creation of weapons of mass destruction, new communities dedicated to the emerging nuclear industries, and a new style of American living that came to fruition after the war.

While the three Manhattan Project communities shared many similarities, Oak Ridge differed from the other two secret locations in its size, social structure, and culture. Unlike Hanford, which was primarily populated by construction workers, engineers, and technicians, and Los Alamos, which served as the hotbed for scientific bomb design, Oak Ridge was something in between. Compared to the other two sites, Oak Ridge was a place that more closely resembled a typical American community, although it was also hidden away and special, hopped up on the speed of the Project, full of PhDs, and gated like Los Alamos. Hanford, by contrast, was never a gated residential community. The managerial class and the higher-ups there tended to live in the bedroom community of Richland, while construction workers and other laborers found housing where they could, in Pasco or other nearby towns.

In addition and multiplication, Oak Ridge was much larger than the other two communities, with five times the population of Richland and thirteen times that of tiny Los Alamos. The sheer number of people in Oak Ridge meant a more diverse community and a more elaborate infrastructure, and also more opportunity for social interaction between different types of folks than was possible at the other sites, although class and racial biases intervened there as well. Within just a few months of its creation, Oak Ridge was filled with thousands and thousands of seemingly ill-assorted people—Ivy League postdocs, hotshot nuclear physicists, expert machinists from the nation's manufacturing centers, laborers from every corner of the country, and recent high school graduates from nearby hills and hollers—all thrown together by the Project and the desperate reshuffling caused by the war. From the beginning there were clear boundaries that marked this place as different from all other places, including both the physical barriers and the culture, in the way that all borders are material and immaterial, but perhaps even more so. Remarkably, out of this chaos a tightly bound and insular community was formed.

Sectioned off from the rest of the country, the inside and outside of the community corpus was marked by a barbed wire fence, which stretched out across the new incision of land like stitches sewn by a surgeon afflicted with palsy. Within these jagged edges, Oak Ridge was ruled by speed and security: a resident's pass was necessary to enter through the city's gates; shotgun-armed guards patrolled the serrated perimeter; gunboats crouched in the ready position in nearby waterways as two small observing planes circled like vultures overhead; lie-detector tests were common; letters were censored; neighbor spied on neighbor; and Nobel Prize–winning scientists skirted around under secret sobriquets while workers of all levels kept the atomic factories going twenty-four hours a day.

By 1943, the city was beating like an overactive pacemaker in the heart of the East Tennessee Valley. Hidden in plain sight, behind the gates and guards, thousands upon thousands of workers labored feverishly, remarkably with very little knowledge of what they were actually working toward. Most of the nearly 80,000 workers—the scores of welders, plumbers, pipe fitters, electricians, engineers, lab technicians, construction workers, couriers, scientists, and dial watchers (known locally as Calutron Girls, named for the special isotope-separating machines they monitored)—knew only that they had signed on to work for a vital war project. They were given only the barest minimum of information needed to do their jobs, and they were sternly instructed not to ask questions and never to talk about their work, not even with close friends or spouses. Being too curious or gabbing about even the most mundane occupational task could result in a pink slip and eviction from the city. If you weren't working on the Manhattan Project, you had no reason to be there. Oak Ridge in those years contained no jails, no courts, no funeral homes, and no cemeteries. Any births or deaths would be recorded as having occurred in nearby towns, so as to not give hints about the size of the population. To further protect anonymity, even high school athletes' last names were absent from the backs of their jerseys. Everything was to be kept secret.

Oak Ridge was constructed during a state of emergency when the nation was on tenterhooks, seeking an end to the terrible war that had already claimed millions of lives. Only the top-flight scientists and the chief military advisers knew the full extent of their mission. The best available estimates indicate that only 5 percent of the workers knew what was going on at their individual work sites, and that no more than 3 percent knew the full operation. Unlike most military endeavors, those who lived in the secret atomic cities were primarily civilians tossed into an adventure they did not expect, doing a job they did not fully understand, though many of them loved it madly. To those of different politics or generations, the thought can seem horrible, even macabre, but to the majority of Oak Ridgers the bomb hastened the end to the war and saved lives on both sides, and the secrecy and security measures, while at times certainly a hassle, also added excitement and mystery to residents' everyday lives. When the bomb was dropped on Hiroshima and the news wires and radio waves shouted the name of their secret city, most Oak Ridgers were shocked. This was the beginning of an atomic America aware of itself.

Although now, lacking the drama of the desert tests, the sand turned to an emerald green glass, or an exploding mushroom cloud, the former secret city of Oak Ridge is often not the first place to appear in the national or international nuclear memory pool. Maybe this is because Oak Ridge is not where Dr. Oppenheimer and his team of star physicists were stationed, but a place where the majority of atomic workers labored in factories, watching dials, checking pipes, and completing other mundane tasks, although there were impressive scientists working in the Tennessee hills as well. Possibly it is also because the story of Oak Ridge is a lesser-known part of the larger story of the Manhattan Project, a topic that remains quite popular in American historical memory.

Writers and readers alike have long been intrigued with narratives about the scientific race to the bomb. They have been drawn toward tales of General Leslie Groves, the taskmaster who pushed the project to stay on schedule, stories of émigré scientists like Enrico Fermi and accounts of the promise of even stronger bombs to come, like those designed by Edward Teller. Perhaps most popular of all are the biographies dissecting the moody and brilliant Oppenheimer—the scientific leader of the Manhattan Project who was later stripped of his security clearance—often written as Shakespearean tragedy.[2] In addition, there are several fine books written about the Manhattan Project communities that have influenced this work, including Peter Bacon Hales's *Atomic Spaces*, John Findlay and Bruce Hevly's *Atomic Frontier Days* and *The Atomic West*, Paul Loeb's *Nuclear Culture*, Joseph Masco's *Nuclear Borderlands*, and Jon Hunner's *Inventing Los Alamos*, along with Charles Johnson and Charles Jackson's *The City behind the Fence* and Russell Olwell's *At Work in the Atomic City*. In addition, Peter C. van Wyck's *The Highway of the Atom* has inspired my thinking about the way atomic materials move, both spatially and temporally. I love these books; I have consumed them with my breakfast yogurt and coffee, at the beach, on the subway, and between writing jags. My hope is that this text will share space with them on the atomic bookshelf. It is not my intention to write a book with a cover of sandpaper, a predatory book that devours those closest to it.[3] Instead, I see *Longing for the Bomb* touching covers with its neighbors, adding something to the story of the Atomic Age by focusing not only on its beginning—not just the age—but also the aging. So far, the case of Oak Ridge has been examined through a brief history, from an architectural and spatial perspective, through a labor history lens, and through personal memoir, but a study from a cultural sociological perspective has not appeared until now.

Although, it almost did. Back in 1946, early Oak Ridge resident Thelma Present wrote to her friend the anthropologist Margaret Mead at her post at the American Museum of Natural History in New York City. Dear Margaret, "I guess it was inevitable that a book be written about Oak Ridge. We have had several discussions as to the manner it is to be written. We considered a serious sociological study for one.... The second idea is... through human-interest stories and folklore get our point across." For reasons not entirely clear, Present's book was never written.[4] Like Present, I have always had enthusiasm for the city and its stories. Here, I have tried to write a serious sociological study that partially fills in the gap in atomic literature, while incorporating folklore and human stories to get my point across.

In addition to materials for atomic bombs, the community design of Oak Ridge and the residential sections of the other Manhattan Project sites produced new thinking about civic organization, giving hints to what a postwar, postnuclear American landscape might look like. Oak Ridge was a canary in the mine of the Atomic Age, confronting the challenges of atomic weapons, atomic energy, and suburban-style living before much of the rest of the United States.[5] I should mention before going any further that here, as elsewhere throughout the book, I use "postnuclear" to mean after the introduction of a nuclear way of life, not that the nuclear age is over. Nuclear is still very much with us: there is still an American arsenal of nuclear weapons; nuclear power remains part of the range of energy sources the nation taps; the disposal and storage of nuclear waste is among the nation's most serious issues; and America continues to worry over nuclear weapons now in the possession of other nations or that they might yet possess, as in President George W. Bush's speech seeking to justify the invasion of Iraq in 2003 ("We cannot wait for the final proof—the smoking gun—that could come in the form of a mushroom cloud"). Postnuclear is meant to signify the rupture between the time before nuclear weapons were put to use in World War II and everything that has come after.

The legacies of the Manhattan Project are traceable in the ruins of rusting uranium factories and contaminated landscapes, in collective memory and nostalgia, as well as in global politics and national energy policies. Compared with the contaminated materials of the Atomic Age, historical memory has a much shorter lifespan; in light of this fact, questions about the nuclear past, present, and future should be viewed as immediate and pressing. Written in the net of the present, this book tries to capture the utopian past of the first city of the Atomic Age and to imagine the shape and texture of the future of atomic remembrance.

Collective Memory and Collective Nostalgia of the Atomic Past

Most Oak Ridgers use memory and nostalgia not primarily to articulate historical authenticity, but to celebrate a glorious past and to grapple with a present moment of uncertainty. Remembering the Manhattan Project allows Oak Ridgers to talk about their sacrifice to the nation, their scientific and intellectual prowess, their cosmopolitanism, and their prominent role in producing the atomic bomb. While for the most part Oak Ridgers' narratives about the past have been celebratory, collective memory and collective nostalgia can also produce critical narratives when "memory flashes up."[6] As Fredric Jameson writes, "There is no reason why a nostalgia conscious of itself, a lucid and remorseless dissatisfaction with the present on the grounds of some remembered plenitude, cannot furnish as adequate a revolutionary stimulus as any other."[7] The key to a more critical nostalgic stance is a collective disappointment or disquietude with "the now" based on historical trajectories and present concerns. In Oak Ridge, there are times when disappointment and uncertainty gather, when the cultural outlook appears as if it might change, but so far a critical mass has not been reached.

The French historian Pierre Nora maintains that "*lieux de mémoire* [places of memory] originate with the sense that there is no spontaneous memory, that we must deliberately create archives, maintain anniversaries, organize celebrations, pronounce eulogies, and notarize bills because such activities no longer occur naturally" (if they ever did).[8] In Oak Ridge, the issue is less that there is no spontaneous memory in the present—to the contrary, the city is suffused with memory—but that in the very near future those who formed the tightly bound community of the 1940s will no longer be around. Most are now octogenarians, nonagenarians, or even centenarians. The aging of the population has led to a communal anxiety over how the community's atomic past will be remembered when those who ushered in the Atomic Age are no longer around. Combined with this anxiety is a powerful atomic nostalgia for the prelapsarian days when Oak Ridgers labored together, sacrificing for their neighbors and for the nation, when victory seemed assured and when an atomic utopia seemed possible in its aftermath.

The communities that ushered in the Atomic Age need to be revisited in the postnuclear era in order to understand the creation and continuation of the nuclear United States. It should not be forgotten that nuclear projects, once put into motion, must be sited in actual communities rooted in the geographical landscape. Even now, some sites connected to nuclear history—the historic-future cities of the start of the Atomic Age like Oak Ridge and Los Alamos—are typically the places that say, "Yes, in my backyard!" while most of the rest of the world shouts, "Stay away!" The atomic cities retain some of this old utopianism, a firm belief in their ability to control and contain the power of the atom—from nuclear warheads to radioactive waste products. In Oak Ridge, this sentiment is sometimes called Oak Ridgidness. A city, as Robert Park has pointed out, "is a state of mind, a body of customs and traditions, and of the organized attitudes and sentiments that inhere in these customs and are transmitted with this tradition."[9] The tradition that prevails in the city of Oak Ridge is a particular cultural sensibility based on a utopian vision of nuclear science, a belief in the necessity of a nuclear America, and a sense of expertise, elitism, and specialness that began with the Manhattan Project, continued throughout the Cold War, and persists even today.

The city continues to be a major player in nuclear science and national security, home to the Y-12 National Security Complex and the Oak Ridge National Laboratory. Y-12 produced enriched uranium for the Manhattan Project and is now a key production facility in the National Nuclear Security Administration's Nuclear Security Enterprise that specializes in storing and processing uranium and technologies associated with nuclear industries. The Oak Ridge National Laboratory, originally the X-10 plutonium pilot plant of the Manhattan Project, now specializes in energy systems and nuclear medicine. Most recently, Oak Ridge was granted an enormous project from the National Nuclear Security Administration, which is building an elaborate storage and processing facility for the nation's aging nuclear arsenal, known locally by the grandiose name The Uranium Center of Excellence.

Oak Ridge was once a place of the future, a prototype for an ideal American city designed by the architectural firm of Skidmore, Owings, and Merrill, as well as a new type of scientific community dedicated to producing the fissionable materials of tomorrow. While Oak Ridge is still a destination for world-class physicists and a site of national nuclear storage and research, the city has taken on a much more historic and nostalgic gloss. A former utopia, it is now experiencing its half-life, the slow erosion of cultural significance. This fear of losing their specialness, their atomic glow, is what has Oak Ridgers working to keep their collective memory of the Manhattan Project alive. Without it, the community's identity is in danger. As Svetlana Boym writes in *The Future of Nostalgia*, "Contemporary nostalgia is not so much about the past as about the vanishing present."[10] Originally an amnesic space looking only toward the future, Oak Ridge is now a memory-saturated city, leaning on its past, slowly sallying forth with technocratic visions of a future conceived in yesteryear.

Nostalgia

Nostalgia is a pining for times in a particular place, but more than that it is a state of mind and a moment of perception that actually "melds time and space," creating a vertiginous space of temporal disruption.[11] Derived from the Greek *nostros*, meaning to return home, and *algia*, a painful condition, nostalgia has traditionally been linked to homesickness. The phrase was first coined by the Swiss physician Johannes Hofer in his medical dissertation written in the late seventeenth century wherein he ascribed the condition to Swiss soldiers fighting away from home and at war and sick for their Alpine beginnings.[12] Unlike melancholia, which was perceived as a condition that afflicted the poetic, artistic, intellectual, antisocial, and deep-thinking types, nostalgia was seen as a democratic disease. If melancholia was the type of condition to cling to Charles Baudelaire, nostalgia was the illness that would cloy onto a Swiss infantryman. Nostalgia, then, could potentially affect anyone, but it had the connotation of affecting the rural, simple-minded, and uncultured and those most tied to the places from which they came. At the time, nostalgia was not considered a typical emotion that could befall any of us at any time, as it is today, but an abnormal reaction, a pathology.

By the twentieth century, nostalgia had ceased to be seen as a psychological disorder. Nostalgia had become a feeling that could be experienced by anyone; it was placed along the spectrum of emotions that included sadness, fear, or joy. To feel nostalgic became an experience of the modern condition. No longer tied only to soldiers longing for home, modern nostalgia is connected with a more complex state of mind. This mindset carries with it the awareness of the acceleration of social change, an awareness that says, "Even if you go back home, you can never go home again—that home is gone." It is this impossibility of return that rests at the painful core of contemporary nostalgia.

Commonly known as hypochondria of the heart, nostalgia fills the aching chest of those who long for home. Symptoms include hopelessness, despondency, and lack of emotion and appetite. Historically, side effects have leaned to the more fantastic, such as a heightened sense of smell, taste, and hearing, as well as the ability to see and commune with ghosts. The symptoms of nostalgia, including sharpened sense perceptions, allow for an experience with the past that can lead the modern nostalgic to critical thinking. During my research for this book, I experienced the nostalgic-ghostly connection firsthand. In fact, I regularly communed with the ghosts of Oak Ridge. I did not hold a séance or utilize a Ouija board, although on occasion I did go looking for the Ghost of Wheat, a spirit rumored to be an ex-farmer who was kicked off his land to make room for the Manhattan Project. (I never saw him.) Instead, historical and imagined figures of the city's past showed up through Oak Ridgers' narratives and through my own daydreams and dreams from REM sleep. Thinking with the ghost stories of this place, why they appeared, again and again, allowed for speculative thinking on alternative pasts: the Oak Ridge that happened versus all the Oak Ridges that never did. I am not the only one who practices this kind of thought experiment; many of those who live and lived in Oak Ridge do the same thing.

Nostalgia is often mistakenly believed to be a solely individual experience, but like memory it is also a deeply social phenomenon. Nostalgia is sociologically relevant because it works as a conduit to show collective ideas about the present, while simultaneously revealing shared past desires, giving new insights into the practices, structures, and institutions those desires created. The feeling not only disrupts individual emotional connections with the present, but it can also have a disorienting effect on societies, which in extreme cases can destabilize them—preventing its members from imagining a better (or different) present and future as they long for a past, which seems superior and often more secure.

A critical nostalgia can do the opposite. It allows for an imagination of a future that is better, where tradition and history are experienced not as a nightmare, as Karl Marx writes, but as dream-images of possibility, capable of embracing a bit of healthy disorientation and destabilization on the way to something better.[13] A nostalgic state of mind could also lead to a critical reflection of history, making room for new perspectives on the past, present, and future. It is precisely this messy nature of nostalgia—its "power to stir things up"—that makes it sociologically interesting and robust.[14] We can be drawn in by the allure of better days that have passed us by into a place of thinking how to redeem our present and alter our course of future action. Without the magnetic quality of the lost past, this space is much less likely to be entered, and therefore much less likely to produce a critical lens.

Critical nostalgia allows for change, while letting us "keep on nodding terms with the people we used to be, whether we find them attractive company or not," as Joan Didion writes.[15] Nostalgic spaces lure us in by inviting us to indulge in the past, either as witnesses to bygone days or as participants in their reconstruction. Nostalgia is alive in social practices, such as storytelling, tourism, and consumption of the past through memoirs, photographs, film, and souvenirs. While nostalgic practices often adhere to established cultural customs and traditions, they are not predetermined through their connection to specific pasts; they are socially constructed and performed in the present. As Kathleen Stewart has argued, nostalgia is "cultural practice, not given content."[16] Outcomes are not certain.

Atomic Nostalgia

Oak Ridge wants to be remembered for its science, its process, its "progress"—the Manhattan Project—which is still in motion, spinning backward and forward simultaneously: fear of a German bomb—atomic utopia—fear of nuclear winter—the Cold War—fear of the Soviet

Union—atomic nostalgia—fear of an Iranian bomb—Uranium Center of Excellence—fear of a North Korean bomb—atomic nostalgia.

Today, "nostalgia isn't what it used to be," a sentiment captured so expertly in the title of the French actress Simone Signoret's autobiography. Still, is it actually possible in the twenty-first century to be nostalgic for the atomic bomb? Are good memories of the Project and its resulting mushroom clouds still possible, amidst all the terrible nightmares and the mounting evidence of destruction? If Oak Ridge, Tennessee, one of the key production sites for the Manhattan Project, is any indication, then, yes, it is possible. Atomic nostalgia is a new form of longing, a distinctively American, postnuclear, industrial-scientific vision of a lost utopia. It can be experienced anywhere, but it vibrates most strongly in places dedicated to nuclear industries, places like Oak Ridge and Los Alamos.

Atomic nostalgia, like the atomic utopianism that came before, masks real-life realities of destruction and atrocity. The fog under the happy mushroom cloud creates an environment where critical thought is smothered. The result is a loss in the potential to engage in debates regarding many important issues facing the United States and the world at large, such as the use of nuclear weapons, the cleanup of "hot," radioactive spaces, and the power of the federal government to reshape and reorganize the landscape as it sees fit. Celebratory atomic nostalgia should be watched closely; it is a dodgy prospect that threatens to highjack nuclear historiography and to choke opportunities to examine important nuclear issues facing the United States and beyond, such as the storage, use, and proliferation of nuclear weapons.

As uranium and plutonium factories erode or undergo the processes of decommission and decontamination, as waste is buried in steel-lined canisters and stored inside the hollowed out hulls of mountains or in Oak Ridge's own Uranium Center of Excellence, the Atomic Age is burying its most important material—the people who participated in the Manhattan Project. "Oak Ridge seems to be losing its elderly citizens at an alarmingly increasing pace," writes D. Ray Smith in the "Historically Speaking" column of the city's newspaper. "These are the individuals who lived Oak Ridge history. Some who were here from the very beginning are still with us, but they are becoming fewer and fewer in number."[17]

Another danger if the Manhattan Project legacy is not critically explored is that the only stories that will remain in historical accounts and in institutional settings, such as museums and monuments, will be elsewhen tales of celebratory nostalgia—atomic back-slapping and job-well-done stories of the production and dissemination of uranium- and plutonium-fueled bombs over the cities of Japan and the American desert. As postnuclear forms of social organization rewrite the Manhattan Project cities of the past, the old atomic social order continues to haunt as ruins, memories, myths, and nostalgic imaginings. This haunting produces an atomic nostalgia, a shared disposition experienced in the postnuclear present that focuses longingly on the Atomic Age. At the moment, atomic nostalgia rests in a mostly conservative and celebratory grove, but it doesn't have to stay there.

Theoretical Underpinnings, Methods, and Craft

The archives, collective memory, and institutional structures of Oak Ridge make certain researches easy. Other investigations prove more difficult as discourses and voices are obscured, omitted, or silenced from official narratives, as well as everyday speech and storytelling. The community, its institutions, and its memory brokers play censor with the past, as does every community, institution, and individual.

During the Manhattan Project, Oak Ridgers were constrained by fields of power; they were relentlessly surveilled and dominated by panoptic spaces, not only at work, but also throughout their everyday lives. Yet within these fields they found their own ways of operating that were not predetermined. I want to think here about the everyday Oak Ridgers who engaged in self-discipline but also in resistances or ruses to their regimented and bureaucratized existence. To this end, Michel de Certeau proves a nimble thought companion. His concepts of strategy and tactics came into play in the Manhattan Project, where strategies were mobilized by institutions and hierarchies of power and where tactics were the practices of the everyday Oak Ridgers. For de Certeau, the average individual moves through the world by poaching, by operating in ways that are influenced but not entirely determined by the rules and regulations initiated by the given culture and structures of power.[18]

De Certeau writes against the completely surveilled and dominated panoptic space of Jeremy Bentham's architectural design and Michel Foucault's vision of modern society to insist that there are some blind spots— and, if not wholly blind, then at least ignored nooks and crannies, spaces for resistance and creativity, unable to truly be seen through the gluttony of watching. In Oak Ridge, poaching occurred through breaking the rules of secrecy and curfew and by smuggling contraband. Skirting small rules and rubbing up against authority helped to create the culture of Oak Ridge as much as the overarching systems of compartmentalization and constraint did. It was part of the fun, although one had to be careful not to go too far.

Also from de Certeau, along with Roland Barthes, Georges Bataille, and Walter Benjamin, this study takes the role of myth seriously in the formation of collective memory in modern life. Myths of the Atomic Age are intrinsic to the stories Oak Ridgers tell themselves and others about their own pasts. From these myths and their retelling, atomic nostalgia emerges, adapts, and lingers.

Lastly, I am perhaps most influenced by Benjamin's redemptive potentiality of the past, his understanding that memory could be a defense to the often totalitarian nature of official history and his insistence in the ability to rediscover bits and scraps of what was once thought lost and to use these discoveries for the future.[19] The idea is to present a narrative that overcomes the ideology of progress to think of a non-linear model of history, in Benjaminian terms a "constellation," that can provide an "awakening" of history that exposes myth and brings forward the "not-yet-conscious knowledge of what has been."[20] This text is driven by Benjamin's notion of the "state of emergency" as not the exception but the rule for modernity, which is perhaps the perfect metaphor for the postnuclear landscape—stretching from the Manhattan Project and the beginning of the Atomic Age to the Cold War and the aftermaths of Chernobyl and Fukushima and still stretching toward what may yet come. The state of emergency is always there in the background, but it becomes more present and urgent in moments of acute political, technological, and ecological crisis.

In this research, I employ the popular Benjaminian tool of "brushing history against the grain." My sensibilities and sociological training demand this effort, although my relationship to Oak Ridge, at times, makes this practice uncomfortable. The folks I have spoken to, who have been so kind and generous, who have given me coffee and cookies and told me stories, will not universally agree with what I have written about their city. It might cause some sore feelings and tense conversations. I am prepared for the splinters I will incur from brushing this history against its grain, hoping that Theodor Adorno was right when he wrote that "the splinter in your eye is the best magnifying glass."[21]

This is the burden of the sociologist, of the outsider who studies a place. In the opening pages of *Let Us Now Praise Famous Men*, James Agee goes so far as to call himself a "spy." The spy metaphor pops up again in Peter Berger's *Invitation to Sociology*. My relationship to Oak Ridge has sometimes felt this way. My insider-outsider status has occasionally made me feel like a double agent, critical and understanding by turns, as I have tried to make sense of this place as it confronts its atomic past and nuclear legacy.

In following Benjamin, I have tried to develop a kind of "mental atomic fission" and a way of looking at multiple time periods simultaneously, where patterns of social practices and social outlooks could be observed.[22]

I have found in the secret city of Oak Ridge what Italo Calvino found in his *Invisible Cities*: "The city is redundant: it repeats itself so that something will stick in the mind," and also that "memory is redundant: it repeats signs so that the city can begin to exist."[23] From my grandfather and grandmother—to my mother and uncle—to me—the stories of the Atomic City repeat. As Benjamin writes in *The Storyteller*, "Memory creates the chain of tradition which passes a happening on from generation to generation." Although each new storyteller tells the story of the happening a bit differently, "traces of the storyteller cling to the story the way the handprints of the potter cling to the clay vessel."[24]

Through my research I found that one of the best ways to see the redundancy of the city and its memory alongside the storytelling of the community was through spaces of atomic tourism as a critical tourist. Critical tourism is a social practice, first defined by Lucy Lippard in her study of touristic practices, *On the Beaten Track*. Here, my position as a researcher is also informed by Dean MacCannell's figure of the "tourist-ethnographer" as elaborated in *The Tourist*. Following Lippard and MacCannell, I enter these spaces with preconceived knowledge of their constructedness and a sense of what has been hidden from view, cognizant that the disjuncture of what is on display as compared to what remains hidden is part of the experience (and pleasure) of the space. Critical tourism, in addition to being a social practice that could be exercised by anyone, is also a method of sociological inquiry, which seeks to recognize, interrogate, and expose power relations behind touristic performances and displays.

In my years of studying Oak Ridge, I have visited tourist sites such as museums and monuments, but I have also visited mothballed nuclear factories; I have been chased by squatters out of the aging Oak Ridge Guest House, now known as the Alexander Inn, which housed traveling dignitaries and star atom splitters during the Manhattan Project; I have tramped through the woods getting brambles stuck to my jeans to get a look at ruins of the former trailer park community where the Manhattan Project construction workers were housed; and I have also done less dramatic things, such as going to the archives and drinking coffee with my grandmother in her Manhattan Project–era house while she told me stories.

This research attempts not only to understand and articulate one small city's connection with the Bomb, but also to provide a piece of a larger story that remains to be written: the story of the American relationship to the decline of the Atomic Age. I have approached this study with more discipline and sociological training since 2005, but it has been an ongoing obsession for me since the 1980s.

CHAPTER ONE

The Atomic Prophecy

I've seen it. It's coming.
—John Hendrix, atomic prophet

When we receive this text, an operation has already been
performed: it has eliminated otherness and its dangers in order to retain
only those fragments of the past which are locked into the puzzle
of a present time, integrated into the stories that an entire
society tells during evenings at the fireside.
—Michel de Certeau, *The Writing of History*

All we really know is that John Hendrix lived and died and that eight dollars was paid for his coffin, but the myth of the atomic prophet states that
at the turn of the twentieth century in a rural section of East Tennessee at
a fog-prone edge of the Smoky Mountains, Hendrix, a local logger with no
formal education, began hearing voices and having visions that the valley
where he lived would be transformed into a bustling city that would provide the key to winning a horrible war in the future. Just prior to his experience of these visions, Hendrix suffered extreme loss. Ethel, his youngest
child, died of diphtheria, and following her death Hendrix's wife left him
and set off for Arkansas with their three remaining children in tow. In a
state of unbearable grief over the loss of his family, Hendrix began hearing
voices telling him to head into the woods for forty days and forty nights
to pray for guidance. He did as the voices suggested, persevering through
near starvation and extreme cold; it is said that one morning he woke to
find his hair frozen to the ground, stiffly braided into the frosty under-
growth of the forest. When the forty days were up and he emerged from his
Mosaic journey, the voices and the visions continued. Hendrix believed he
could see the future and felt that it was his duty to tell everyone who would
listen (or at least everyone within earshot) what would transpire along the
Black Oak Ridge. Around the year 1900 he is thought to have said, "Bear
Creek Valley some day will be filled with great buildings and factories, and
they will help toward winning the greatest war that will ever be. There will

be a city on Black Oak Ridge, and the center of authority will be on a point midway between Sevier Tadlock's farm and Joe Pyatt's Place. A railroad spur will branch off the main L&N line, run down toward Robertsville and then branch off and turn toward Scarboro. Big engines will dig big ditches and thousands of people will be running to and fro. They will be building things, there will be great noise and confusion, and the earth will shake. I've seen it. It's coming."[1]

Hendrix would repeat his proclamations to locals and those passing through while holding court at a crossroads market called Key's store, which was conveniently located right across the road from Bill Locketts's store. At the time of his prophecies most people in his community thought he was mad. He was even institutionalized for a time.[2] Yet in the early 1940s Hendrix's visions seemed to come to life. During World War II, the area surrounding the Bear Creek Valley was chosen by the federal government as a top-secret site for the Manhattan Project. When the five small hillside communities were evacuated and replaced with several gigantic atomic factories and the city of Oak Ridge, the chief administrative building or "center of authority" for the site was placed at the point described in Hendrix's proclamation, as was the railroad spur. The sudden appearance of the instant city of Oak Ridge with its busy populace, massive factories, and new railroad branch lines closely resembled the precise description of the "great city" of Hendrix's visions. Of course this is no coincidence; it's the reason why the myth of the atomic prophet is ever present in the narratives of the city. The story of Oak Ridge is told in a way that cites the place itself as the ultimate proof of the myth's truth.

It is curious that Oak Ridge, the Atomic City, a place that sees itself as a stronghold of high culture, would trace its origin to a notorious hillbilly; it is perhaps even more curious that a city devoted to science would rely so heavily on a mythic prophecy to tell the story of its beginning. In histories of Oak Ridge, a stark contrast is drawn between the earlier residents who are presented as believing in mystics and visions and the Oak Ridgers, who by contrast are supposedly steeped in a modern rational tradition of science. Yet it is the Oak Ridgers and not the pre-atomic citizens who were removed from the area who utilize the myth of John Hendrix to justify their place in the landscape. As Georges Bataille wrote in the twentieth century, perhaps the grandest myth is that there is an "absence of myth" in modern times.[3]

After World War II, the Hendrix myth becomes a key component in the story of Oak Ridge's beginning. Its repetition creates a prophetic spectacle of the past by circumventing and screening out other, more complicated and ruthless histories of the area, including the forced removal of the pre-atomic residents from their land, as well as the grisly details of the World War II atomic bomb attacks. The story of John Hendrix makes what transpired in Oak Ridge and the bombed-out cities of Japan seem inevitable: an atomic manifest destiny.

This thread from Oak Ridge's prehistory is part of a larger quilt of myths that make up the backstory of an American atomic inevitable that is characteristic of Manhattan Project storytelling. Among the Atomic Age's most powerful myths, this notion is reflected even in Oppenheimer's farewell address to the Association of Los Alamos Scientists. On November 2, 1945, the former scientific director of the Project said frankly, "When you come right down to it the reason that we did this job is because it was an organic necessity. If you are a scientist you cannot stop such a thing." Oppenheimer also famously said, "When you see something that is technically sweet, you go ahead and do it and you argue about what to do about it only after you have had your technical success. This is the way it was with the atomic bomb."[4]

Going back to the Oak Ridge story, what is at stake here is not the accuracy or inaccuracy of the script of Hendrix's visionary rantings and ravings, which could certainly be debated; what is far more important is how this myth has been passed down through time by members of the Oak Ridge community and what use it has for those who choose to repeat it. What follows is an explanation of how a city without a past creates one, not out of thin air, but rather by plucking a story from an earlier time period and bending it to reflect a desired origin story.

Declaration of Taking

In 1942, as World War II raged overseas, General Leslie Groves, fresh from his latest project overseeing the Pentagon from an idea to a blueprint to military theory in three dimensions, was given a new stateside assignment as the U.S. government's military taskmaster for the secret mission to create an atomic bomb. The mission was more than urgent. There was intelligence that Hitler's scientists were also working to create atomic weapons. Rumors of heavy water, an essential component of some nuclear reactors, weighed on the minds of Allied scientists. They would need to work fast. This would be a difficult and dangerous race, made all the more harried by the fact that it was not known exactly where the opposing runners were on the track.

On September 19 of that same year, a cohort of powerful men, high-ranking officers from the Army Corps of Engineers and officials from the

Stone & Webster Engineering Corporation arrived at the railroad whistle stop in Elza, Tennessee. After a brief on-site consultation, it was decided that the area, as they had thought, would be an excellent choice for a key location of the Manhattan Project. The government needed cheap land and easy access to water, but at a distance from the coast, as well as abundant electricity and transportation outlets. The neighboring Tennessee Valley Authority (TVA) power center of Norris Dam and the Louisville & Nashville (L&N) railroad line were key deciding factors. The chosen section of East Tennessee proved more than adequate for the Project's needs.[5]

In Oak Ridge, there is another widely circulated story about the positioning of the site, which involves pact making between the powerful: I'll pat your back if you pat mine. In this version, President Franklin D. Roosevelt wanted to shuffle large amounts of funds for the atomic bomb project without Congress and the American people knowing what it would be used for. To this end, the president asked Senate Budget Committee chairman Kenneth McKellar of Tennessee if he could help to keep the expenditures for the Project as quiet as possible. McKellar, possibly motivated by the desire to bring wartime jobs to his state, is said to have responded, "Yes, Mr. President, I can do that for you.... Now where in Tennessee are you going to put that thang?"[6]

In 1942–43, approximately forty years after Hendrix's predictions, the federal government of the United States evacuated the communities of Elza, Robertsville, Scarboro, Wheat, and New Hope. The land acquisition process was set in motion on October 6, 1942, when an attorney from the Real Estate Branch of the Ohio River Division of the Corps of Engineers filed a "declaration of taking" at the Federal Court in Knoxville.[7] The result of this declaration was that nearly 4,000 residents of the area were ordered to leave their homes or be removed by force if necessary.[8] Through the power of eminent domain the land was seized; if the owners were not home when the government officers visited their property, evacuation notices neatly typed on onionskin paper would be hammered to fence posts, front doors, or any surface that could hold a nail.[9] Typically, residents were allowed less than three weeks to relocate.[10] The most important areas to the Manhattan Project were designated "hot spots"—a term that now carries a radioactive or contaminated connotation, but at the time meant desirable. Residents of these areas were given only fourteen days to vacate their property. For many in the region, this would be their third forced removal for federal projects, after the clearing of homesteads for the Great Smoky Mountains National Park in the 1920s and for the creation of Norris Dam by the TVA in 1933. And all these removals scraped the surface of the same topography from which the Cherokee were swept in the prior century.

To Be Rid of the Old Place

Initially, scientists believed that atomic weapons could be created only from uranium-235, but by the middle of 1941 the future Nobel Prize winner Glenn Seaborg and his team discovered that plutonium-239 was also fissionable.[11] The scientists now had two possibilities, but they did not know which would be optimal. Afraid of making the wrong choice, it was decided that the Manhattan Project would pursue both simultaneously. Originally, Groves thought he could try the two types of processes in one spot, but following Enrico Fermi's successful plutonium pile experiment at the University of Chicago on December 2, 1942, it became clear that a huge area was necessary to situate the massive reactors needed to produce enough plutonium. Groves felt the Oak Ridge site was already being pushed to its limits. On top of this, plutonium production seemed highly dangerous and Groves thought that the area around Oak Ridge was too populated to risk it. Just as the Project did not want to chance blowing up Chicago, the sizeable city of Knoxville felt too close for comfort. Another site would be needed.[12] When I tell this story to Knoxvillians, they often beam with a reluctant pride. The city retains a kind of rivalry with and suspicion of its atomic neighbor, and even today it retains imaginings of mad scientists tinkering in the labs. Sometimes this attitude seems more put on, sometimes more deeply felt.

To spare Knoxville and to avoid further overtaxing Oak Ridge, the Manhattan Project looked westward for the plutonium-focused site. The higher-ups in the Project considered their methods for choosing space and obtaining the land for Oak Ridge to have been successful, so they replicated their practices for the new site. Like the five evacuated pre-atomic communities in Tennessee, the towns of White Bluffs and Hanford were effectively disappeared from the state of Washington. And like its eastern counterpart, the Hanford site was desirable because of its proximity to a large New Deal project, the Grand Coulee Dam.[13] This was the modus operandi of the Project: kick out the people, clear the land, and bulldoze it to the point where newcomers might even suspect that they had landed in a territory that had never been settled before.

Unlike the TVA evacuations, the Manhattan Project provided little assistance to the evacuees, either with help moving their belongings or with finding new homes in other areas. Some were paid for their land prior to their relocation, but most were not. This left many of the pre-atomic citizens with no money, no land, and often no job prospects. As surgical as the government tried to make this process, it was not without its mess.

Transportation shortages and the speed with which the previous residents were forced to evacuate led to the abandonment of many possessions not deemed absolutely essential. Anyone who has ever moved even under the best circumstances knows this. Things are left behind, sometimes by accident, sometimes in haste, sometimes because the damned thing won't fit in the truck. This happened in the space that was to become Oak Ridge as well, leaving workers engaged in the grunt work of clearing out to discover photo albums, kitchen items, farming tools, canned vegetables and fruit preserves, gingham curtains, confused livestock, and other flotsam and jetsam abandoned in the rush as the Appalachian valley gave itself over, mostly unconsciously, but not without effort, to the Atomic Age.

Most of the evicted left without serious challenges to the government beyond some sass and idle threats, although a few brought legal action to dispute the sums paid for their land. In 1943, the House Military Affairs Committee launched an investigation into the land acquisition practices of the War Department. Leading the charge was Representative John Jennings Jr. of Knoxville, who argued provocatively, "The Secretary of War has assumed the guise of an invader."[14] In the end, the Manhattan Project was deemed of too great importance to be more than mildly affected by these claims,[15] although in a few rare cases the land was reappraised and landowners received second offers. In the final settlements, the average cost of an acre of land was forty-five dollars, considered by most to be much less than what it was worth. As if to sum up the ease with which the pre-atomic citizens were excised from their properties, James Marshall, an official for the Corps of Engineers, described the land acquisition process as "child's play."[16]

As Dorathy Moneymaker, a local historian of the Wheat community, which became the area surrounding the K-25 gaseous diffusion plant, wrote, "When a new place is to be built, the first thing that must be done is to be rid of the old place. Even though all buildings are removed, the impression of the people who lived in the old place cannot be erased."[17] While Moneymaker expresses a nice sentiment, the truth is that the impression of those who came before is often in the hands of those who come afterward. The effect can be thought of much like a toy drawing pad wrestled away from a younger sibling. Here the impression or memory of the pre-atomic communities can be compared less to impressions left upon Sigmund Freud's *Wunderblock*, where past markings are recorded in wax to be rediscovered at will, and more akin to designs created on an Etch A Sketch, which can be erased by a vigorous shake of the wrist.[18]

After the land grab, the federal government had in their hands a rough and hilly jagged rectangle of 59,000 acres, a houndstooth-shaped swath of earth measuring seventeen miles long and approximately seven miles wide; at first, the newcomers referred to it derogatively as "Dogpatch."[19] The area was protracted through the geometry of military and political power in accordance with the natural landscape. Chosen in part for its seclusion and its distance from the coast, the site was nestled in green valleys of lush grass and fruit trees hemmed in by the Clinch River and a series of ridges. The topographic layout ensured that the various atomic plants could be separated, with each tucked in its own valley, so that in case of an accident at one site the damage could theoretically be contained, avoiding a dangerous game of radioactive dominoes.[20]

Once the inhabitants of the pre-atomic communities were scattered into neighboring towns, states, and beyond, the Manhattan Project was free to usher in a new panoptic aesthetic of power based on spatial, social, and visual control. Since no official records were kept, it is difficult to say where people moved once they were evacuated from the area.[21] One of the most devastating effects of the forced removal of the residents who were pushed off their land was that many went to work on the Manhattan Project, becoming tenants on the very land they once owned.

In a matter of months Oak Ridge began to take shape, most of the city was newly built, but portions of the new space contained scraps of the old. In light of wartime shortages, the Army Corps of Engineers sometimes incorporated abandoned buildings into the construction of the factories of the Clinton Engineer Works. The effect was a rustic military aesthetic, a bricolage of Appalachian elements combined with government drab. For example, the abandoned New Bethel Baptist Church was taken over by the x-10 site and was converted into a storage building, abandoned log cabins were used as recreation and picnic centers, and the fence around the perimeter of the city was laced with barbed wire scavenged from abandoned farms.[22] To add insult to injury the menacing material, which once helped to protect the pre-atomic citizens' property from would-be thieves or wild animals, was then used to keep them out.

What is simply amazing is that the land was commandeered, residents were removed, and construction of facilities was begun without so much as a phone call to Tennessee governor Prentice Cooper. General Groves had received permission from President Roosevelt to set up Oak Ridge as a federal military reservation, giving the military freedom from both federal and state laws. When high-ranking officers were finally dispatched to inform the governor, he was livid and reportedly tore the memo to shreds. He felt that the land and roads had been seized and stolen for an "experiment in socialism." Governor Cooper may have been onto something. Throughout the war years, Oak Ridge had universal healthcare, zero unemployment, and state-owned housing. In the 1950s, during the heights of McCarthyism, charges of socialism would rise again, and that favored insult of those consumed with the Red Scare—"un-American"—would be aimed at Oak Ridge and other Manhattan Project sites. By contrast in the 1940s, moving to Oak Ridge to work for the war effort was lauded by the Manhattan Project recruiters as a highly American act, one of patriotism. Still, something about it rankled the governor.

Cooper believed the takeover of the land was a trick by the "New Dealers cloaked under the guise of a war project."[23] When the governor finally visited the Oak Ridge site, he was shown only the factories' facades and had to trust his guides that he was seeing a vital war project and not a Potemkin village. According to military accounts, the governor was reportedly "placated by whiskey," while the importance of secrecy, his patriotic duty, and security was impressed upon him until he softened.[24] In actuality, any smooth talking or pressuring on the part of the military was superfluous: the president had already written the order, the factories were in construction, and Governor Cooper really had no choice in the matter. General Groves, known for his aggressive and brusque demeanor, later admitted that this situation should have been handled with more finesse.[25]

It was not only Tennessee's governor who was perturbed by the seizure of this particular plot of land. David Lilienthal, the chairman of the TVA who was known as Mr. TVA, was also resistant to the Project's site choice.[26] Lilienthal objected because portions of the land chosen had already been set aside as part of a TVA agricultural improvement program. He tried to steer the Manhattan Project into western Kentucky close to Paducah but to no avail. The physicist Arthur Compton, working for the Manhattan Project site selection team, refused Lilienthal's pleas and authorized the court seizure of the land. Lilienthal argued, "It was a bad precedent. That particular site was not essential; another involving far less disruption in people's lives would have served as well, but arbitrary bureaucracy, made doubly powerful by military secrecy, had its way."[27]

Whereas the goal of the TVA was always to involve local populations in new modernization developments, the way the federal government dealt with Governor Cooper, as well as the forced removal of residents from their land, shows the focus of the Manhattan Project was to be directed away from the local and toward a more national and international view.[28] The strategy could be summed up as "the more imbedded in the local, the more difficult to persuade."[29] This logic persisted until after the war. Following the war, there was a new "local" population—those who worked in

Oak Ridge for the duration and decided to stay on—who were in large part "persuaded" by the goals and outcomes of the Manhattan Project.

Once Oak Ridgers began to think of their city as something more than a temporary war project, and when it was clear that Cold War security needs would keep the labs open, many chose to remain in the city and make it their permanent home. This terrain, both imagined and lived, helped to shape the way Oak Ridgers remember and retell their past. In the late 1940s, the situation in Oak Ridge began to change as the city was slowly weaned from total federal control. In 1949 the gates of the city opened with great fanfare, and by 1959 the city was a fully incorporated entity in the state of Tennessee. With each of these changes, in order to think about the future, the community began to turn inward and backward, looking for a way to tell its story to explain and justify its place in the world, both geographically and historically. The myths of John Hendrix and of the unproblematic volunteer exodus from the pre-atomic communities dominate this storytelling.

John Hendrix as Synecdoche

After 1945, a curious process occurred where those who remained in Oak Ridge began to tie their histories to those who had inhabited the geographical space in which they were now situated. From this point forward the myth of John Hendrix, the atomic prophet, took on greater significance, often as the lead story in the city's history. The Hendrix myth is historical stenography, a kind of shorthand for telling a story of the region both to outsiders and to Oak Ridgers themselves. Accounts of area history do not simply herald the glories of scientific prowess, they also suture Appalachian heritage to the Atomic Age.

Even though the genres are sometimes used interchangeably by Oak Ridgers, the story of John Hendrix should be considered a myth rather than a legend. The anthropologist and folklorist William Bascom has defined myths as "prose narratives which in the society in which they are told are considered to be truthful accounts of what happened in the remote past."[30] He goes on to define legends as "prose narratives which like myths are regarded as true by the narrator and his audience, but they are set in a period less remote when the world was much as it is today."[31] While these definitions seem to point the Hendrix story toward legend rather than myth, I argue the opposite. Even though the time period between Hendrix's visions and the realization of Oak Ridge was only a few decades, the narrative is told in a way that stretches time, making it seem as if there is actually a much deeper temporal gap between the two forms of social organization—in other words, the world of Hendrix is *not very much as it is today* in Oak Ridge.

Myths both gigantisize and miniaturize the people and pasts with which they come into contact. Through the myth of the prophecy of John Hendrix the history of Oak Ridge grows large; it unfolds with a message from God, disseminated through a local prophet. Oak Ridge emerges from the tale as a heroic city built of speed with a robust and intelligent citizenry destined for greatness. Meanwhile, the history of the communities that were removed to make room for Oak Ridge is reduced and distorted. Through the telling of the myth, John Hendrix functions as synecdoche, where the entire population of the pre-atomic communities is compressed into a caricature, a man who had premonitions of what was to come. The earlier inhabitants of the valley are then dismissed as willing participants in their own exodus, making the story altogether too neat. The pre-atomic citizens of the hills and valleys are mentioned, but they are "half-amputated, they are deprived of memory," as Barthes writes of the figures portrayed in myth.[32]

Not only are the histories of the earlier communities flattened, but they are also victim to a temporal pause. By focusing on Hendrix, the narratives fix the pre-atomic residents at a time before 1915 when he passed away, thus canceling out nearly thirty years of area history. Like a thief who manipulates a security system to show a fixed, constant time while he is pilfering in a dynamic flow of time, the narratives of Oak Ridge halt the prior communities' history and take the parts they desire for their own. By portraying the people of Wheat, Elza, Scarboro, New Hope, and Robertsville as from another era, the historical narratives are able to move Oak Ridgers beyond these locales, as if the two forms of social organization did not exist simultaneously but instead as nodes on a linear timeline, the pre-atomic followed by the atomic, thus implying progress—inevitable, preordained progress. In fact, "piling their goods on trucks or wagons, or in some cases leaving them behind, outgoing residents crossed paths with the thousands of construction workers pouring in."[33] In Oak Ridge in the 1940s it was possible to look for ruins of a lost civilization—one that had just been eradicated—and one that was oddly contemporaneous with the secret atomic city that had taken its place.

Along with the bulldozing of the physical structures, the barns and homes, the Manhattan Project nearly obliterated the memory and culture of the pre-atomic communities. Of Wheat, all that was left was the George Jones Memorial Church and a smattering of cemeteries, which were maintained by the federal government and remain so even today under the Department of Energy. Before the erasure of the pre-atomic communities, the city of Wheat was the educational seat of the region, home to a well-respected high school that in modern parlance would be called a magnet school; it drew students from the surrounding areas who wanted to go to college. The community could also boast Roane College, one of the earliest accredited four-year liberal arts colleges in the region.[34] Yet in local history, the images and narratives that dominate are of rustic cabins and moonshine stills peopled by "old-timers," "wandering hill folk," and "pioneers of another era" who voluntarily gave up their land and homes to a "new type of pioneer" who could "bring about a New Age."[35]

These myths fit snugly into yet another myth of the area, a myth woven into Tennessee's nickname: the Volunteer State. Some say the name arose to celebrate the volunteer soldiers who fought bravely in the War of 1812 under General Andrew Jackson, while others link the moniker to those who fought in the Battle of the Alamo. Regardless of its origin, it is used in the area as a celebration of Tennesseans' willingness to sacrifice for the greater good—to pitch in and to fight for the right side.

Through mythic storytelling the history of Wheat and the other pre-atomic communities lose their dynamism; they are arrested. Former Wheat resident Grace Raby Crawford, the step-granddaughter of John Hendrix, balks at this representation. In an interview with D. Ray Smith, she bristled: "It has been said of the Oak Ridge area, ' . . . from a wilderness to an atomic city,' but many people do not realize that a growing and thriving community existed there. There were many acres of cultivated fertile fields, beautiful farm homes, churches, schools, post offices, lumber mills, grain mills and at one time an ammunition (powder) mill. Various other small businesses were also in the community. . . . None of these are found in a 'wilderness.' "[36] Not only do some former residents of the pre-atomic communities take issue with the way they are represented as caricatures; they also wish the evacuation story to be told with more nuance and for some responsibility to be taken for the rough treatment dealt by the government.

John Rice Irwin, historian and founder of the Museum of Appalachia, was twelve years old when his family received notice that they would have to vacate their land, land that had been in the family for generations. Shedding light on the psychological effects of the move, Irwin writes, "The economic and technical problems inherent in such hurried-up moving, monumental as they were, did not compare to the mental trauma. One has to understand the cultural and ancestral roots to which rural folk become attached to the land after a few generations in order to understand the shock which results from such uprooting."[37]

Another, more colorful narrative on the forced evacuation comes from Hendrix's own son, Curtis, who laid his resentment down in a poem titled "The Planned and Organized Society (Sponsored by Elinoir)," referring to Eleanor Roosevelt. Here is an excerpt:

I had a home in Robertsville
They call it Oak Ridge now
T'was home for all my younguns
and their chickens and the cow
One day a bunch of men rode in
With papers in their hands
And great big shining badges
They came and took our land.[38]

An aspect of the eviction story that is not often highlighted is the fact than many of the men between eighteen and fifty years of age were off fighting in the war, leaving families split with women, older folks, and children working to pick up the slack. It is on top of this hardship that many families were forced to pack up and begin a new life elsewhere.

While Wheat citizen Dorathy Moneymaker's husband was not overseas but only a few miles away and already working in the rapidly developing Oak Ridge site, her story illustrates the type of interaction that happened between government agents and the pre-atomic residents. She reminisced: "They came to evict us, and the man come up to the door and he wanted to know where my husband was, and I said he was at work. . . . He said, 'Well, I come to evict, serve eviction papers on you, so I'll just serve them on you.' Now, I was expecting our first baby . . . and he weighed well over eight pounds. So, you know very good and well I was showing. I stepped back and I said to him, 'Did you know that there is a law in the state of Tennessee that will not allow you to evict a pregnant woman?' And he was so amazed, he almost stepped off the front porch. He never did come back. I didn't know that there was a law and I just made it up, but come to find out there was one."[39] That particular officer didn't come back, but despite Dorathy's spunk and crafty ability to make up laws on the spot, the Moneymakers had to move out all the same. Eventually they would settle in Oak Ridge and Dorathy would become my grandmother's Sunday school teacher at Robertsville Baptist Church and a lifelong advocate and chronicler of her lost community. In the Benjaminian sense, she "narrate[d] events without distinguishing between major and minor ones," operating with "the following truth: nothing that has ever happened should be regarded as lost to history."[40] With grand narratives and notes of minutiae she battled the bulldozing of her area's history, leaving behind a strange, slim volume that gives some texture to Wheat's past.[41] Rumor has it that she was once invited to appear on *Good Morning America* but became ill and couldn't make the trip to New York City. Would more people know of Wheat if its backstory had been televised?

The process of establishing the Oak Ridge site was much more complicated, brutal, and not as widely accepted as many of the dominant narratives of the city suggest. The myth of a peaceful and enthusiastic exodus, which is in line with the trumpeted volunteer spirit of the region, is actually a violent way of telling this story, infused with the "false aliveness of the past-made-present, the elimination of every echo of a 'lament' from history."[42] The acquisitiveness of the federal government is often whitewashed with patriotic anecdotes. To battle these one-dimensional stories, counter-mythic accounts or "back talk" are important in that they trouble the simplified story of the area by "open[ing] a gap in the order of myth itself."[43] Myth, of course is not benign; it has a "type of social usage."[44]

When myth is put into action, a great deal of violence is caused to the richer histories it upends. For example, if you were to consult newspapers from wartime, you might find something like this report from October 18, 1942, in the *Knoxville News-Sentinel*, complete with shouting capital letters: "Prospects of short-notice wholesale exodus have naturally loosened their tongues. Their stories pathetic, humorous or tragic go to make up the picture. The humor may have been studied but not the pathos. These valley and ridgeside families speak their piece in straight-forward matter-of-fact fashion. AND EACH AND EVERY EVACUEE, WITHOUT EXCEPTION, DECLARED A WILLINGNESS TO LEAVE 'IF IT WILL HELP WIN THIS WAR.'"[45]

And if you were to turn on the radio in the immediate postwar years, you might hear something like this report from William Gallaher from the nationwide radio show *We the People*, which aired on February 9, 1947:

All the folks in these parts were farmers. They worked the ground and minded their own business, peaceful folks living a simple life. Of course, when the Civil War came along, we sent a few of our boys out to fight. And then in World War I we did our share. But other than that, we didn't pay much attention to the outside world and they didn't bother with us. That was up to 1942, anyway, when one day a man came to our house and said he was from the Government. "We're going to buy up your land," he said to me. "All of it?" I asked. "Yes, sir," he said, "we're going to buy all the land in this section. Everyone has to go." I went outside the house with the visitor and looked around me . . . up at the green hills my grandfather had come across 100 years earlier, and I looked at the farm I'd worked for half a century. I asked the visitor what the Government was going to do and he said he didn't rightfully know, but it was for winning the war. I had three sons in the Service—two overseas—and I figured if giving up my home and my land would help bring them home sooner, I'd be happy to do it.[46]

At the time, the newspapers and radio stations were patriotic boosters and nothing critical regarding the war effort in general or the Manhattan Project more specifically would be given ink or airtime. In fact, any article pertaining to Oak Ridge in the *Knoxville News-Sentinel* carried the tag, "In accordance with censorship regulations, the accompanying article has been referred to a proper military authority in this region—EDITOR." The danger is that these are the reports that have mostly been taken up by historians and memoirists and incorporated into their work. When no dissenting voices are represented, these accounts are the only ones repeated until they appear as natural history, as common sense.

The Ubiquity of the Hendrix Myth

Myths of the Atomic Age pile up. Mythic stories featuring Oppenheimer and other star atom-splitters, myths of traitorous spies, myths of brave volunteers sacrificing their land for the war effort, and myths of gruesome radioactive experiments and disasters are among the myths that have captured the most attention on a national level (of course, there have been some spies, volunteers, disasters, and experiments in reality as well). Yet, at a local level, no myth has surpassed the popularity of the John Hendrix story, which is lodged in the collective memory of Oak Ridgers. The story of the atomic prophet is ubiquitous, repeated in local histories, memoirs, poems, films, and museum displays.

On November 2, 1944, the Hendrix myth made its first print appearance in the *Oak Ridge Journal*, the local newspaper.[47] Initially, the military resisted publishing the article for fear that the dynamism of the story and its depiction of frenzied construction would draw too much attention to the Oak Ridge site. Ed Westcott, who photographed the remains of the Hendrix homestead and his rough-hewn gravestone for the article, explained: "The lid was placed on Dick's story and my photographs because intelligence wanted to prevent any attention to be attracted to the concentration of industry in Oak Ridge."[48] Security was a priority during wartime, so much so that the newspaper was not even supposed to leave the city. The *Journal* carried a staunch warning just below its masthead: "KEEP THIS COPY HERE PLEASE. NOT TO BE TAKEN OR MAILED FROM THIS AREA."[49] Eventually, the story proved too alluring and was published under the pseudonym "Joe Oakes, Journal Prophecy Expert"; the writer was actually Richard (Dick) Gehman. Drafted by the U.S. Army in 1942, Gehman was sent to Oak Ridge, where he was assigned the wartime duty of editor of the *Oak Ridge Journal*. After the war, he had a vibrant career as a writer and journalist, working for *Playboy, Cosmopolitan, Good Housekeeping, Time, Life,* and *Esquire,* among other publications.

Gehman began the atomic prophet article with an air of suspicion: "There is no written proof that John Hendrix actually made these predictions, no Hagiographa, no Doomesday book, no local Book of Mormon. He never bothered to write them down, but simply told them to everyone he knew and met."[50] The reporter first heard the story from Guard Force lieutenant James Braden, who grew up in the area and told Gehman, "I got the last whipping I ever got from my mother for believin' John Hendrix prophesyin'."[51] In the article, Braden gave the script of the Hendrix prophecy, a script that is repeated verbatim in nearly every account of Oak Ridge history. Here I am also guilty. I have repeated this same block of sentences at the beginning of this chapter. As Barthes has argued, this is "the major power of myth: its recurrence."[52]

The next mention of the Hendrix myth in print can be found in former Project worker George O. Robinson's *The Oak Ridge Story: The Saga of a People Who Share in History,* a hybrid and at times grandiose text of local history and memoir; it is subtitled as a "saga," after all. Robinson's account suggests that Hendrix "found his most ready audiences at the crossroads' store near his home and to them he solemnly voiced his prophecies."[53] Robinson concludes that these folks and their kin who listened to Hendrix at the trading post and then passed on the story give the myth its authority. This is the only link to Hendrix, the author stresses, as "there was no historian to put his stories to paper," but still, "fragments of information remain which give accounts of John's speculations of the future."[54]

Accompanying Robinson's text are photographs by official Manhattan Project photographer Ed Westcott. Black-and-white images of Hendrix's gravestone and ramshackle home complete with an empty rocking chair make for a scene straight out of James Agee's and Walker Evans's Great Depression era *Let Us Now Praise Famous Men.* These are the same photographs that appeared in the original Hendrix newspaper article. This is not surprising in that Westcott was the only Oak Ridger authorized to

Joe and Dorathy Moneymaker (courtesy of Oak Ridge National
Laboratory, U.S. Department of Energy, from the collection of Barbara Elys)

photograph the secret military site during wartime. These photographs are a bit of a trick because they tend to suggest that this broken-down condition of Hendrix's home was how it looked when he lived there, when in fact what Westcott has captured on film is a ruin. The images show what was left after the Project procured the land and kicked everyone out, which was twenty-eight years after Hendrix died. Also, even though there are existing photographs of the Wheat school and other flourishing examples of pre-atomic community life, the images utilized in area histories are typically of "old-timers" dressed in overalls and wrinkled by a life lived working in the fields. The fact that these are the only images that consistently appear in the early histories of Oak Ridge makes Westcott's photographs that much more powerful; like the Hendrix myth itself, they repeat. By contrast, you can see the photograph of Joe and Dorathy Moneymaker of Wheat embracing in 1936, dressed smartly and modernly, despite the Great Depression.

The John Hendrix Myth in the Museum

In the first three decades of the American Museum of Atomic Energy (1949–78), which later became the American Museum of Science and Energy (AMSE), a mannequin of John Hendrix sat in a rocking chair at the entrance to the "Oak Ridge Story" section of the museum.[55] The display of the dummy Hendrix might have seemed out of place next to the mostly technical and scientific displays devoted to the uses of medical isotopes, the process of nuclear fusion, and the machinations of the calutrons, which made up the majority of the museum. The poet Marilou Awiakta, whose childhood was spent in Oak Ridge, captured the odd juxtaposition in these lines from a poem about the prophet: "John would feel proud. . . . He's in the Museum. By a giant atom with electrons whirling round it like tiny azure stars, there he sits—leaning on his cane. His prophecy came true. They've hung pictures to show it's so. And I can go out the museum door and see the great city strung along Black Oak Ridge, waiting."[56] Since 1978, the Hendrix mannequin is no longer a permanent feature of the museum; in his place, a wax statue of Albert Einstein greets visitors. AMSE deputy director Ken Mayes credits the Department of Energy with the mandate to remove Hendrix from the museum because of the dearth of proof of his predictions. Meanwhile, a local historian reports that the Hendrix "display was removed when a Washington, D.C. bureaucrat felt the folklore had no place in a 'prestigious museum of science,' and the museum staff was coerced into removing the display."[57] But, as Mayes suggests, the issue may be cloudier still: "The reasoning for having to pull the exhibit has become as much folklore within the museum as John's story has to the history of Oak Ridge."[58] The switch from Hendrix to Einstein illustrates the tension in the museum between local history and the broader national and international story of physics and nuclear science that the community wishes to tell. Sometimes Oak Ridgers want to be thought of as southerners steeped in Appalachian heritage, and sometimes they want to be thought of as existing in the realms of high science; often they want both simultaneously.

Recently, the museum chose to forefront local history as the city of Oak Ridge was afflicted with John Hendrix mania. In 2010, the atomic prophet returned to the AMSE with a new exhibit, "Prophet of Oak Ridge,"[59] as well as a new book, *The John Hendrix Story*, and two short films. The John Hendrix exhibit at the AMSE was a collaborative effort of the museum staff, along with local Hendrix enthusiasts Jack and Myra Mansfield and newspaper columnist and local historian D. Ray Smith.

The exhibit was composed of text from Hendrix family records, transcriptions of oral history, a short film, and nineteenth-century artifacts. The artifacts were examples of objects that Hendrix may have used and had around him rather than authentic relics of the man himself, although some of the objects on display ensconced in plastic cubes were found on the grounds of Hendrix's abandoned homestead: a rusty saw, a canning jar, and a weathered washboard. Aromatic bales of hay and a rough-hewn fence enclosed the exhibit, making it seem more like a display from the Museum of Appalachia in nearby Norris, Tennessee, than a national museum dedicated to science and energy. Despite the fact that the AMSE is a Smithsonian affiliate, there was no opposition from Washington, D.C., and no local controversy over the Hendrix exhibit of 2010.[60] The museum reflects the sensibility of the city, one that has always vacillated between playing up its futuristic scientific mission and its southern Appalachian frontier tradition. The Hendrix myth works so well for Oak Ridgers because it is a synthesis and an explanation of the relationship of the two.

The centerpiece of the Hendrix exhibit was the short video *John Hendrix as Portrayed by Jack Mansfield*, by the documentary filmmaker Keith McDaniel.[61] The video presents the standard script of the Hendrix myth but also adds some theatrical flourishes. Mansfield begins his performance, "Howdy, my name is John Hendrix. I was born in 1865 over in Bear Creek Valley, of what is now Oak Ridge just at the end of the 'War of Northern Aggression' which as you know was a war between the Yankees and the Americans." Dressed in a period costume, a simple cotton shirt, suspenders, and a farmer's hat, the actor portrays Hendrix by peppering his soliloquy with folksy phrases, southern pride, and religious vernacular.

The video shows how Oak Ridgers use the story of Hendrix not only as a period piece or means to justify their nuclear past, but also as a vehicle to express their views about the present. Mansfield veers from the mythic script as he ends the six-minute monologue with this pronouncement: "It was God's plan to build a weapon to stop that war and there hasn't been another big one since. What took place here was an awesome miracle. Only a desperate situation would warrant dropping another bomb like that one and I pray it doesn't happen. Since then God has allowed this nation to prosper and to help keep the rest of the world in order. So keep praying for this nation. Especially, for us to return to our Christian heritage on which we were founded."[62] In this telling of the myth—from Adam to the atom bomb—not only is Oak Ridge a product of providence, but atomic bombs are as well![63]

While Jack and Myra Mansfield focus primarily on the religious meaning of the Hendrix story, another short film produced in 2010, *Prophet of Oak Ridge*, links the myth more closely to institutional power. The film, narrated by the official Y-12 National Security Complex historian D. Ray Smith, includes dramatic reenactment and voiceovers combined with black-and-white images to tell the story of Hendrix. Even though the Y-12 film was not the one on display in the AMSE, the text on the wall of the exhibit was provided by Smith and geared more toward the institutional justification version of the myth: "The story of John Hendrix must be appreciated for the wonder it brings. Y-12 is more than just a place and more than mere historical fact. Y-12, in the truest sense, is a vision brought to reality. Over 40 years before it was conceived in the minds of government officials, it was seen in a true-to-life vision by John Hendrix. In the 1940s, [when] Y-12 was a monumental national triumph over seemingly insurmountable obstacles, it succeeded in producing a new material so powerful that it changed the world forever and it represented the epitome of an idea transformed into spectacular and tremendous action."

Smith describes the Hendrix myth as a "memory hook," which helps visitors to tie the atomic past to the city of Oak Ridge.[64] The Hendrix story also functions as a "usable past" for Y-12 that helps paint a desirable picture of national history.[65] The Y-12 National Security Complex's "Our Hidden Past" film series, of which *Prophet of Oak Ridge* is a part, is an outreach program designed by the institution to foster a stronger relationship with the community. These videos can be seen at the Complex's New Hope Center, which also includes artifacts from Y-12's past and explanatory display boards. The videos are handed out to visitors for free along with promotional and educational brochures.

Y-12 is self-conscious about its image and works hard to control the memory of its operations by always presenting itself, now and in the past, as virtuous and reliable. As the anthropologist Mary Douglas has written in *How Institutions Think*, "An institution causes its members 'to forget' experiences incompatible with its righteous image and brings to their minds events which sustain the view . . . that is complementary to itself."[66] What could be more righteous than the myth of John Hendrix with its direct proclamation from God, which seemed to unfold so true to form?

While it is not entirely clear why Hendrix mania struck when it did, a few factors could be said to contribute. First, it should be mentioned that the Hendrix myth has been used in the telling of the story of Oak Ridge, more or less consistently, from 1945 onward. Why the atomic prophecy has become more of a spectacle in recent years is partially attributable to Smith, the Y-12 historian and newspaper columnist, who is one of the main atomic storytellers of the community. In 2010, he finished a volume on the Hendrix myth that he had been working on for several years. This led to the short film produced by Y-12, mentioned above, as well as the exhibit in the AMSE. Oak Ridge is a small city obsessed with its atomic memory. Once a memory theme appears in one cultural venue, such as the local newspaper, it tends to be picked up by various local cultural outlets, such as the AMSE, the Oak Ridge Heritage and Preservation Association, and the annual Secret City Festival, which is dedicated to celebrating the city's role in the Manhattan Project, as well as everyday life in the community.

Oak Ridge remains a community with strong ties to the federal government (still its largest employer) as well as a scientific center with a huge corporate science presence. It is therefore not surprising that the Department of Energy and the large-scale scientific corporations anchored in Oak Ridge are among the most powerful entities shaping the collective memory of the city today. The philosopher Avishai Margalit points out that "shared memory is built on a division of mnemonic labor."[67] Yes, but it should be noted that these labors are not equal; the same powerful institutions that shaped the city now shape the dominant collective memory.

Of course there are dissenting voices, counter-memories, and alternative histories, but these are mostly quieted behind other stories, such as the prophetic myth of John Hendrix and the patriotic myth of land volunteerism, stories that obscure and distort the richer histories that rest behind them. If the counter-stories are not altogether silenced, they are sometimes tamed. Still, a bit of wildness emerges from these tellings. Through these stories, likeable rascals such as Dorathy Moneymaker are uncovered: those who resisted in small ways, even though they moved within the larger constraints of Manhattan Project living. Just as their tactics troubled the strategies of the Manhattan Project authorities to impose order in the 1940s, their memories trouble the official institutional histories that those orders have written and continue to write.

The Ghost of Wheat

Alongside rascal narratives, another way that an uneasy relationship to the past receives voice in the region is through ghost stories. Even around the perimeter of the Atomic City, revenants hover. "There is no place that is not haunted by many different spirits hidden there in silence, spirits one can 'invoke' or not,"[68] writes de Certeau. In and around Oak Ridge, local lore holds that the last remaining structure in what used to be the pre-atomic community of Wheat, the George Jones Memorial Baptist Church, is haunted. No one knows who the spirit is, but it has been widely speculated that it is the ghost of a displaced person forced off their land in the 1940s to make room for Oak Ridge. The ghost of Wheat circulates through and around the church like a circuit rider—what folks used to call itinerant preachers who came through town on a semi-regular basis. The ghost is thought to be seeking revenge, although no physical harm toward humans, beasts, or fowl has been reported. Wheat's phantom is sometimes seen dressed as an overall-clad farmer, sometimes as a flame-shaped mass composed of colorful orbs, and sometimes as a fantastic swirl of vapor resembling the collective exhalation of a team of horses on a cool morning, a ghostly cloud that easily blends with the low-lying fog the valley is known for.

The circulation of this ghost story troubles the uncomplicated narrative of volunteerism and sacrifice of those who lived in the pre-atomic communities. The angry ghost betrays the tidy pastness of the place by allowing an expression of guilt, or at least a gesture of compassion and understanding of the plight of those who had to go.[69] The Wheat ghost story expresses a sleight-of-hand admission that some went not in a spirit of patriotism, but against their will.

Driving on the backcountry roads on a muggy Tennessee summer night, wheels neatly tucked between the fog lines, I can't help but wonder what the unknown ghost of Wheat might say to the atomic prophet John Hendrix if they were to have a chance meeting at some crepuscular hour, when both are known to appear. Maybe one would convince the other of a righteous mission and they would team up. Or maybe there would be arguing and fisticuffs: two frail old farmers dislodged from the time-space continuum wailing on each other. I wonder if one might find the other insane, and which would be more likely. In my favorite fantasy, Oak Ridgers would use these otherworldly messengers against each other in a kind of boxing match with the past: the "it had to happen this way" of Hendrix duking it out with the "it didn't have to happen this way" of the Wheat ghost.

The truth is that it almost didn't happen this way. At the end of the war, there was barely enough fissionable uranium to make the bomb that was dropped on Hiroshima. They didn't even test it beforehand. They knew they had the plutonium bomb as well, the one they tried out in New Mexico, lying in wait. Oak Ridge almost failed to fulfill Hendrix's prophecy. If that had happened, Hendrix would have long been forgotten by now. Of course, the Wheat ghost would still have reason to be angry, the pre-atomic residents' land and homes would have been taken all the same; but the fate of the area after the war would have been very different. Certainly, Oak Ridgers would not celebrate their city with great pride through festivals and museum displays as the Atomic City or the Secret City. In fact, there would not be a museum or festival at all. It would be a secret city with a lowercase *s* and a lowercase *c*. I often wonder about these alternative Oak Ridges that never were, but I fail to create a full picture, only mental sketches. Like Italo Calvino in *Invisible Cities*, "I am collecting the ashes of the other possible cities that vanish to make room for it, cities that can never be rebuilt or remembered."[70] These ashes pile up next to those of Wheat, New Hope, Robertsville, Scarboro, and Elza.

Nostalgic Bridging, Historical Robbery

The Hendrix myth expresses only confidence that the Manhattan Project would meet its desired goals. This is what makes me suspicious. When the myth is employed, it teaches Oak Ridgers to be nostalgic for the future they have already fulfilled through the process of nostalgic bridging.[71] Through this operation, the residents of the Atomic City can be nostalgic because they can see themselves as the product of a deeper past, a past that they have created by linking themselves to the history of those who lived in the geographical space before them. Nostalgic bridging is a historical robbery that causes longing for a golden age not entirely deserved but seen by those pining as justified, a culmination of an inevitable chain of events, the sweeping away of local farms as prophesized rather than as a near-instant industrialization via government fiat. Myths not only mark the boundaries of times but also "have the function of founding and articulating spaces."[72] The Hendrix myth is a narrative with much plasticity—it can be bent to illustrate how the city without a past became a continuation of the American pioneering story, or it can be bent to explain how the city without history is actually the fulfillment of its preordained destiny.

"Perhaps the absence of myth is the ground that seems so stable beneath my feet, yet gives way without warning," wrote Georges Bataille in 1947.[73] In the aftermath of World War II, Bataille understood that society had not fully realized Max Weber's great fears of being completely rationalized and disenchanted. Devastated, yes; disenchanted, not yet. As he wrote his essays on surrealism in the late 1940s and early 1950s, Bataille argued that there is still a deep social desire for myth and a social function for myth to play. He only wished that myth didn't always serve the powerful or provide justification for war as it so often does, and as it did in the case of Oak Ridge.

While the myth of the atomic prophet is alive and well, John Hendrix lies buried in the city of Oak Ridge in an area now called Hendrix Creek Subdivision. The rude gravestone captured in Ed Westcott's snapshot is long gone, replaced by a new headstone, a gift of Dorothy Bruce's 1966–67 Jefferson Junior High School students. The lot adjacent to Hendrix's gravestone, which falls on land owned by a man named Bobby Ledford, is caught in a tug-of-war between the past and the present. Ledford aims to build a house on the plot, but some historical preservationists and city leaders worry about construction on what they consider at most a sacred site and at least an important civic historical marker. The Oak Ridge Heritage and Preservation Association is fighting for a fifteen-foot monument to be erected onsite. They worry that without a site indicator, the Hendrix grave will be dwarfed by the new home construction and come to resemble "nothing more than a yard ornament."[74] And so the battle over the memory of the pre-atomic citizens and John Hendrix, the man chosen as their representative, continues, as does the struggle over land rights and the historical weight of the past.

CHAPTER TWO

Brahms and Bombs
on the Atomic Frontier

*To the frontier the American intellect owes its striking characteristics.
That coarseness and strength combined with acuteness and
inquisitiveness; that practical, inventive turn of mind, quick to find
expedients; that masterful grasp of material things, lacking in the artistic
but powerful to effect great ends; that restless, nervous energy; that
dominant individualism, working for good and for evil; and withal,
that buoyancy and exuberance which comes with freedom
—these are traits of the frontier, or traits called out elsewhere
because of the existence of the frontier.*
—Frederick Jackson Turner,
"The Significance of the Frontier in American History"

*You definitely decide that Oak Ridge is the most
cosmopolitan spot in the world.*
—Theodore Rockwell,
"Frontier Life among the Atom Splitters"

Despite the fact that Oak Ridge was built at a furious pace for an urgent war project and was meant to be invisible, great care was taken with the design of the city and the organization of community activities. Oak Ridge was socially engineered as an atomic utopia, an atomic Levittown before Levittown.[1] On its way to ideal living, there are two interlocking tropes that are primarily used to describe the city's early construction and design: the frontier and utopia.[2] In Oak Ridge, the frontier and utopian imaginations do not compete so much as nestle alongside and within each other. Of course, these imaginations are not unique to the former secret atomic city of Oak Ridge but characteristic of other regional and national myths as well. What is unique is how these common tropes are used to tell the story of a particular city at the emergence of the Atomic Age.

The Atomic Frontier

Frederick Jackson Turner argued that America's collective identity was wrapped in the collective imagination of the frontier, the moving line that brought new experiences and new challenges to a growing nation. He worried that when the frontier was dissipated, there would be something intrinsic to the American character that would be irrevocably lost. When he was young, this same anxiety plagued General Leslie Groves, the military director of the Manhattan Project, but after the first test of an atomic bomb in the desert of New Mexico in July 1945, his fears were alleviated. Groves wrote in his memoir, "When I was a boy, I lived with my father at a number of the Army posts that had sprung up during the Indian wars throughout the western United States. There I came to know many of the old soldiers and scouts who had devoted their active lives to winning the West. And as I listened to the stories of their deeds, I grew somewhat dismayed, wondering what was left for me to do now that the West was won. I am sure that many others of my generation shared this feeling. Yet those of us who saw the dawn of the Atomic Age that early morning at Alamogordo will never hold such doubts again."[3] On the one hand, Groves's words illustrate that Turner need not have worried; the frontier is always being reinvented, and when imagination fails, the frontier is remembered, nostalgically. Yet, on the other hand, Turner linked the frontier to American individualism and democratic pursuits, not to secret war projects where citizens would live tightly monitored and restricted lives under military control.

Whether critical or unquestioning, nostalgic expression of the past always involves a multi-chronic experience of time. To feel nostalgic, time must be experienced in at least two temporal zones simultaneously: the actual time situated in "the now," and the past time, which you remember and long for, "the then." The now, as Walter Benjamin theorized, is the "actual site of history."[4] As the atomic pioneers tell their stories of the past, they (re)create their identity in the present. When describing these dual and dueling temporalities, Oak Ridgers use both circular and linear narratives. They are regenerated through a circular narrative as the latest version of a national pioneering tradition, creating a "symbolic continuity" with the traditional American pioneer myth.[5] In the second sense, wartime Oak Ridgers are the products of a linear progressive narrative, which creates an entirely new type of pioneer, a member of the vanguard in the realms of science, engineering, and nuclear weapons technology. Thus, by employing this line of thinking and storytelling, the Oak Ridgers are able to see themselves as pioneers, to emerge trailblazing, as products of social regeneration and as products of cultural and scientific evolution.

Just as the geography of the frontier is kinetic, so is nostalgia for each new frontier that is traversed, transformed, and settled or abandoned. Oak Ridgers describe themselves as pioneers, as striking out in uncharted territory, but in one obvious sense this is difficult to do when established communities had already existed in the geographical space they "settled." Theodore Roosevelt's cocky and assured notion of the "Winning of the West" in the eighteenth century functioned in a similar way, by imagining the American Indians as sparsely present, roving in the lands white settlers wished to take for their own.[6] By the mid-twentieth century this colonist view had become exposed and unusable as metaphor and framing device, especially in a space once inhabited by the Cherokee people. As a way around this problem of history and representation, Oak Ridge narratives stress a tradition of pioneering, of which the Atomic City is but the latest manifestation of an ever-evolving America that is a place of constant and dramatic change.[7] An example of this strategy can be seen in Martha Cardwell Sparrow's thesis: "The real pioneers of Anderson and Roane counties [the counties where Oak Ridge is situated] left the rural land which had been their ancestral home. A group of modern pioneers replaced them almost immediately. . . . Their settlement was to have its own share of hardships, as pioneer settlements generally do. The pioneer spirit which had been so much a part of the experience of the early settlers, *manifested itself anew*."[8] The real pioneers, according to Sparrow, were the Scots-Irish who settled the area, bringing their freckles, hill music, whiskey-making skills, and Protestant work ethic.[9]

When pioneering came to be seen not as a one-off but as tradition, a radical shift in the thinking about "progress" and space occurred. When there was no farther west to go, the idea of the frontier resurfaced, often in the same places it had been imagined historically, but the new imagination of the frontier was linked to technological and scientific development and was no longer primarily a spatial project. At the end of World War II the American concept of the frontier became even more expansive. Vannevar Bush, the director of the Office of Scientific Research and Development, went so far as to declare Science as "the endless frontier."[10]

This change in the perception of the frontier alters both the spatial aspect of pioneering and destabilizes linear temporal notions of the concept. The frontier is not only something that occurred in the distant past; the frontier is also a modern condition. In a collection of essays written by early Oak Ridgers, poet and professor of languages James Wayne Miller argues this position explicitly: "The 'frontier' and 'pioneer' situations we associate with settlement and pre-settlement in the United States are not old-fashioned situations, but the result of modern thinking. Frontiers are created by modern ideas and attitudes. The frontier experience is not only a modern experience, but is now itself a tradition. Oak Ridge is a part of that tradition of the frontier experience in America."[11] Miller's point that the frontier is always already modern is an important intervention in shaking off the sepia-toned imagination of the pioneering process.

An echo can be found in the words of the poet Gellete Burgess, who writes of the modern pioneer living in a time made queer through change and technological speed: "In addition to gaining all this experience that trained the pioneers of old, [the new pioneer] has, while living at the confines of civilization, kept in touch with the world, and has tasted the exhilarating flavor of the old and new in one mouthful. For, in this century, distance is swept away and no land is really isolate. The pioneer lives like a god above distinctions of time, at once in the past, the present and the future."[12]

The new pioneer is a product of old mythologies but also carries new potentials. Gone is the image of the Davy Crockett frontiersman with a raccoon hat and moccasins; in is the image of the nuclear physicist, like J. Robert Oppenheimer, a new type of twentieth-century frontiersman (although occasionally with "Western" aesthetics), but this time positioned in front of a chalkboard of equations rather than a row of buffalo hides. Yet, unlike Crockett, as all good southern children know from singing "The Ballad of Davy Crockett," the majority of the new atomic pioneers were not "born on a mountaintop in Tennessee, the greenest state in the land of the free," but relocated there for the Manhattan Project.

The major frontier imagery that emerges from Oak Ridgers' descriptions of the city's early days is of pine boardwalks and red clay mud. Even with the breakneck speed of the construction crews, it took awhile for the city to fully develop, lending some credence to the frontier aesthetics of Oak Ridgers' collective memory. Before roads were built, pine boards were the city's major passageways: "Boardwalks are the subways, streetcars and taxi system of Oak Ridge. They drift for miles through the woods, without touching or spoiling them, like an abstract plane intersecting an abstract plane, an abstract surface in geometrical text."[13] The viscous East Tennessee red clay mud also finds its way into nearly every early Oak Ridgers' recollections. As an example, here is a poem by an atomic worker at the x-10 factory; the poet's name has been lost in the shuffle of time:

> In order not to check in late,
> I've had to lose a lot of weight,
> From swimming through a fair-sized flood
> And wading through the goddam mud.
> I've lost my rubbers and my shoes
> Perpetually I have the blues
> My spirits tumble with a thud
> Because of all the goddam mud.
> It's in my system so that when
> I cut my finger now and then
> Instead of bleeding just plain blood
> Out pours a stream of goddam mud.[14]

Other Oak Ridgers remember carrying ladies dangling high heels across the mud, wearing yellow knee-high rubbers to tamp down the unruly muck, and helping fellow pioneers who got stuck push their cars through the stubborn substance. Life on the edge of the Atomic Age was muddy, dusty, and hectic. Workers sometimes complained about dust swirling around, getting stuck in their lungs and causing respiratory problems, leading to the diagnosis of a new condition—the Oak Ridge croup.

The American pioneer experience once had a clear destination: the West. The Manhattan Project created a new version of pioneering by placing atomic trailblazers in one of three key destinations, two in the West, one in the East. After 1945, with the benefit of hindsight, the connection of the frontier imagination with modern sensibilities allowed for an imagined American atomic landscape that was cosmopolitan and sophisticated, yet at the same time dangerous and uncertain. Over time, the idea of national progress gallops across the land, rears up, and doubles back; notions of time and space are scrambled and reordered, allowing for multiple readings of the frontier.

Atomic Utopia

In addition to the new atomic frontier, the history of Oak Ridge is also told as the history of utopia achieved.[15] Utopia, like ideology or culture, is a word with multiple, even contradictory meanings, making it notoriously hard to define. As its etymology shows, this confusion was built into the term from the very beginning, when in 1516 Thomas More deliberately

Seal of the City of Oak Ridge

called his ideal country "utopia," meaning "good place" and/or "no place." Despite its nebulousness, the term had legs. Nearly five centuries later the concept of utopia is still used to describe human attempts to reach perfection through social organization.

The twentieth century is rife with varied utopian attempts: religious communities, hippie communes, feminist collectives, lesbian separatist sects, Soviet worker towns, and scientific and technologically focused ideal communities, just to name a few. Oak Ridge falls into this last category but carries its own peculiarities, as all utopias do. Many Oak Ridgers are deeply committed to the idea that their city is the perfect combination of a pastoral and urban utopian landscape birthed by science, a magic geography where the plan was destined to come into being at the necessary moment, as Hendrix had predicted. The Icelandic artist Björk captures the utopian logic at the heart of magic geography when she sings in "Modern Things," "All the modern things, like cars and such have always existed. They've just been waiting in a mountain for the right moment" to emerge and "take over." The seal of the city of Oak Ridge illustrates this action, where an atom with an acorn heart is emerging from within the handsome purple ridgeline animating the landscape.

After the war, the notion of Oak Ridge as the capital of a new Atomic Appalachia, a place fulfilling its atomic manifest destiny as predicted by its own prophet, makes for a strong utopian foundation. But this idea and the need for effort to bring it to fruition have been intrinsic to the formation of the Oak Ridge community, at least in part, from the beginning. The town manager, Captain Samuel S. Baxter of the Corps of Engineers, indicated as much in the second edition of the community's newspaper on September

11, 1943: "Rather than ponder on what may seem hardships, it would be well to wonder at the skills and hard work which have carved the beginnings of a town out of virgin hillside. Let us all pull one way with our thoughts and labor. The magical result from such concerted effort will amaze everyone."[16] In celebration of Oak Ridge's bucolic setting, the community has been described by a variety of utopian monikers. At one point the suggested name for the city was Shangri-La, after the fictional paradise located in a mystical valley that is isolated and protected from mankind, specifically from warfare.[17] Ironically, it was the wartime Manhattan Project that destroyed the pastoral land that existed before the atomic factories were built. "Having now reached the far shore of the twentieth century and portaged into the grainy noir of the twenty-first," writes Peter C. van Wyck, "nature is no longer where or what we thought it was. And perhaps it is not there at all."[18] The atomic prophecy warned this transformation was coming—magic geography made it so.

The utopian history of the United States is dominated by religious enclaves, transcendental communities, and the counter-cultural communes of the 1960s and 1970s, places such as the Oneida Community, Brook Farm, and Drop City.[19] These utopias existed outside of the dominant American culture, either by actively resisting the state or by choosing to live independent lives alongside the prevailing sociopolitical apparatuses of federal, state, and local governments. Oak Ridge marks a distinct break with this tradition in American utopianism in that it was actually established by the federal government. Residents of Oak Ridge were not seeking an alternative from mainstream American culture; in fact, the city was originally a place of heightened patriotism dedicated to the Allied cause of World War II and ever since has been a site of national nuclear optimism. In *The Last Reunion*, early Oak Ridger Jay Searcy sums up this sentiment: "There was a time when America was a team, when the free world had the tremors and looked to us for help. There was a time when we made sacrifices without complaint, supported our president without question and honored the standards of decency. There was a time of American patriotism and pride, of hope and love and humanity. It was World War II and the nation was one. . . . In Oak Ridge thousands upon thousands of everyday Americans . . . joined hands as strangers in a near classless society and secretly pulled off the greatest scientific experiment in history. . . . We have never let go."[20] As Searcy's enthusiastic prose shows, Oak Ridgers sought not to smash the dominant American value system or to skirt the cultural norms, but to celebrate and defend them. During the war, the folks of the Secret City lived in a fast-paced, muddy, cosmopolitan environment full of mystery and meaning. They knew they were working to win the war; most of them just did not know how. It was a place where simply leaving the house carried a sense of adventure. There was no telling who you might meet or what you might see. The war had shaken up social ties, allowing for new freedoms and possibilities, paradoxically in a secret place where folks were watched carefully and where so much could not be said.

Writing in 1968, the anthropologist Margaret Mead recognized that what she found in the small city of Tennessee was a new type of living arrangement, not yet seen in the United States, a new variety of utopia, the first scientific community. In her essay "The Crucial Role of the Small City in Meeting the Urban Crisis," she wrote, "The segregation of those with special interests is an old tradition in the United States in the form of communities of the religiously dedicated, communities of artists, communities in which the political Utopians have experimented. But the community of scientists and technicians specifically, concerned with such problems as the development of atomic energy, the instrumental bases of automation, the space sciences, is new—only as old as Oak Ridge, Tennessee."[21]

The quest for utopia has been an American tradition, one that has often taken place on the "frontier" or at least at the edge of what has been considered by some as "civilization." Sociologist John Hannigan describes the quest for utopia in *Fantasy City*: "Pioneers head out of the cities in order to create a new Eden on the physical edge of the landscape (the frontier). Here they would forge a new restorative synthesis by merging the best features of both urban and rural living: the machine and the garden."[22] While nature was a focus and prime feature of the utopian vision of Oak Ridge, it was not the back-to-nature sensibility found in many utopian communities; instead, it was a view of the natural world in awe of and in the service of science.

Despite the restrictions placed on residents, including the inability to talk about their jobs, security checks at city gates, and the possibility that whomever you socialized with could be a government informer, many people describe this period of life in the Atomic City as idyllic. As long as Oak Ridge remained "the city behind the fence," many of its residents saw it as utopian, an island of culture, prestige, and intelligence tucked away from the surrounding communities and the outside world. Oak Ridge was an ideal city where unemployment was nonexistent, where the school system set up by educators from Columbia University was far above the national average, and where universal health care provided the most advanced medical services available. Meanwhile, a free bus system crisscrossed the city, taking residents not only to work but also to the plethora of cultural opportunities available at nearly all hours, from theatrical performances to dances to organized sports leagues. Oak Ridge was a place where you could work on the vital stuff for the first atomic bomb during the week, swim in the largest swimming pool in the South on Sunday, and then towel off to attend a performance by the Oak Ridge Symphony Orchestra later that evening. "We were so special," says my mom; "It was a super time, a super place," says my uncle; Jay Searcy says it was like growing up in a "magic kingdom."[23]

In this special atomic enclave, residential, occupational, and commercial structures were designed from the top down by the military or federally employed private enterprise. Beyond design, the Army also ran the city with everyday services outsourced to the Roane Anderson Company (named for the neighboring counties), which operated as an agent of the federal government. The Army had complete control over housing, medical care, and recreation, as well as the authority to approve or deny proposals for commercial businesses. Federal money to run the high-tech labs also flowed into the community, allowing Oak Ridgers to enjoy a higher standard of living than their neighbors.

While it would have been easy for the Army to produce Oak Ridge on the model of a military base, they instead opted for a design they hoped would be more pleasing to civilians. The architectural firm of Skidmore, Owings, and Merrill (SOM), with offices in New York and Chicago, was called in to create an ideal American community. SOM was not the government's first choice. Initially, the Boston engineering corporation of Stone & Webster was given the task. The plan they designed turned out to be so dull and uninspiring that the contract was passed on to the ambitious upstarts—SOM.[24] This shift illustrates that speed alone was not the sole consideration of the Project, at least not at the beginning, but that community development was also in the minds of the planners and managers.

In the interest of secrecy, the architects and engineers of SOM were not initially given direct access to the site and were only shown aerial photographs of the topography. They were told to design for a population of 3,000, which at the time was the estimate of the number of workers needed to complete the assignment. It soon became clear that a huge labor force would be necessary to complete the task at hand. Hiring enough workers was a challenge during wartime with competing war industries at home and much of the workforce fighting overseas.[25] Manhattan Project leaders knew that in order to recruit workers they would have to offer more than just high wages. Influenced by the Garden City Movement, the Secret City was planned with an immense greenbelt and parks surrounding every neighborhood.[26] Echoing the ethos of the American architect and utopian Frank Lloyd Wright, the architect in charge of the Oak Ridge project, Ambrose Richardson, insisted that "a building cannot be better than the setting that it is in."[27] Meanwhile, Owings envisioned Oak Ridge as a tabula rasa, "a kind of clean and uncluttered, uncommitted area with nothing to stand in the way of an ideal plan."[28] At the beginning there was not a lot of time spent on what Leo Marx would call pastoralism: sentimentalizing the life and culture of the valley as it existed before its atomic industrialization would not come until much later.[29] Thinking about the area as a kind of nowhere space, a sparse nook ready for development, was characteristic of the Manhattan Project's design in Oak Ridge.[30]

Once the Project started spinning, though, the valley was peopled with quickness. The initial calculation of 3,000 workers was proven drastically inadequate, and by the end of the war the population of Oak Ridge reached 75,000. No matter how large the city grew, the idea was always to keep the scientists and skilled workers happy enough to be productive. With this in mind, the architects created "a plan not for any city but for a particular city, a city located at a particular point in the United States for good reason and a city living a particular sort of life because of its location and the reasons behind it . . . planned as a place of good living for people who are depended upon to do good work. . . . For that reason the physical facilities that serve the people of Oak Ridge cannot be reduced to a few standard categories designed for the average man and his average likes and dislikes."[31] The city plan and housing schemata were designed most of all to appeal to the elites of the Project, those with intellectual and aesthetic tastes that were deemed above average.

Atomic Domiciles

The crown jewels of the community housing landscape were the single-family homes. These homes were called "Cemestos" because they were constructed with a new building material made from cement and asbestos sandwiched together.[32] Cemestos came in five variations, each distinguished alphabetically: A, B, C, D, and F. The A's were the smallest and the F's the largest. Each home came equipped with floor-to-ceiling bookcases, a fireplace, and a porch. These flourishes were considered mostly aesthetic and psychological; they were features that would appeal to the scientists and engineers that the Project wished to attract. The wife of a physicist at the x-10 lab, who felt comfortably at home in a Cemesto B, remarked, "I was especially intrigued with the fireplace, surrounded by red brick in the spacious living room."[33] Care was taken even with the smallest design detail, and the rooms would not have looked out of place in a Bauhaus catalog or, as one resident suggested, "a plan . . . such as you might see in the Museum of Modern Art."[34] In Oak Ridge, modern atomic design was forward thinking with respect to material choices and furniture construction but maintained the status quo in following the segregated interior design practices of the region—the largest Cemestos came with separate living quarters for black maids.[35]

The Cemestos went to the most valued employees, including scientists and high-level military personnel; prefabricated wooden homes (or "prefabs," as they were called) went to mid-level employees. And when housing needs outpaced production, the Tennessee Valley Authority came to the rescue with more prefabricated houses, referred to as "TVAs" or "flattops" because of their box-like appearance. The prefab homes were churned out with fordist proficiency; "one of these dwelling units could be assembled and ready for occupancy in about eight hours."[36] Although they were thrown together quickly, they had been designed well, one resident remembered: "When I think about the tiny appearance of the house from the outside and the spaciousness inside, I sing the praises of the genius who designed the flattop."[37]

In addition, there were dormitories for all levels of unmarried workers, and trailers, sometimes called "victory cottages," were used as temporary homes while workers were placed on a waiting list for prefabs or if they were in town on a temporary job. The trailers had electricity, but workers had to use communal outhouses. Lastly, there were the barely livable hutments for the black and unskilled white laborers. The hutments were dirty, crowded, and by all accounts unpleasant quarters with substandard cafeterias and bathhouses. Most hutments were outfitted with only an oil stove in the center of the floor and four or five single beds. Better hutments might also have steel lockers, dressers, and chairs, but one couldn't count on such luxuries. Each unit was designed to house four workers, although it was not uncommon to find five or even six crammed into the tiny space. The rent was six dollars per occupant, no matter how many persons were sardined therein.

In contrast to the hutments, in the dormitories care was taken to make the living environments aesthetically pleasing. Early Oak Ridger and city historian Bill Wilcox remembers: "The furniture was of simple, modernistic design and very functional, most of it maple."[38] Beyond design, dormitories provided camaraderie for the young single workers of Oak Ridge, but they were not without their unpleasantries. Dorms were overcrowded and loud, and residents were often subject to theft.[39] Early Oak Ridger Bettie Levy remarked, "It looked as if beer parties and pie throwing had gone on in a room they gave me. It was not inspiring. . . . It was primitive, like a summer camp that had been inhabited by degenerates."[40] At least structurally, the women's dormitories resembled the college dormitories of that time: each residence had a housemother on duty, and men were not allowed in ladies' rooms. A dating parlor was located on the ground floor where suitors could pick up their dates, chat, and sometimes dance. There were also reports of "an occasional homosexual gang."[41] But downstairs, in the parlor out in the open, it was mostly a heterosexual affair, with spaces crowded with men looking for dates—in the early days of Oak Ridge, men outnumbered women twenty to one.

Some single workers had more luck in the housing lottery and were able to share homes. One such lucky resident, Earline Banic, who worked for a spell in a chemistry lab, fondly remembered sharing a house with five other single women during the Manhattan Project, but only after she was able to convince the housing authorities that the dormitories were too wild for "a little Southern girl like me." The scene she described seemed to have her residing on an almost feral edge, as if the young women she lived with when she first moved to Oak Ridge had escaped from domestication and become wild in the Tennessee foothills. Even in the shared house, Earline recalled lots of courting, lots of dancing, and a high turnover rate for roommates: "When one of the girls would marry and move out, another girl would move in."[42] By the time Banic herself had married, she was the thirteenth resident in that D house on Venus Road.

From the beginning, Oak Ridge was intended by the planners to be a community with distinct neighborhoods.[43] While houses were uniform in their construction, streets were mapped out in undulating lines that matched the shape of the topography, where the "location of each house was a specialized operation, since many units had to be turned a few degrees to fit on ridge shoulders."[44] This was partially an aesthetic decision, but mostly because clearing and evening out the land would have taken unnecessary time, time that could have been spent producing materials for the Bomb.

In the early days of Oak Ridge, the city was in a frenzied state of construction, where roads and homes nonexistent in the morning would appear fully formed in the evening. One resident remembered a city official telling her that they did not intend to build a road in front of her home; that afternoon she called the town manager: "That road you weren't going to build—well, they're driving on it now."[45] Another resident remembered that because of the vertigo of constant change, "parents often marked their Monopoly-like houses with colored ribbons or some marker so their children would know where to get off the bus."[46] Despite the need to build the city as quickly as possible, neighborhoods for mid- and upper-level employees were designed with care, each with its own park, shopping center, and elementary school.

On the other side of the city, the trailer communities, which housed mostly construction workers and other blue-collar laborers, also had their own neighborhoods, but they had quite a different flavor from those created for single-family homes. Helen Jernigan, a resident of the Happy Valley trailer community, remembers: "There were no nights there. There were bright spotlights and loudspeakers on high poles. The music played all night, the lights illuminated everything all night, and there was activity all night. The cafeterias never closed. It was an adventuresome place, a boom town."[47]

In addition to the cafeterias, a food cart would sometimes roll through, offering a chance to grab a quick bite. With its own stores, entertainment, and housing, the trailer area was so self-contained that Colleen Black, a worker at the K-25 said, "Some people in Happy Valley didn't even know about Oak Ridge," referring to the main townsite area.[48] Happy Valley even boasted its own U.S. post office, named Trailer City Branch, and its own amusement park, Coney Island. With the wooden boardwalks and raucous crowds, if you closed your eyes it might have sounded and felt a lot like its namesake in Brooklyn, only with the hum of atomic factories instead of crashing waves as a sonic backdrop.

Helen Jernigan worked as a bookkeeper for Coney Island, which had "games and basketball hoops like a carnival . . . like an arcade where you shop for things and you got prizes, and the prizes were mostly cigarettes," although she went on to add, "We had some prizes besides the cigarettes. We had these little figurines that glowed in the dark."[49] The lucent prizes from the 1940s Secret City amusement park were not unlike items in contemporary atomic souvenir shops, which nearly always contain some glow-in-the-dark goods. Helen Jernigan has written about her experiences working at the Coney Island amusement area in Happy Valley in the collected volume *These Are Our Voices*, edited by James Overholt. In an oral history recorded later, Jernigan explains that Overholt took out her account of the glowing toys because "he thought there was something spooky and irradiated about those."[50] And there was. After the fact, as a ragpicker of history, I have put them back in here.

In Oak Ridge, recreation was one thing, but finding housing for the ever-increasing flow of workers was quite another and proved to be a constant problem for the Project. Neighboring towns were overrun, guesthouses doubled up, homeowners took in boarders, and tent cities sprouted outside the fence. Of all the creative planning and lodging schemes, the Louisville & Nashville Railroad Company contrived one of the most inventive housing solutions. Since there were no accommodations available in town for the railroad people, the L&N simply extended a railroad spur just past the gates and set up boxcar apartments. There was one boxcar issued per family, and people became very creative with the tiny spaces—there were closets, bedrooms, and kitchens, but no indoor plumbing. Those who lived in the boxcar apartments were typically clerks and operators, but even members from upper management experienced this unique living situation.[51] It was a kind of hobo chic. Each type of housing in the Secret City was placed in its own "neighborhood" and had its own community; the result was class and racial segregation. Utopian planning in Oak Ridge stretched only so far.

Snob Hill

Accounts of early history by Oak Ridgers reveal a tension between the collective memory of elitism and the collective memory of social equality. Oak Ridgers tend to focus on the city as a social leveler. For example, in her memoir *Oak Ridge and Me*, Joanne Gailar describes Oak Ridge as a place where individuals could be judged not on their past or wealth, but on their own merits.[52] Others remember a similar situation where "everyone lived in the same types of homes," where "the drab sameness of government housing blurred class differences" and "even if you had money, you couldn't show it."[53] More accurately, if you had money, you could not show it in the same ways as you could in places "outside the fence." You could not, for example, build a gigantic house exactly to your specificities or brag about the promotion you received at the office. Dick Smyser, the former editor of the *Oak Ridger*, the city's newspaper, recalled, "We used to say we were totally 'class-unconscious.' Some people say, as we philosophize now, that was really never true. Maybe we were not so economically class conscious, but there always has been, to some extent, an education class consciousness."[54] Class, of course, is not just about wealth.

The city, new as it was and dedicated to its single purpose, did not have prominent businessmen, landed gentry, or other professional classes that usually occupy the upper echelons of society. Yet Oak Ridge was class-conscious, but in a different way from most cities. Those at the top of the social hierarchy were the scientists, followed by engineers and the highest-ranking Army officials. When they tell stories of their past, inequalities are revealed. As one early resident remarked, "For once the scientists, most of them former professors and commonly called eggheads, were the privileged and highest paid members of the community!"[55] This was a place you could "live very well if you belong."[56] Physicists and their wives tended to hang out together, and the same with engineers, GIs, and on down the social ladder—groups were diverse only in terms of geographical origin. An engineer's wife recalled that although "[we] came from all over the United States (Illinois, Georgia, Louisiana, New York, Massachusetts, Pennsylvania, Ohio, California), we still formed what the sociologist would call an in-group, because we had so much in common."[57]

In families, the societal position was in almost all cases dictated by the occupational position of the eldest male member of the household. One Oak Ridger remarked, "One of the first questions people ask you here is 'What does your husband do?'"[58] Although, many women worked on the Project, in the earliest days there were few female scientists, engineers, or military officers. In fact, to indicate social status wives often referred to their husband's profession—"So, I am a physicist," declared one housewife.[59]

There were some tells regarding wealth and class, of course, the most conspicuous having to do with housing. The quality and size of your house and your neighborhood placement gestured toward your importance to the Project, which was often in direct correlation to your social status. Social hierarchy and housing also went hand in hand in Los Alamos, where the most desirable dwellings were clustered in an area called "Bathtub Row," appropriately enough because those were the only homes equipped with a bathtub. The most important were allowed a deep soak in a cast iron tub; the rest had to make do with a shower alone.

In Oak Ridge, there was a distinct social line drawn between those living in "permanent" Cemesto-style homes and those in the more temporary dwellings, the victory cottages and hutments. For example, a neighborhood with some of the best housing and prime views was called Knob Hill, but locally was referred to as "Snob Hill" or "Brain Alley." It was a neighborhood where many world-renowned physicists lived, including the Nobel Prize winner Eugene Wigner. Writing to her friend Margaret Mead, Thelma Present wrote of Knob Hill as a "little Westchester," where "I imagine one can easily forget any of the unpleasant aspects here—such as the Hooverville aspect, segregation, Army control—because you can become absorbed in your own social circle and be quite isolated from general life here."[60] In Oak Ridge there were various rings of segregation and isolation—a barbed wire fence demarcated the city, more fences surrounded the atomic factories, and family neighborhoods were offset from workers' hutments and trailer communities.

The tension around housing assignments created the largest social and cultural schisms in the city. Writing in 1947 in the *New York Times Magazine*, a journalist described the jockeying for Manhattan Project housing as "a spirited social rivalry among the citizens of Oak Ridge and a never-ending headache for its harassed housing officials."[61] Twenty years later in a speech to the East Tennessee Historical Society, A. K. Bissell, an early Oak Ridge resident and former city mayor, channeling George Orwell, admitted, "Although all operating people were equal, some were more equal than others. It soon developed that rank had its privileges and its influence."[62] While on the surface it appeared as if everyone was granted housing equally, certain rules were bent for the people at the top of the military, scientific, or managerial levels. Echoing this sentiment, an Army lieutenant interviewed by the *New Yorker* in September 1945 stressed, "All we wanted to do was take care of the longhairs [the scientists]. You can't expect a high-powered scientific joe . . . to sleep with ants."[63]

Those who mattered most to the Project were catered to, while those who were viewed as more expendable had much rougher living conditions. The poor conditions of the hutments are still downplayed, as a recent book of historic Manhattan Project photographs illustrates. Under a photograph of several hutments a caption reads, "There were few complaints among workers about living conditions at the facilities. Everyone understood the demands of the war effort and simply took everything in stride."[64] Some strides were easier to take. In other words, life on Knob Hill was another world from life in the hutments.

Bowling for Uranium

In 1943, the Recreation and Welfare Association (RWA) was formed to organize social events and activities, to build a sense of community, and to combat anomie, which it was feared would lead to absenteeism or, worse, resignation. The RWA was run by civilians, but like all organizations in Oak Ridge it was overseen by the military, which had to approve all new clubs and official group gatherings. Work in Oak Ridge could be monotonous, and with nearly all workers ignorant of their jobs, and even of the knowledge of what amounted to doing a job well, morale could be a problem. The idea behind the RWA was to provide wholesome and stimulating activities that would keep workers of all stripes happy enough to be productive. The RWA sought to combat malaise with sporting leagues, cultural clubs, and dances.

Y-12 security guard Willie "Little Red" Honeycutt wrote "Atomic City Boogie" in the late 1940s and recorded it in 1952:

ATOMIC CITY BOOGIE

You can talk about your boogie, well now listen to me
I'll tell you 'bout a place down in East Tennessee
Just a little Secret City hid among the trees
They do The Atomic City Boogie from their head to their knees
It's down in Oak Ridge where the moon shines bright
Everyone's a neighbor and they have no fights
Just a Secret City hidden out of sight
They do The Atomic City Boogie every Saturday night.
Boom-boom Boogie every Saturday night!
Everybody boogies to an old guitar
And they get their atoms from an old fruit jar
When that bass fiddle's ringing out a tune,
They do The Atomic City Boogie in the light of the moon.
Boom-boom Boogie in the light of the moon!
Now if you like to boogie and you think you're too old
Go down to Oak Ridge where the atoms grow
Just drink you some atoms from an old fruit jar
And you'll be doin' that Boogie eight to the bar
Everybody there is so happy and gay
They all look forward to the old pay day
When they can go out on a Saturday night
And do The Atomic City Boogie 'til the broad daylight.
Swayin' in the morning, boogyin' at night
In the little Secret City hidden out of sight.

From 1943 to 1945, factories operated twenty-four hours a day, and it was not rare for Oak Ridgers of all occupations to work eighty hours a week. Even with all the hours put in on the job, the hard-working atomic citizens did manage to get out on the town. There was dancing somewhere every night, often on tennis courts, moonlight cruises on the lake, bowling leagues, croquet tournaments, chess and checkers clubs, an orchid club, seven movie theaters, a symphony orchestra, an all-girl orchestra, a playhouse, an officer's wives club, a music listener's club, plus various athletic teams including baseball, basketball, softball, touch football, roller hockey, boxing, and much more.

During the war, none of these clubs could be affiliated with national organizations, so as to keep anyone from guessing the number of inhabitants in the Secret City. Thus, while the leisure activities did not connect Oak Ridgers to the outside world, the teams and social clubs succeeded in creating nodes of interaction for those who came to work on the Manhattan Project from various areas of the country. My grandmother still talks about her bowling league highs and lows, over seventy years later.

While class division within leisure practices was not strictly enforced and most clubs were advertised in the local paper, which was delivered to every doorstep free of charge, opportunities for recreation were formed around communities, and thus social clubs rarely cut across occupational levels and socioeconomic lines. For example, it would not be likely to find a nuclear physicist dancing in the trailer community on a Saturday night, as it would be equally unlikely to find a construction worker from the hutments at a rehearsal for the musical group the Rhythm Engineers.

One of the few places that it was possible to find a cross-section of the (white) population of Oak Ridge was at one of the many religious services that took place at the Chapel-on-the-Hill.[65] In early Oak Ridge, there were no formal religious institutions, so each denomination took turns holding their services at different hours in the shared building. It is often said that there was only one official church in Oak Ridge, the Chapel-on-the-Hill, but there were actually two; the other was located in the black community and was off-limits to the white workers.

All these activities going on twenty-four hours a day gave early Oak Ridgers, particularly young singles, the feeling that anything could happen. It is this sense of excitement and possibility that is reflected in the nostalgic storytelling of the city's beginnings. "Did you know that I took tennis lessons from a world famous physicist?" my mother asked me on more than one occasion. "Oh! We had all kinds of brains here," my grandmother liked to say. "You wouldn't believe it. We'd see 'em at the grocery store, at the pharmacy, playin' softball, wherever. I'm not sure I ever saw one that could beat me at bowlin', though."

Stories of "class unconsciousness," as the former mayor defined the term, coexist with stories of pride in the elitism of certain social circles. Other accounts reveal distinct efforts to set up a community where high culture would be readily available. In 1943, as the community was developing, Atomic City librarian Elizabeth Edwards wrote in the local newspaper of the collection's growing pains: "Has our face been red when for almost six weeks we had to admit 'No Shakespeare!' Thus there has been as much rejoicing over the arrival of the 'Comedies,' the 'Tragedies,' and the 'Histories.' "[66] James Wayne Miller remembers, "[Despite] living under the frontier conditions of mud, crowds, and shortages, many Oak Ridgers still considered themselves the guardians of culture," an atmosphere they nick-named "Brahms and bombs."[67] Other Oak Ridgers describe a "facade of uranium and privilege," a city with "the Mensa set's prodigal offspring," and a class of people referred to as the "nuclear bourgeoisie."[68] Media activist, Paper Tiger Television founder, and second-generation Oak Ridger DeeDee Halleck describes the place as an Army town where "many of the scientists were refugees from war-torn Europe, or MIT and Princeton postdocs who were accustomed to elite high culture. To help fill this cultural vacuum, my parents were part of a group that started a symphony orchestra. It wasn't hard to fill the second violin section. And there were probably more oboe players in Oak Ridge than in all of Eastern Tennessee at that time."[69]

The Oak Ridge Symphony Orchestra is credited to the biochemist and cellist Waldo Cohn, who formed the group in 1943 after being inspired by an advertisement in the *Oak Ridge Journal* calling for musicians to get together. Initially, the group was made up of anyone who showed up, but very quickly it became clear that a great number of the attendees had been classically trained and could play at a very high level. Once they figured this out the group became more selective. Oak Ridgers, when given the chance, tend to gravitate toward the celebration of their ideas of excellence above activity for activity's sake.

Oak Ridge was a cosmopolitan place, with most of the scientists coming from metropolitan areas or university towns. While there was not much mingling of classes or races, the Atomic City was a place where those of different cultures and ethnic backgrounds socialized, as they would have in New York City or on the campuses of the University of Chicago or the University of California at Berkeley. If Oak Ridge was a utopian community, it was one without social, racial, and economic equality.

Atomic Shangri-La Was Not for Everyone

Despite the nostalgic narrative that many Oak Ridge residents share of social harmony and a city free of social class, it was not an atomic Shangri-La for everyone. Racial division of leisure, for example, was practiced with vigilance. "It's common for someone who's lived in the city for years to get misty-eyed when reminiscing about the old days of Oak Ridge—when everything was mud and great pains were taken to maintain security," writes journalist Libby Morse.[70] She goes on to illustrate how this wet-eyed response is not universally shared by all citizens of the city and that especially for many black Manhattan Project workers, "there just doesn't seem to be much to get nostalgic about."[71]

While the dominant view depicted in mid-twentieth-century accounts of Oak Ridge during the Manhattan Project era is overwhelmingly positive and nostalgic, there were dissenting voices, especially from outside the city. As part of a 1945–46 series of articles for the *Chicago Defender*, journalist Enoc Waters penned a scathing report of the Atomic City's treatment of the black population: "Oak Ridge is the first community I have ever seen with slums that were deliberately planned. The concept back of the planning and operation of this small city is as backward sociologically as the atomic bomb is scientifically advanced."[72] Inequality could be found most sharply with respect to housing. White workers could expect to move to better homes as they advanced in their careers, married, or had children; the same could not be said for Oak Ridge's black population. During the war, only hutment housing made of flimsy plywood was available for black workers.[73] While great care was taken to make the single-family homes and dormitories as pleasant as possible (with varying degrees of success), no appeal to beauty or creature comfort could be found in the construction of hutment neighborhoods. Waters, the best gadfly journalist for black workers in Oak Ridge, captured the contrast of spaces in the Atomic City: "Here, cloaked in mystery, inanimate gadgets of steel and glass are housed in concrete palaces where temperatures are controlled to a fraction of a degree but Negro workers must live in flimsy packing box structures set flush on the muddy earth. Here millions of dollars are marshaled to exploit atomic theory but not enough pennies can be corralled to provide for the welfare and comfort of a few thousand Negro workers."[74] If other Oak Ridge domiciles were the epitome of modernist design, examples of Le Corbusier's "machines for living," the hutments were of the most primitive sort of dwelling.

The hutment areas were divided along gender and racial lines into "neighborhoods," including the whimsically named Happy Valley and Gamble Valley. Oak Ridge's black workers lived in hutments under difficult conditions until 1950. And while unskilled white male workers also lived in hutments, they did so only until 1945. It should be noted that white women never lived in the rude dwellings, and what's more, they were not even allowed to set foot inside. After a visit to the site, the muckraking Waters referred to the hutment area as "a modernized Hooverville."[75] He went on: "During my overseas experience I saw army mess halls in the jungles of New Guinea much better than the cafeteria provided in the colored hutment area."[76]

Unlike for white couples, no housing was available for black couples in the early days of Oak Ridge.[77] As one worker remembered, "Couples had to slip and see each other when they could."[78] They had to create spaces for their love, spaces to be together, by poaching on the eros-blind territory of Project design. It wasn't easy. Black women lived in hutments in an area called "the pen," which carried a curfew of 10:00 PM and was surrounded by barbed wire, an electric fence, and armed guards "for the protection of the women."[79] It is not entirely clear just what or whom this militaristic stance was protecting the women from, although the assumption was that they were being protected from the black men housed in the adjacent hutment area.[80] Still, from time to time the workers found their way around the security measures to meet spouses or lovers.

On a visit to Oak Ridge in 1946, Waters found evidence of such practices: "Footprints on the ground and chairs leaning against the fence would suggest that the traffic from the men's to the women's area has not always been through the guarded gate which is the official entrance to the sacrosanct confines."[81] Like all pedestrians, as de Certeau tells us, "their story begins on ground level, with footsteps. They are myriad, but do not compose a series. They cannot be counted because each unit has a qualitative character. . . . Their intertwined paths give their shape to spaces. They weave places together."[82] The illicit character of these weavings added an element of danger and excitement if a meeting was successful, of frustration, resentment, and disappointment if it was not. When lovers' paths connected, a kind of third conjugal space for affection was created between and betwixt the hutments. In the secret cities of the Manhattan Project, many secret meetings took place. It is rumored that in Los Alamos lovers copulated clandestinely through the openings in the chain-link fence.

For black workers, sex—secret or otherwise—could produce additional challenges for life in Oak Ridge. Black children were not allowed on the federal reservation until 1945. And it has been reported that any black woman who was discovered to be pregnant lost her job and was escorted off the reservation to wait for a bus.[83] Meanwhile, the situation for white women was quite different. As one former Project worker reported, "Unexpected pregnancies did not keep most [white] women from their jobs. Thanks to meticulous planning, an untroubled birth, and a company grace period, a friend of mind successfully made it back to her demanding job within a few months."[84] In light of these conditions, most black families chose to live in Knoxville, twenty miles away, where there was adequate housing and also schools for their children to attend, but this also meant a more difficult commute to the job.[85]

In addition to the unpleasant living conditions, workers who resided in the hutments also had to deal with the stigmatization that came with their housing assignments. Rumors circulated wildly; it was said, for example, that in the hutments there was at least one homicide per day.[86] These numbers are impossible to verify because all the police records of that time were destroyed after the war. This may explain why these rumors persist. Even in fiction published recently, negative myths of the black hutment area proliferate. In *Bones of Betrayal*, a mystery authored by the writing team known as Jefferson Bass and set in Oak Ridge during the Manhattan Project era, a character goes to the black hutments to procure an illegal abortion.[87] The hutments are portrayed in Oak Ridge histories and memoirs as a breeding ground for unsavory and unlawful conduct, accounts of prostitution, dice games, knife fights, and even murderous religious cults abound.[88] When early Oak Ridgers nostalgically recall their atomic utopia, they leave out the part about the hutments.

The original design of the city did include an area with the working title "Negro Village," which included dormitories as well as fifty single-family homes, a cafeteria, a church, a school, and a knot of stores, but the plan was scrapped and officials ultimately decided to build another "white village" to house additional white workers.[89] Since housing was based on employment and black workers were systematically denied high-level job posts, Army officials could claim that there was a housing shortage for skilled workers and that black workers were simply given housing appropriate for their rank. Shamefully, it was also rumored that the black workers would not like or feel comfortable in the nicer housing.

Although black workers and white workers were paid the same wage for the same job, and sometimes worked side by side, at the end of their shifts they would head home to completely separate worlds. Valerie Steele remembers: "For the black person in Oak Ridge, segregation was total. Blacks lived day in and out under oppressive conditions. There were separate communities, cafeterias, recreational houses, churches, and water fountains, and blacks had to ride on the back of the buses and suffer other indignities like being served food at the bus station through a pigeon hole."[90] As evidence of the racial segregation of the community, one Oak Ridger recalled, "Most white townspeople were never aware of the blacks' living conditions. We saw them mostly in their workplace."[91] Another white resident refers to the traditionally black neighborhood of Scarboro by saying, "*Of course* we didn't know about Scarboro or any of that."[92]

Black citizens were invisible after work hours to most of the white population because they were often not permitted in the same leisure and consumption spaces. A concrete finisher who worked to pour the foundations for the mammoth atomic factories remembered that "there wasn't no place black folks could go for entertainment."[93] They were denied many of the best features of Oak Ridge, including high-paying jobs, top housing assignments, and access to the prime social and cultural spaces, such as libraries, movie theaters, the symphony, and the Olympic-size swimming pool, which was still wonderfully impressive in the 1980s when my grandmother took me there and when everyone, thankfully, was allowed to cannonball off the high dive, if they were brave enough. Sometimes I was, and sometimes I wasn't.

The deplorable situation for black workers in Oak Ridge parallels the highly stratified design found in many company towns. Historian J. D. Porteous sums up this point rather succinctly: "Whereas elsewhere the social segregation of housing has developed through a variety of socio-economic pressures, in the company town it was possible to impose ready-made ghettos from the beginning."[94] The deliberateness with which the slum-like hutment areas were preplanned belies both the nostalgic frontier and utopian imaginations of early Oak Ridge. Still, these historic imaginations persist for those who experienced the better sides of Atomic City living.

Atomic Nostalgia

At the end of World War II, the average Oak Ridger was twenty-seven years old. The fact that most residents were quite young when they were working on the Manhattan Project undoubtedly contributes to their nostalgia. Still, beyond youth, Oak Ridge was for many the culmination of the utopian and frontier imaginations, a place shaped by a feverish belief in the combined powers of science, technology, and nation. On top of this, the secrecy and specialness of the Manhattan Project added layers to the meaning Oak Ridgers applied to their work during and especially after the war.

While it could be assumed that the pioneer narrative was applied after the fact when Oak Ridgers think about the past, both residents and the military utilized the pioneer analogy during the war. Atomic workers were initially drawn from all corners of the United States and had little common history, but what they shared was an experience of the Manhattan Project and a well of American mythology to draw from. The frontier provided a perfect trope, an easily recognized scenario with which to communicate with each other about the unique experience of living and working in a rough-hewn secret city "in the middle of nowhere."[95] The military utilized the pioneer analogy as both a motivational strategy and as a way of cutting down on complaints from residents unaccustomed to or unhappy with the rustic conditions of the community.[96] The pioneer rhetoric of the early Oak

Ridgers and the military may have even worked as a pre-nostalgia narrative that residents internalized and drew upon after the war.

Despite its effectiveness as a metaphor, there were some aspects of Oak Ridge that are hard to reconcile with a frontier imagination: the vigilant state security apparatus, the advanced nuclear physics that was happening in the labs, the fact that the city was using one-sixth of the electricity of the entire country, that it contained the largest building in the world at the time, and that the fifth largest bus route in the nation circled on a twenty-four-hour schedule to accommodate shift workers. In addition, it is unlikely that in other frontier boomtowns residents were subject to a military intelligence background check before gaining employment, or that they were given frequent lie-detector tests, or that one in four adults was a government informant.

Oak Ridge, in the words of one writer, was a "raw and regimented city."[97] Yet it was a city. Other large-scale federal government projects that had been developed in the region had concentrated on building villages, such as the TVA dam communities of Norris, Wheeler, Pickwick, Fontana, and Watts Bar, but those places were more regionally focused and lacked the cosmopolitanism and sheer size of Oak Ridge.[98] Despite its initial rustic facade, no other frontier community in history could match the bureaucratization and organization that existed in Oak Ridge during the 1940s. In the Atomic City everyday life was engineered—living and working were compartmentalized, ordered, coded, and covert.

Many people loved it. Their love is expressed through their longing for bygone days and in the stories they relay. The telling of atomic nostalgia unfolds in layers. Oak Ridgers begin by describing an experience of wartime sacrifice; then they move to postwar pride and tell about the Bomb, often in low, serious tones. Then they talk of the speed and excitement of life, of the pressures of work, the release found in dancing, music, bowling, or social clubs; they go into details of how they met their husband or wife on the Project. The feeling of pride that Oak Ridgers experience is not a direct identification with the Bomb alone, but a sense of wonder about the Atomic City as a whole, a task-oriented community that worked as a machine with so many moving parts, engineered for a specific mission. The atomic workers were all caught up in the wheels and gears of this specialized and mechanized urbanity, like the Charlie Chaplin character in *Modern Times*; but unlike the singular tramp, together they felt the mash and pull-push of the machine together.

CHAPTER THREE

At Work in the Atomic Beehive

Worked in what looked like a rush and a rage. . . . Possessed with the
business, jamming it all into the days and nights.
—Walker Evans, "James Agee in 1936"

While it was theoretically feasible to produce an atomic bomb in the early 1940s, the creation of a large-scale sustained atomic production apparatus was still considered a gamble. So much so that the nuclear physicist Niels Bohr insisted that building an atomic bomb "can never be done unless you turn the United States into one huge factory."[1] With the Manhattan Project, the federal government initiated a process nearly along those lines, creating a system of *atomic fordism* that stretched across the country with the nation's major highways functioning as a conveyor belt of nuclear knowledge, nuclear secrets, and fissionable uranium and plutonium. Along this route, secret locations were built as the primary nodes of atomic production that worked with universities such as Columbia University, the University of Chicago, and the University of California at Berkeley. These sites engaged in an enormous scientific and industrial project larger than the Ford Corporation—in fact, larger than the entire U.S. automobile industry.[2]

In Henry Ford's 1923 autobiography, *My Life and Work*, the automaker cataloged the number of workers needed for the production of the Model T wherein each worker would complete one task. The full production required 7,882 distinct tasks; out of these, 949 required "strong, able-bodied, and practically physically perfect men. . . . 670 could be filled by legless men, 2,637 by one-legged men, two by armless men, 715 by one-armed men and ten by blind men."[3] While not as precise in the limb-count department, the Manhattan Project was also highly segmented and task-specific. In the Project, the tasks requiring the smallest number of personnel were not reserved for the blind but for the ones who saw everything—those privy to the secrets of the entire operation.

For most, the work was heavily compartmentalized, where each worker according to each site was responsible for a very specific part of the process and often required to perform a set of repetitive, monotonous tasks. The purpose of separation in atomic fordism was for speed and efficiency just as in Henry Ford's organization, but with the added understanding that this way of working would aid in the Project's desire to prevent the flow of information. Also following the fordist model, wages were good and workers tended to buy into the system. In Oak Ridge, this meant the ideology of patriotic work and the necessity for secrecy.

The Clinton Engineer Works and Compartmentalization

If the townsite of Oak Ridge with its cosmopolitan air can be thought of as the "Manhattan" component of the endeavor, the Clinton Engineer Works (CEW), the codename given to the austere atomic factories located on the other end of the reservation, can be thought of as the "Project." As previously described, the upstart architectural firm of Skidmore, Owings, and Merrill designed the residential sections of Oak Ridge with new modes of everyday life in mind—the aesthetic could be summed up as Walter Gropius for Robert Oppenheimer. On the other end of the design spectrum, the atomic factories resembled (from afar) established forms of industrial design.[4] While the new atomic plants may have outwardly resembled other industrial factories across the country, the most advanced scientific processes were being employed inside.

Unlike the large-scale federal projects of the TVA, including the nearby Norris Dam and its corresponding village, the atomic factories' design and complex layouts were never meant to draw attention to the area or to inspire those outside the fence of the secret atomic city.[5] Instead, the purpose of the design of the Manhattan Project factories was to camouflage and confuse. From the beginning, the atomic landscape was intended as an "invisible landscape," simultaneously created and designed to disappear.[6]

Since no one knew which if any of the methods of isotope separation would be the most successful for large-scale production, three separate atomic factories were created, employing different techniques: X-10 utilized a graphite reactor and was also a pilot plant for plutonium production; Y-12 used an electromagnetic separation method to gather fissionable uranium; and K-25 employed a gaseous diffusion method to separate isotopes of uranium. The alphanumerical code names are not completely decipherable. X and Y, I was told, might be a nod to the mathematical symbols of the unknown, while K stood for the Kellex Corporation, the initial contractor of the plant. Not all the numbers had significance, but 25 was supposed to be shorthand for uranium-235 (U-235). In calmer times each method of isotope separation would have been subject to extensive pilot testing before full-scale production laboratories were built, but in the race to beat the Nazis, testing was bypassed.

Equally important to the Project, atomic factories and workers were separated in order to protect regimes of scientific knowledge and to prevent knowledge dissemination. Unless you were at the top of the Manhattan Project ladder, you were not allowed to know what went on in the other plants. During World War II, this division marched under the official term "compartmentalization." General Groves described the policy in his memoir *Now It Can Be Told*: "Compartmentalization . . . was the very heart of security. My rule was simple and not capable of misinterpretation—each man should know everything he needed to know to do his job and nothing else. Adherence to this rule not only provided an adequate measure of security, but it greatly improved over-all efficiency by making our people stick to their knitting. And it made quite clear to all concerned that the Project existed to produce a specific end product—not to enable individuals to satisfy their curiosity and to increase their scientific knowledge."[7] As the mechanical heart of atomic fordism, compartmentalization beat and pulsed beyond the factory gates, keeping the townsite apart from the factories, the construction sites from the production sites, the chemists from the engineers from the physicists, and so on down to the lowest level of workers. In the atomic factories, it was not only isotopes that were separated but also teams of workers and, at the lower production levels, each individual worker from another. The policy was extremely unpopular with scientists, who felt this was antithetical to the way they worked; they protested that science demanded the free exchange of ideas. Toward the close of the Manhattan Project, the head-cracking, get-things-done Groves had to ease up a bit, allowing the scientists, especially in Los Alamos, to work more according to their own logics. This was less the case in Oak Ridge.

General Groves wanted each worker to "stick to their knitting," but to do so blindly and silently. For the atomic worker, the very mode of being was separation and abstraction. As the Y-12 plant manager Mr. Connie Bollings remembers, "My lady cubicle operators were always keeping the best production by carefully adjusting the M, G, K, and J voltage symbols that meant nothing to us at the time beyond the technical task at hand."[8] In the coded language of the Manhattan Project, the operators' everyday task was "not to lose our Z," which meant to never let production levels drop.[9] What the cubicle operators were actually monitoring in this alphabet soup of symbolic speech was the electromagnetic separation of isotopes of uranium. As Bollings's comment illustrates, under the Manhattan Project specific labor practices were abstracted along with the general abstraction of the entire production process. In the making of the first uranium atomic bomb, the everyday worker had no idea what she was producing, or even *how* she was producing.

The Buzzing Atomic Hives

The atomic factories must be thought of in terms of constant movement, not only as static buildings embedded in a landscape. The factories were structures of time, not only of space, equally made of speed as well as matter. Operating on a twenty-four-hour schedule with shift changes occurring at 7:00 AM, 3:00 PM, and 11:00 PM, the masses of workers punching in and punching out created a staccato rhythm that reverberated through the atomic plants. To be at work in Oak Ridge during the Manhattan Project was to be a part of a buzzing hive of atomic activity, a sonorous, whirling, meditative pounding for the war machine.

The busy x-10, y-12, and k-25 atomic plants were gargantuan, labyrinthine structures located behind electrified barbed wire fences and armed with rifle-ready guards. Smokestacks, which never smoked, adorned the buildings, causing workers to question not only the specific purpose of the architectural mystery but also the entire Clinton Engineer Works operation. The stacks were actually for inhalation; they were sucking fresh air in that was circulated throughout the plants, rather than pushing air out, as most smokestacks do. To many workers the stacks seemed suspicious, even menacing.[10] Also troubling was the stream of empty railroad cars heading out of town; workers "would see huge quantities of material going into the plants, but nothing coming out," creating "an atmosphere of unreality, in which plants operated feverishly day and night to produce nothing that could be seen or touched."[11] After dark, Oak Ridgers sometimes stared out at the luminescent factories glowing in the blue-black Tennessee night, as people elsewhere gazed at constellations.

Inside the factories, workers participated in what seemed to be magical labor, "eerie work," where even mundane tasks were charged with urgency, secrecy, and often fear.[12] Perhaps one of the strangest jobs, if done without any understanding of its purpose, was tasked to women who worked in the laundry for the Monsanto Chemical Corporation, which operated the x-10 plant. In the atomic launderette, workers would count, wash, and iron each uniform and then carefully sew on all new buttons. The garment would then be handed to a laundress whose specific job was to wave a special instrument like a magic wand over the garment and listen for a clicking sound. If one was heard, the uniform was passed back to be relaundered.[13] Of course, we know now that the worker was using a Geiger counter to check for radioactivity.

For those who knew the aims of the Project, they were involved in a massive science experiment that they hoped would yield unprecedented results. For those who knew only that they were working on a vital war project, the clandestine environment made for a work experience that was at times incredibly boring, at times exciting, at times vexatious, and at times repressive. The pressure to show up and to work hard was unremitting. For those at the top of the Manhattan Project hierarchy, it was a laboratory race, not for grant money or tenure or publication in a scientific journal, but to beat Hitler and his team of Nazi scientists and develop an atomic weapon first. Despite the pressures of the work and its anxiety-inducing pace, most workers describe their time in the atomic factories and laboratories as an exhilarating, even cherished experience. "It was a real lark!" early Oak Ridger Earline Banic told me.[14]

X-10 Graphite Reactor

In 1942, in an abandoned squash court under the west bleachers of the University of Chicago's Stagg Field, Enrico Fermi and his team of approximately fifty scientists from the Metallurgical Laboratory (Met Lab) gathered for a historic experiment. In the space where players once whacked a small hollow (squashable) rubber ball against four wicked walls, Fermi and his scientific group tested the world's first controlled nuclear reactor. After the first self-sustained nuclear chain reaction was achieved, the head of Met Lab, Arthur Holly Compton, called the chairman of the National Defense Research Committee, James B. Conant, and reported, "You'll be interested to know that the Italian navigator just landed in the new world. . . . The earth was not as large as he had estimated, and he arrived at the new world sooner than he had expected." "Is that so, were the natives friendly?" asked Conant. "Everyone landed safe and happy," Compton replied.[15]

Much to the chagrin of many of the scientists working in Chicago, the second nuclear reactor was not assembled nearby at the Argonne Laboratory but, rather, hundreds of miles away in East Tennessee at X-10. A mere eleven months after the Chicago experiment, on the morning of November 4, 1943, the Nobel laureates Compton and Fermi, who were staying at the Oak Ridge Guest House under their rustic aliases Mr. Holley and Mr.

Farmer, were roused from their beds in order to witness the graphite reactor go critical. By the end of the month, x-10 had a significant amount of fissionable plutonium, which was enough to fill a container the size of a penlight to ship out via secret courier.[16] This yield was an early indication that the Manhattan Project could be a success. x-10 was unique in Oak Ridge in that it was a plutonium research facility, whereas the other laboratories there were devoted to separating isotopes of uranium. Large-scale plutonium production for the Manhattan Project took place at the Hanford site.

Y-12 Electromagnetic Separation Plant

The second atomic factory to go online in November 1943 was the Y-12 plant, built by the engineering firm of Stone and Webster and operated by Tennessee Eastman, a subsidiary of the Eastman Kodak Corporation. Y-12 was a virtual labyrinth, composed of 268 buildings that spread out over several miles. The plant was further divided into laboratories and 1,728 individual cubicles, where workers managed a complicated set of levers and dials that determined how much of the fissionable uranium-235 was being separated from the much more common uranium-238 (U-238).

At Y-12, U-235 was separated from U-238 by a process of propulsion through a series of mass spectrometers called calutrons. Each moved in a circular path with a radius that was determined by the atom's mass. U-235 is slightly lighter than U-238 and could be collected by putting a kind of pocket in its path. The calutrons were then organized into specialized lanes known as racetracks, an appropriate name considering the essence of the Project was always speed. This whole process required massive amounts of electricity and conducting metal. During the busiest times of the Manhattan Project, more electrical power was used in Oak Ridge than in all of New York City.[17] All the wattage of Broadway and more was applied to smashing atoms instead of illuminating stars. Wartime shortages of copper meant massive amounts of silver were needed for conducting purposes; to that end, 14,700 tons of silver worth $300 million were borrowed from the U.S. Treasury. Oak Ridgers are proud to say that 99.9 percent of the silver was returned to Fort Knox after the war. One-tenth of 1 percent fell beneath the cushions into the folds of atomic Appalachia, never to be seen again.

Filled with immense machines and thousands of workers, Y-12 could overwhelm the senses. Like Ford's famous River Rouge Plant, "everything trembled in the enormous building[s], and we ourselves, from our ears to the soles of our feet, were gathered into this trembling, which came from the windows, the floor. . . . Tremors . . . shook the whole building from top to bottom. We ourselves became machines, our flesh trembled in the furious din, it gripped us around our heads and in our bowels and rose up to the eyes in quick continuous jolts."[18] As it was for fordism, so it was for atomic fordism, except more secret.

As Louis-Ferdinand Céline writes, "You give in to noise as you give in to war."[19] Y-12 literally buzzed with electricity, which could be heard miles away in the townsite. And the huge magnets that were employed in the separation of isotopes pulled on anything metallic, including absentminded workers who neglected to remove their loose pocket change or bobby pins. The scientific explanations behind these sensations, the electric hum and the magnetic pull that affected workers' experiences of their bodies in space, were never given. The result of this tight-lipped policy was that many workers reported being afraid, and not without reason. For example, an employee at the Y-12 plant recalled a time when a co-worker was carrying a metal plate too close to the magnetic field: "Whammo! There he was pinned to the magnet. Everybody is yelling, 'Shut off the magnet! Shut off the magnet!' What I'm about to tell you sounds like it comes right out of Hollywood, but I watched it myself. . . . So this guy was pinned to the wall, and people were saying, 'Shut down the magnet!' The foreman says, 'I'm not going to do it.' He says, 'We've been told that there are three hundred people an hour being killed in the war. If I shut down a magnet, it might take as long as a week to get it back up and stabilized again and production during a period of instability could be pretty worthless production.' "[20] The pinned worker was eventually released, not because the magnet was turned off, but because co-workers pried his body free using two-by-fours, like a pair of giant chopsticks.

More gruesome stories include workers who brought metal tools into the magnetic field and lost fingers, and even a few who lost their lives. There was a red line painted on the floor. To cross it could be disastrous. It is safe to assume that a brief explanation of the scientific processes at work in the plants could have alleviated worker anxiety without giving away atomic secrets, but the government's official policy was always to keep as quiet about the job as possible.

In fact, for the soldiers stationed in Oak Ridge who died in factory or construction accidents, notes were sent to their families that simply stated "killed in the line of duty," with no further explanation.[21] This notice reveals more than just secrecy methods; it also shows how Project leaders viewed Oak Ridge as another theater of war—the laboratory as battlefield on the Appalachian front. Oak Ridgers adopted this notion in the postwar years and even went a bit further to assign their particular battle site as the cause for ultimate victory. Sometimes they say this straight out; sometimes they tell you through stories. One of the most common anecdotes told in this spirit is of Japan's General Tomoyuki, who was asked after the surrender why his nation had lost the war: "Science," he reportedly said. Another story told is of a Japanese roundup of persons suspected as threats in the Philippines during the war. A Japanese officer asked each person collected, "Where are you from?" An elderly American who had been living in the Philippines responded, "Tennessee." The officer then let the man go free: "We have no war with that nation." Oak Ridgers tell this story with a wink. Little did that officer know, they say.

K-25 Gaseous Diffusion Plant

During the Manhattan Project, 12,000 atomic workers filled the huge K-25 gaseous diffusion plant operated by the Carbide and Carbon Corporation. Although there is no evidence to support this, I have often fantasized that the building's contour was a thumbed nose to the enemy, an architectural taunt: In this giant building shaped like a U, we separate isotopes of uranium. Catch us if you can.

A behemoth in the landscape, K-25 was dragonlike, exhaling steam that could be observed miles away. Not only the largest building in Oak Ridge, but the largest roofed structure in the world at that time—2,450 feet long and an average of 400 feet wide and 60 feet high—K-25 was so monumental that workers had to bicycle from one section to another to deliver files or hold meetings. Sometimes workers used the bikes as a way to escape, to steal a moment, an act of poaching on work time, as de Certeau might say. Joanne Gailar, a clerical worker at the K-25 plant, remembered her wartime cycling jaunts with fondness: "Because of the distances between offices, most supervisors were assigned a bicycle, to be used by any group member who needed it. All were women's models. Whether this was because both sexes could ride them or because men's bikes were in short supply or because Uncle Sam got an especially good deal on women's bikes, I never knew. But I did know that an escape vehicle stood right outside our office to be used when work was slow or when I simply couldn't stand to type another line."[22] At times, the perimeter of K-25 could resemble a velodrome with racers replaced by scientists and secretaries, and with sleek racing kits replaced with flapping lab coats and sensible shoes.

The inside of K-25 resembled a drawing by Dr. Seuss, with an elaborate and complicated system of sealed pipes and busy pumps. Maintenance of the pipes was a constant job, as any leakage would slow down production, not to mention release highly toxic substances into the air. The pipes had to be completely clean and completely sealed, because any grease or dirt would confound the system. Eventually, a material was invented that allowed for this type of sealing capability. After the war the material gained fame as Teflon, becoming a darling of the kitchen as it graced non-stick frying pans.

Backtracking to the 1940s, sealing was a real problem and a job that required human attention, even with the liberal use of ur-Teflon. The job of the leak detector was monotonous but of great importance. Colleen Black, who worked for a time at this key post, remembered, "I don't know exactly what they were doing, but sometimes they would send me down there to find leaks, and you had to climb up real high . . . and you had to climb all over these pipes and find the leak. I didn't know what they were doing. I didn't ask. I know one time one of the GIs told me, 'If you ever smell anything, get out of here.' So I thought something must be going through these pipes that smells bad."[23] Flowing through the miles of pipes of K-25 were very dangerous and highly toxic gases; a malodorous experience should have been the least of workers' concerns. While it is unclear exactly what the supervisor knew in this situation, what is clear is that he knew more than Colleen.

Atomic Workers

World War II put the nation on the go, not only by sending soldiers overseas, but also by encouraging movement at home. During the war years, nearly 25 million people relocated and 15 million new workers entered the workforce.[24] New factories, many of them dedicated to war-related industries, mushroomed across the country. New skills were needed as even established industries changed course; typewriter factories assembled rifles, and the automotive industry abandoned coupe production for tank construction. Industry was hungry for workers to fill the vacancies left by men fighting in the war, as well as the newly created occupational roles. Many of the new industrial workers were women or older workers who were past fighting age and had previously retired but had returned to the workforce to contribute to the war effort.

From 1942 to 1945, thousands of workers came from all corners of the United States to join an international cohort of scientists to work in the brand-new atomic weapons industry in Oak Ridge, Tennessee, a city that did not yet exist. Cultures clashed and accents jousted for recognition in the daily competition of communication. Chemists, physicists, and engineers were recruited from university campuses and scientific labs. As previously noted, young women were enlisted from the valleys and foothills of Appalachia to work as Calutron Girls, leak detectors and secret-aries, among other jobs, and skilled and unskilled laborers came from all over the United States, many moving from war industry job to war industry job. Over the course of the Manhattan Project, 125,000 workers labored in the secret atomic city nestled betwixt and between the Cumberland and Smoky Mountains. While demographic information for specific occupations can only be speculated upon, it has been suggested that skilled laborers came from areas of the country where those skills were most practiced—"From Pittsburgh came the iron and steel workers; from Grand Rapids the woodworkers, from Detroit the machinists; from TVA the electrical experts."[25]

High wages, cheap housing, and draft avoidance attracted workers to the mysterious city of Oak Ridge in hordes. Sometimes entire train cars of the Southern or Louisville & Nashville Railroad would be filled with people headed to work for the Manhattan Project. Often the riders were not fully aware of exactly where they were going. Many were told, "You'll be met at the station in Knoxville and you'll be taken to your place of employment." Rolling into the train stop could be a dramatic experience; the station was stunning. James Agee noted its beauty in *A Death in the Family*: "The stained glass of the L&N Depot smoldered like an exhausted butterfly."[26] Its beauty might have delivered a false aesthetic hope for those who would then travel on to Oak Ridge, a rangy city in progress, nowhere near the polished urban center that was 1940s Knoxville. Years later, the L&N railroad station was turned into a restaurant where I would occasionally eat with my family. My grandmother and I delighted in standing below our initials in the old proud railroad sign, that tired butterfly still working its magic, L for Lindsey and N for Nan. We mugged for camera snaps but mostly for each other. The Manhattan Project that had delivered so many others to this building also brought us here through decades and generations hungry for nourishment.

Absenteeism

Until the war was over, the appetite of the Project was insatiable. Even with the steady supply of workers flowing in, recruiting and keeping enough skilled employees was a constant problem, especially in the construction trades. Absenteeism was a common practice, often used to protest the working and living conditions in Oak Ridge. To combat absenteeism, management created a "presenteeism" campaign. Extra ration tickets and weekly war bond raffles were used as added incentives for workers to keep a good attendance record. Social pressure was also applied: Manhattan Project employees who took time off or called in sick were labeled unpatriotic, whereas those who worked through vacations and put in overtime were lauded as doing service to the nation. They were soldiers on the home front, at a distance from the enemy.

There was a brief moment when this distance might have been lessened and the enemy might have been brought closer. The problem of absenteeism was so severe that General Groves considered using Italian and German prisoners of war as forced labor, but he backed down when the problem of housing and controlling these separate populations grew too complicated.[27] There are so many Oak Ridges that never happened swirling just under the surface of the Oak Ridge that did: unlived atomic legacies that remind us things did not have to go quite this way.

Computers, Chauffeurettes, and Calutron Girls

During the war, being a good citizen meant sacrificing, planting victory gardens, buying war bonds, going without nylons, and donating scrap metal, but in Oak Ridge citizenship also involved going along with Project management by not questioning orders, housing placement, or work conditions, and above all by not talking about the job (even though all these things happened from time to time). If outsiders asked about their jobs or the city behind the fence, Oak Ridgers often gave clever replies. Q: "What are they making out there in Oak Ridge?" A: "O, about eighty cents an hour." Q: "How many people are working out there?" A: "O, about half of 'em."

The notion of sacrifice also meant that women entered industrial work in droves, filling the positions vacated by men fighting overseas, as well as the new jobs created by the developing war industries. Whereas the image of Rosie the Riveter has made a strong impression in the national historical memory, appearing almost as a superhero, the everyday "heroines" of the atomic bomb project are less known. The Manhattan Project hired women to work at almost every occupational level in the production and service sectors. They worked as chemists, leak detectors, typists, secretaries, retail clerks, janitors, and maids, among other jobs, but the largest group was the Calutron Girls.[28] Although they were unaware of the science behind their jobs, these young women monitored the mass spectrometers, known as calutrons, used for separating isotopes of uranium at the Y-12 plant. Former Calutron Girl Willie Baker remarked, "Even when somebody let it slip that we were building a bomb, I didn't know what they meant. I was just a country girl. I had no understanding of what an atomic bomb was."[29]

General Groves was keen on hiring lots of local women, who he thought would be an asset to the Project because they were readily available and accustomed to hard work in mining or farming operations. There was also another reason: Groves felt that they would have no understanding and no interest in the more technical aspects of the Project and would not ask too many questions.[30] The questions would come later. Calutron Girl Gladys Owens asked after the fact, "Why on earth did they have all these high-school girls running this machinery? We could have blown up the whole of Tennessee!"[31] The answer was that, in general, the Manhattan Project liked to draw from labor pools it felt would be the most loyal or, perhaps, even the most docile, which is where Groves lumped these young women. In the end Groves was right about their loyalty. As far as their docility, he might have been less right, judging from the stories I've heard of their adventures and carryin' on.

From 1943 to 1945, the Tennessee Eastman Company, the corporate contractor that managed the Y-12 plant during the war, hired around 10,000 young women to work as Calutron Girls.[32] In order to attract workers, a mass local advertising campaign was launched. One ad read, "When you're a grandmother you'll brag about working at Tennessee Eastman." The advertisement was prescient; I've heard many a grandmother do just that. My grandmother, who was a stay-at-home mom, told me she wished she had been a Calutron Girl because "those ol' girls are famous now." The calutron operators were recruited mostly from areas close to Oak Ridge, although some were from as far as a hundred miles away. The Clinton Engineer Works' bus service extended this distance, picking up workers who did not live on the Oak Ridge reservation. For the farthest away, this meant a bus pickup at 3:30 in the morning, which would land them at the Y-12 gates at 6:45, just in time to clock in for the 7:00 AM shift. Thousands of workers were delivered in this way to the buzzing, electricity-sucking hive that was the electromagnetic separation plant. Once inside, the experience could be all-consuming, made more dramatic by the contrast between workers' home lives and work lives. I've been told that some of these women had no electricity in their own homes, even in 1944.

In training the Calutron Girls, Tennessee Eastman is credited with performing one of the largest civilian training programs in history. Instruction for the job was extensive and lasted several weeks. Up to this point, only advanced graduate students in physics at the University of California at Berkeley or their professors had operated these machines, whereas more than half of the Calutron Girls did not have their high school diplomas.[33] This hiring practice did not sit well with all parties involved in the Manhattan Project. Some scientists were understandably nervous about employing young southern women for such an important task. In order to put their minds at ease, a contest was set up in which for one week a group of scientists would control a set of dials operating a calutron and a group of Calutron Girls would operate a second set to see which group worked more efficiently. It was a contest of dueling calutrons.

At the end of the week, it was revealed that the Calutron Girls had won hands down, producing considerably more enriched uranium than the PhDs.[34] This victory proved the capability of the young women working in Oak Ridge to doubting scientists and also worked as a morale booster for the women themselves. Despite the celebratory nature of this story and its underdog appeal, it must be pointed out that there was a major difference between these two groups. The scientists knew exactly what they were doing as they wielded levers and turned knobs; the women had no idea what their mechanical manipulations were producing. "We were robots," Gladys Owens recalled.[35]

The robotic self-description does not simply denote that the women had become less human, rule-following drones; although they did for the most part follow orders, "robots" also conveys that the women felt as if they had become more like machines. As Richard Sennett writes in *The Craftsman*, "A robotic machine is ourselves enlarged: it is stronger, works faster, and never tires."[36] During the Manhattan Project, many of the Calutron Girls felt themselves more powerful and productive than before or after the war. They had developed what Donna Haraway later called a cyborg identity, before such a thing ever existed. It is implicit in the nickname Calutron Girl: part isotope-separating machine, part young woman. "I'd rather be a cyborg than a goddess," writes Haraway; thousands of Calutron Girls concur.[37]

Another plum position that local women held during the Manhattan Project was the job of Chauffeurette. Instead of the bicycles used at K-25, the Y-12 plant employed "trustworthy" women with good driving skills to chauffeur managers and scientists with high clearance levels to the various buildings in the complex, or sometimes from one plant to another. Local women who were accustomed to working on farms and managing tractors were particularly appealing to Project management for this task. In addition, it was felt that scientists could gab about the Project (in code, of course) in the back of these vehicles without their lady drivers guessing what they were talking about. In these backseat conversations, all matter of *noms de guerre* were used: "the gadget" referred to the A-bomb, "tops" to atoms, and "tubealloy" to uranium.

While the Chauffeurettes and Calutron Girls were essentially unskilled laborers who were trained as operators and technicians, the Manhattan Project also hired women with advanced degrees in chemistry, physics, engineering, and especially mathematics. In the early 1940s, computers, as we know them today, had not been invented yet, and complicated calculations required a lot of pencil-and-paper labor. The people who worked on these projects of applied mathematics were called "Calculators" or "Computers."[38] There were several female Computers in Oak Ridge, but a much greater number were employed by the Theoretical Division at Los Alamos, where a manager was reported to have said, "We hire girls because they work better and they're cheaper."[39]

Part of the expansive system of atomic fordism, the Computers would be seated in neat rows in order to calculate "how the neutron collided with a plutonium atom; whether it was gobbled up; how many new neutrons if any were released in the process; how many neutrons those in turn released, and so on." It was an assembly line for atomic number crunching. Historian George Dyson called this process building bombs "numerically, neutron by neutron, nanosecond by nanosecond . . . statistical approximation whereby a random sampling of events . . . is followed through a series of representative slices in time, answering the otherwise incalculable question of whether a configuration would go thermonuclear."[40] In Los Alamos and Oak Ridge, it was often scientists' wives who were well versed in physics, chemistry, or statistics that held this job.

Whereas the story of local women employed on the Manhattan Project is often told in the spirit of the empowerment of women and Appalachian folks, this was not the aim of the bulldozer-like General Groves. He merely wanted to complete his mission as quickly as possible. That is not to say that the higher wages and job experience that these workers received did not in many cases benefit the workers and their families, but rather that those results were unintended consequences of the Project. Still, as the examples of the Calutron Girls, Chauffeurettes, and Computers show, women played a vital role in the atomic production machine of Oak Ridge, although their jobs were often of lower status and lower pay than those of their male counterparts. Shirley Woods, a clerical worker at Y-12, rationalized the gendered division of labor: "We women did certain jobs and men did other jobs."[41] While this is for the most part true, it should be remembered that, as the example of the Computers shows, even when occupations were separated by gender it was sometimes the case that women were selected for their intelligence and advanced training, not only for their suspected naivete and docility.

The Least Desirable and the Most Dangerous Jobs

While the population of Oak Ridge was incredibly diverse, with workers coming from all over the United States and the world, the approximately 7,000 black workers who ended up in Oak Ridge came largely from the southern United States, mostly from Alabama, Georgia, Mississippi, and Tennessee. To encourage these workers to sign on, recruiters for the Project organized labor trains or paid the bus fare for new hires, giving free transportation to the secret city.

A young recruit, Hal Williams, remembered the process:

> Here's how that worked: My work boss told me to be down at this government building in Memphis at 10 o'clock on Monday morning if I wanted to work. He said it was good money, but he didn't say nothing about where we was going. I lived about twenty miles outside Memphis in Mississippi, so I hitchhiked to get there. I had to come in the highway where Elvis Presley's place is now. It wasn't nothing but a cotton field then. There was a bunch of us black folks waiting at the government building and when they got there they just gave us a ticket and put us on a bus and I still didn't know where we was going. . . . There wasn't no Oak Ridge. . . . I didn't have no idea what was going on.[42]

The buses were so crowded bringing workers to Oak Ridge that riders stood in the aisles. They arrived in the secret city with feet numbed from the vibrations of rough country roads and stiff joints from trying to hold their bodies so as to respect others' personal space while the jolting, rambling work buses traveled to their clandestine destination "People looking for work are very compressible," writes Céline in *Journey to the End of the Night*. His musing on the compactability of persons comes directly from his experience of waiting to get hired on at Ford.[43] He saw men lined up and ready to be slotted into the fordist machinery. Even in wait they are subjected to the psychology of the assembly line. As it was for fordism, so it was for atomic fordism, except more secret.

Even though all workers were caught up in the atomic assembly line and the machinery of the Manhattan Project, black and white workers had different experiences from the very beginning of their tenures working on the Bomb, but it did not necessarily have to be this way. In 1941, President Roosevelt signed Executive Order 8802, which stated, "There shall be no discrimination in the employment of workers in defense industries of Government because of race, creed, color or national origin." Despite this decree, Oak Ridge in the 1940s, like the rest of the southern United States, maintained a segregated social landscape. The official policy of the federal government at that time was to conform with the laws and social customs of the states and communities in which federal installations are located. And conform they did. Segregation was aggressively practiced throughout the Project as yet another form of compartmentalization. Evidence of this practice could be found in all the places the civil rights movement would highlight in the following decades, including housing, schools, buses, lunch counters, and water fountains. Segregation practices in Oak Ridge drew heavily from those of other large-scale federal practices in the area, particularly those of the TVA, where black workers also had subpar and separate housing.

Black workers were hired in large numbers but given the least desirable and most dangerous jobs.[44] They worked largely in construction, hauling coal or waste, and in janitorial or maid service. They were often uneducated, which was paradoxically seen as an asset to Project management. Illiterate workers were strategically given janitorial positions so that potentially confidential office correspondence would not be deciphered by those emptying rubbish bins. Like the Calutron Girls, black workers were thought to be a great asset because of their assumed compliancy. The Project seemed to believe all poor southerners would do just what they were asked.

In addition to the unequal housing opportunities afforded to black residents of Oak Ridge, the treatment of black laborers on the job raises issues of racism and illustrates the sometimes fractured ethical environment of the Project. As an example, labor historian Russell Olwell brings to light a horrifying experiment conducted in March 1945 on Ebb Cade, an African American cement truck driver. Cade fractured his arms and leg in an accident, which landed him in the Oak Ridge hospital. As Olwell tells the story, "The Manhattan Project Medical Division selected Cade to be a subject in the first plutonium injection experiments, to test the dangers of the new element inside the human body. . . . Cade was injected with 4.7 micrograms of plutonium in April and monitored for adverse effects. When his bones were set, samples were taken for biopsy, and when his teeth and gums were found to be infected, fifteen were extracted and tested for plutonium residue. Cade was never asked his consent to participate in the experiment and was never told what happened to him. Instead, he simply left the hospital on his own power and disappeared. . . . He died in 1953 in North Carolina of a heart attack."[45] The report from the federal government's Advisory Committee on Human Radiation Experiments, which was issued in 1995, revealed many more cases such as Cade's, workers who were unknowingly used as human guinea pigs. It is hard to read statements such as Oak Ridge health physicist Karl Morgan's account of a Project official telling him the story of Ebb Cade and not see something exceedingly racist and beyond sinister, wherein the official remarked, "Remember that nigger truck driver that had the accident some time ago? . . . He was rushed to the military hospital in Oak Ridge and has multiple fractures . . . so this was an opportunity we had been waiting for. We gave him an injection of Pu-239 [plutonium]."[46] These horrible experiments show the harmful extension of the Manhattan Project's culture of secrecy into the medical field. The experiments were performed on workers who were seen as more dispensable than others, illustrating the skewed and often racist vision of the Manhattan Project and the nuclear endeavors that followed.

In light of this discriminatory and sometimes racially charged environment, why did black workers come to Oak Ridge? Just like their white counterparts, black workers were drawn to the secret city for a variety of reasons: high wages, job opportunities, patriotism, and the chance for upward mobility and/or adventure. For example, the former K-25 worker R. L. Ayers saw her move to Oak Ridge as a ticket out of her rural hamlet. For her, working on the Manhattan Project "was one way of getting out of the Mississippi Delta, one way of getting away."[47] Kattie Harris took the job in Oak Ridge in order to support her children when she had a hard time finding work in Alabama.[48] And Leroy White was lured by the promise of high wages and by the appeal to his patriotism: "If your government supports you in what you are doing, then you've got to go along with it."[49]

Even with overt discrimination in housing and occupation, World War II brought some opportunities for some black workers to learn new skill sets and to earn higher paychecks than they had previously. These benefits, like those afforded to white Appalachian and female workers, were side effects of the Project's need for labor rather than intended social consequences.

Alvin Smith

After the war, my grandfather continued driving along the atomic highway for the Atomic Energy Commission (AEC). His driving partner on these expansive, secret trips was a light-skinned African American man named Alvin Smith. He was my grandfather's best friend. They shared the space of an atomic-toting machine careening across the postnuclear landscape of America and back again. They talked. They were close. Despite their camaraderie, my grandfather called him Nigger Smith, as did everyone else driving for the AEC. People called him this to his face. Alvin was well liked and respected; people thought he was a good guy. They used this terrible nickname for him anyway, carrying this racist way of talking into the Atomic Age.

Sometimes when they were driving and they would stop to rest, my grandfather would stay in a hotel and Alvin would sleep in the truck. On rare occasions the opposite would transpire if Alvin wanted to try to pass as white. I met Alvin in 1987 at my grandfather's funeral when I was nine. He was introduced to me as Alvin. I didn't understand he was the same friend I had heard about because I had known him only through stories that obscured his identity with racist language. The atomic frontier's racist policies, practices, and ways of thinking had bled into the postnuclear landscape. They saturated the cab of my grandfather's eighteen-wheeler and circulated along with my familial stories. They disrupted the transmission from the past to the present, making folks unrecognizable. It makes me wonder how many other Oak Ridgers have been distorted through atomic storytelling.

Although Oak Ridge was ahead of the mark in nuclear physics and atomic engineering, race relations during the Manhattan Project were not always good. This is one area that tends to be glossed over or that receives a quick explanation when it comes up in the otherwise nostalgic storytelling of the town's past. Discussions of racial inequality are suppressed in order to maintain the imagined utopian atomic landscape. Questions about the treatment of the black population often elicit what I call the "fevered wartime explanation," in which the need for expediency is used to explain away mistakes and unfair policy decisions. That is, having "a war to win" justified a lot of what went on in Oak Ridge; it was a phrase used both as explanation for progressive actions and for maintaining the existing state of affairs, depending on what suited Project needs at the moment. But it didn't stop there. As the story of Alvin Smith shows, the Manhattan Project's culture of racism was couriered by the AEC right along with fissionable materials and plans for new weapons into the Atomic Age.

Dreaming Atomic Nostalgia

Perhaps as an unconscious corrective both to the gender and racial discrimination of the times and to the piggishness of General Groves, on a research trip to Oak Ridge I had a dream that echoed the competition of the Calutron Girls versus the Berkeley PhDs. Although in my dream the Computers battled each other, there was no more worthy competition for their figuring. In the dream, the Computers, who were not all white but from many diverse backgrounds, emerged out of little doorways to individual theme songs, dressed in satin capes like boxers, brandishing calculators and pencils. One bounded out to the song "Neutron Dance" by the Pointer Sisters: "I'm just burning / doin' the neutron dance / whoo, oooh / whoo, ooh."[50] This one was Pinky the Numerator. They all had names like this, like tough girls from a roller derby: Sally the Subtractor, Lee-thal Long Division, Moe-Numbers, etc. I woke up, abruptly, the results of the dream contest unclear.

Then I went to have "real" coffee with my grandmother, as she calls it, and we talked about the old days. When I'm not around she drinks Sanka, which I find unacceptable. She suggested I take a look at the newspaper. The morning's headline: "Oak Ridge Reveals World's Fastest Supercomputer, Titan."[51] In 2012, the fastest computer was a machine, no longer a woman, no longer dressed in satin, but very, very fast. I felt proud and then almost immediately nostalgic for the super-Computers of my dream. I was dreaming atomic nostalgia as I was writing it.

CHAPTER FOUR

We Didn't Exactly Live in a Democracy

The space of a tactic is the space of the other. . . . It must vigilantly make use of the cracks that particular conjunctions open in the surveillance of the proprietary powers. It poaches in them. It creates surprises in them. It can be where it is least expected. It is a guileful ruse.
—Michel de Certeau, *The Practice of Everyday Life*

Workers who arrived in Oak Ridge had been recruited in the name of freedom and democracy, yet paradoxically they found themselves inside a restrictive federal reservation surrounded by barbed wire, armed guards, and monitored gates. Even a trip to the movies did not provide a reprieve from surveillance; security agents would walk the carpeted aisles like hyper-vigilant ushers, making sure no one was talking (about the Project). There were no local elections, no free press, and no freedom of assembly. As early Oak Ridger Barbara Lyon put it: "Well, we didn't exactly live in a democracy."[1] Workers were even forbidden to keep a journal that mentioned anything about Oak Ridge. Some of them did anyway. I've seen them. Defiant sentences typed or scrawled, formed with ink, machines, and digits, rogue narratives written across dominated time, examples of de Certeauian poaching in tactical spaces.

Security in Oak Ridge was pervasive and invasive. Still, no system is without its gaps. The system contained spaces subject to manipulation where moments of occasional evasion were possible. One such site of poaching was x-10's rooftop—a favored place where lovers could meet for trysts during lunch breaks, at odd hours, and between shifts. Journalist Jay Searcy writes, "Next to the atomic bomb, that roof was the best-kept secret of the war."[2] Small resistances were like pinprick release valves for Oak Ridgers against the intense pressure to keep quiet on the job. Still, taking chances was risky, which of course was part of the excitement. Billboards watched and warned from the roadside: "Loose lips sink ships."

Lie-detector test (photo by Ed Westcott, courtesy of
U.S. Department of Energy Photo Archives)

One of the very first tasks Oak Ridgers had to complete was to sign an official Declaration of Secrecy, a promise not to scupper the whole operation. This document was meant to make new employees aware of the need for secrecy and the penalties under the Espionage Act for any violations. Workers were not supposed to share with their co-workers or even their spouses any information about their job, letters were heavily censored, and lie-detector tests were commonly employed. If a worker resigned or was fired, he or she would be reminded (some might say threatened) of this pledge in an exit interview. Many Oak Ridgers took this declaration to heart and refused to ever talk about their role in the Manhattan Project, keeping mute on atomic matters for the rest of their lives, their signed secret oaths treasured like love letters tucked away, sweetly and intimately. Other workers in the postwar years loved talking about the Manhattan Project any chance they got, big and bold and free skywriting their atomic histories for the largest audiences possible.

Those floating and hidden stories stand in contrast to the reminders to keep silent that were everywhere during the Manhattan Project, from billboards to grocery receipts to newspaper columns, whispering or shouting, trying to hammer home the message every way possible: "What you see

Billboard in Oak Ridge, 1943 (photo by Ed Westcott, courtesy of
U.S. Department of Energy Photo Archives)

here, what you do here, what you hear here, when you leave here, let it stay here." The visual landscape of Oak Ridge was dotted with strident warnings to keep silent, to work hard, to identify with soldiers fighting overseas, and to remember who the enemy was. Although war propaganda posters were common at all war industry sites, Oak Ridge was "like another world," as Thelma Present wrote to Margaret Mead: "[Elsewhere] the billboards display polar bears sitting on ice cubes drinking Pepsi-Cola and magnificent cars driving up the highest mountains with Esso. Here they show wise old owls telling you to keep your mouth shut, or Uncle Sam pointing at you to BE CAREFUL."[3]

There was even a semi-regular editorial in the *Oak Ridge Journal* called "Silence Means Security." An example of this weekly feature shows the wartime anxiety that dominated the Atomic City:

Last April an editorial in the Oak Ridge Journal entitled "Does Your Tongue Wag?" outlined in some detail the methods a Nazi might use if he were attempting to get information from gullible Americans employed by this and other vital war projects. The editorial was predicated on experiences in situations of which many of us were not aware. The apprehension in Knoxville last week of Waldemar Othmer, a Nazi espionage agent, awakens us to the realities of the dangers that confront us. Waldemar Othmer was a pleasant man. He lived at the YMCA; he was a member of a Knoxville church, where he met many of the people employed here. He went on picnics with them, played croquet, was an all round good fellow. He was a friendly, understanding, intelligent man. It was interesting to go out with him socially, and fun to speculate with him on what local war projects were accomplishing. That was just what he desired: talk, gossip of what, where, how, and who is concerned with war production. The news of Waldemar Othmer's presence in Knoxville should serve one excellent purpose. It reminds all of us here that security slogans and programs are neither for decoration nor amusement, that it is important to remember "What you see here, What you do here, What you hear here, When you leave here, Let It Stay Here." It is very probable that there are other foreign agents in the environs of Oak Ridge, with friendly smiles and avid ears, eagerly collecting any bits of information we might casually mention. It is up to us to be security conscious, alert, mindful that careless talk is dangerous. By refusing to talk about our work, we form a positive shield of security, making the work of these agents a frustrating and disappointing process. Remember, Silence means Security![4]

The shush factor sometimes caused interpersonal tension, especially between husbands and wives. In response, a whole framework was developed in which to talk about the ways Oak Ridgers could not talk about the Project. As a result, repression helped to make secrecy a core component of not only the culture of the place, but of Oak Ridgers' collective identity as well, whether they completely followed the secrecy doctrine or if they operated occasionally outside its guidelines.[5] The self-disciplining and self-silencing of Oak Ridgers did not end with the Manhattan Project. The practice continues in the former Secret City and elsewhere in the postnuclear landscape.[6]

Of course, many Oak Ridgers did talk about the Project, especially to their spouses. J. H. Rush confessed, "Like many another scientist, I disregarded security regulations to the extent of telling my wife what the project was about. I would not have been willing to go to such an out-of-the-way place for the duration if I had not known what I would be working on, and I saw no reason to expect that she should, either."[7] Other couples found their relationships changed through talking about new things, once work was off the table for possible discussion. Others found their dinner conversations grinding to an uncomfortable halt, like a saltshaker with no more granules to release.

The Security Apparatus

Oak Ridgers were often halted unexpectedly as they went about their everyday lives. It was quite common to be stopped at random for security checks and required to show a resident's badge. Wearing and showing identification became such a habitual activity that scientists and workers remembered flashing their badges to the minister when leaving church on Sunday mornings.[8] *A new way to witness.* My grandmother told me that my grandfather would occasionally flash his badge to her as well, sometimes in jest, sometimes in reflex. Perhaps this is not so strange. Some badges contained dosimeters and were to be worn close to the heart to monitor radiation. Holding out your badge was like holding out your heart.

Identification badges indicated security clearance levels and what parts of the factories workers had access to. Badges were color-coded and sometimes uniforms were as well, depending on a worker's place in the atomic hierarchy. Clearance levels broke down as follows: Level one was for maintenance workers, who were confined to the basement. Level two designated process workers, such as the Calutron Girls, who worked in cubicles on the main factory floors. Levels three and four were composed of managers and engineers who knew more about the processing methods, but not the ultimate goals of the Project; these workers had greater freedom of mobility. Level five, the highest, bestowed what was known as Q-clearance. The 5-Qs, as they were known, were the most knowledgeable members of the Manhattan Project workforce, the top Army brass and the elite core of physicists. These workers pretty much went wherever they wanted, whenever they wanted, but that does not mean they were not followed. Army counterintelligence agents, known as shadows, tailed top Oak Ridge scientists when they traveled to other stops along the atomic highway.

When the scientist Chris Keim was visiting the Lawrence Radiation Laboratory in Berkeley, California, he boarded a train car. Just as he settled into his seat, the driver said, "Good morning, Dr. Keim. How is everything in Oak Ridge?" The name of the Secret City was not even supposed to be said aloud. This was most likely an attempt by military intelligence to test the scientist's vigilance with secrecy. At the time, he was too shocked to respond. Years later he mentioned the story to fellow Oak Ridge scientists, who reported similar experiences.[9]

Shadows also chased down suspected leaks farther afield. An intelligence agent was once sent to the front lines in Belgium to address an American officer who had written to a friend in Oak Ridge, inquiring if he was in fact working on atomic energy. Another well-traveled story among Oak Ridgers is that of the agent who was dispatched to Brazil to check up on a report of a skin rash filed by a former Manhattan Project worker, who believed his epidermal discomfort was the result of "queer rays" employed by the atomic plant where he worked.[10] There was intelligence invested in the Project, but half-wittedness and paranoia as well.

In addition to assigned security agents, the Project recruited Oak Ridgers to watch and report on each other. Residents and employees would be called in by Intelligence for an "interview." During the course of the meeting the importance of Oak Ridge operations in the war effort and the atomic citizens' patriotic duty would be impressed on them. The new "secret agent" would then be sworn to secrecy, adding another layer of concealment upon the vow of silence already taken. The new agent's job was to pay attention in everyday actions to "loose talk" and anything that could indicate a security breach. Agents were required to report their findings in regular letters, which would be slipped into envelopes provided by Project officials. If they didn't see or hear anything, they simply sent a blank card. The envelopes were addressed to a false company, the Acme Credit Corporation of Knoxville.[11] This practice created some excitement and encouraged amateur sleuthing, while at the same time undoubtedly contributing to the environment of fear and paranoia on the atomic reservation. Many Oak Ridgers suspected their partners were having affairs because they were observed writing clandestine letters and mailing them furtively.

The Oak Ridge post office was an important hub in the security system. Postal workers, who were often FBI agents, recorded magazines received by each resident, as well as the points of origin and destination for every piece of mail. All packages coming in and out were searched for contraband and all letters were combed for sensitive material. If anything remotely suspicious was discovered, workers were hauled in for questioning. Colleen Black remembered a nurse who was brought in for interrogation after she wrote a letter to her mother describing how many appendectomies were performed at the Oak Ridge hospital that week.[12]

The security apparatus of the Manhattan Project was elaborate and far-reaching, sometimes absurd, and often inadequate. In Hanford, the poet Bill Witherup's mother's cherry pie was declared top-secret. Mrs. Witherup, a frugal woman, gifted in baking, decided to try to reel in a bit of extra money by selling desserts, so she advertised in the local paper. Her pies "with Yakima Valley cherries as the nuclear core" became so popular that she was visited one day by military intelligence. The officer did not immediately announce his station, but instead requested a sample of her pie. Mrs. Witherup gladly complied and even offered a coffee chaser, mistaking the officer for a local businessman. Only after completing his slice did he flash his badge. "I'm sorry, Mrs. Witherup, we can't let you advertise your pies. It violates security precautions. But you keep on making these. You can sell these to friends, or by word-of-mouth, but any advertising by Hanford workers or their families is CLASSIFIED. Security, you know—we wouldn't want the Axis to find out what we are up to here, would we?"[13] Any statistical information that could give even the slightest hint of how many people were in the secret atomic sites was considered dangerous information. Witherup refers to these practices as ur–Homeland Security.

The Manhattan Project worked tirelessly to control not only statistical information but language as well. In Oak Ridge, military intelligence forbade a chemist to name his daughter Sarah Uranie, insisting that the birth certificate (which could not even list Oak Ridge as the place of birth) show only "Sarah U" until after the bomb was dropped on Hiroshima. The most striking difference between law enforcement in Oak Ridge compared to that outside the fence was that violations often led to loss of employment and eviction from the site, not only fines or jail time. Those fired were also placed on a blacklist to prevent them from being rehired.

Eviction resulted even when infractions were minor. Often the reason given was suspicion of spying or the possibility that the worker's character would lead him or her to commit espionage. Workers who would fall into this last category were alcoholics, drug addicts, adulterers, workers perceived to have communist friends or tendencies, and people Project managers called "sexual deviants," in most cases meaning homosexuals. It was believed that homosexuals would relinquish project information to avoid blackmail. An example of the firing of a sexual deviant can be found in the case of Mr. Ford, a cement finisher who was fired under the assumption that his sexuality was a threat to national security. While he had threatened his boyfriend with violence after finding him in bed with a woman, physical skirmishes were typical everyday occurrences on the construction sites, and other violators did not lose their jobs.[14]

The fear of the gay spy haunted the Manhattan Project as pre-McCarthyist paranoia. In the contemporary postnuclear landscape, residues of this fear show up in archives, anecdotes, and even mystery novels. In Joseph Kanon's *Los Alamos*, a scientist believed to be queer turns up dead. In the first few pages of the novel we get the description of his autopsy with one of the officers requesting the medical examiner to make sure to check for anal penetration. Upon hearing the news an officer reports to General Groves,

"If he was homosexual, that would constitute a security risk all by itself. You know that." Groves responds, "Yes, I know that." In *Bones of Betrayal*, a mystery of Manhattan Project Oak Ridge, a similar story is told—the book begins with a dead gay scientist and the same rhetoric is repeated: "I don't suppose there's any virtue in guarding his secret any longer. . . . Queer as a three-dollar bill. . . . Today, nobody cares, but things were different then. . . . It was considered a perversion. He'd never have been able to keep his security clearance if they'd known."[15] The Manhattan Project's policies forced gay workers to be clandestine about their romantic and sexual lives, another layer of secrecy heaped upon the others. The result is the near absence of queer life from the atomic archives, which are dominated by the laws of what could be said at the time.[16]

Tension at the Gates

Tension between security and everyday life gathered most visibly at the city's gates. For every vehicle that attempted to enter Oak Ridge, resident or visitor passes had to be presented and inspected. A famous photograph shows even Santa Claus succumbing to guard inspection, the jolly red-suited gift-giver getting the once-over from the guards. Head tilted to one side, white beard flowing in the wind, standing in black shiny boots that make his legs look almost peg-like, Santa holds a stuffed dachshund in his right hand and clings to his oversized sack with his left. A guard is pulling back on the sack, creating a tense scene as we watch Santa get stopped and frisked.[17] The photograph is funny but also contains a streak of menace. What would be said of this image if the guards were not from the American security forces, but Nazis or other Axis members?

These checks and searches could be time consuming and often caused considerable delay and agitation. Dorathy Moneymaker remembers trying to get through the gate when she was in labor. In the hustle to make it to the hospital she had forgotten her resident card, and the guard refused to let her through. Her husband, who had his card, was ushered through the gates and went to fetch the doctor; eventually Moneymaker made it to the hospital, and her baby was born without further incident, although there were some hairy moments.[18]

Not everyone fell subject to the authority of the gates in the same way. At the entry points, the Manhattan Project's security system was poked and prodded by ruses, and the "make-shift creativity of groups or individuals already caught in the nets of 'discipline.'"[19] There were ways of operating that allowed for some getting around the disciplined posts. One example

Santa going through security at Elza Gate, 1944 (photo by Ed Westcott, courtesy of U.S. Department of Energy Photo Archives)

comes from Lois Van Wie, whose husband forgot to leave her visitor's pass at the gate in the days before she was an official Oak Ridge resident. By the time the pass arrived, Lois had missed the bus heading into the reservation—actually several buses, she told me. Another one would not come around for quite some time. Tired of waiting, she hitched a ride into the reservation in a Kraft mayonnaise truck, which was a bit unorthodox but not a major challenge to the authorities on guard, so she got away with it.[20] Getting away with it—committing minor infractions against the sometimes oppressive security system—gave great pleasure to Oak Ridgers and provided them stories they love to tell even today.

Monitoring the gates was a constant and tedious job, so one can imagine that a guard might let a lady or two slip through on a condiment truck from time to time, although they weren't supposed to. When Oak Ridge was at its busiest, an average of 1,500 cars would pass through daily.[21] Each vehicle would get a thorough inspection to check for hidden contraband—things were caught, things were missed. The most common materials seized included weapons, liquor, and binoculars. Anecdotally, the most common materials snuck in were weapons, liquor, and binoculars. Visitors and residents alike often went to great links to smuggle forbidden items past the checkpoints, especially liquor. Tales of whiskey bottles stashed in diapers, moonshine in hollowed out bibles, and rye tucked into hidden auto compartments abound.

Beyond the confiscation of alcohol and the possible ruination of a Saturday night on the atomic reservation, the gates also worked to control the flow of information. They acted not only as physical barriers to the city but also as mental, social, cultural, and even narrative barriers. For example, visitors' passes contained the following statement: "I hereby certify that the above named visitor is not a newspaper or magazine writer or photographer, motion picture photographer, radio commentator, alien, inspector or investigator (State or Federal)."[22] In this way, the gates worked to control what could or could not be said.

In her memoir *Oak Ridge and Me*, Joanne Gailar writes that the gates were "nothing special," a "group of bare, wooden framework structures at which armed military police stood guard to inspect unceremoniously the identification passes of the entrants. That's all it was—nothing more . . . and yet there was something very exciting about the situation."[23] The secrecy of the Project created a mystique around even the most mundane bureaucratic functions of the town. There was a sense that anything could happen at anytime.

Each day, curiosity seekers, usually from nearby communities, tried to finagle their way in to have a look around the secret city. Oftentimes they did not take refusal to be let on the grounds well. Usually this would only lead to verbal threats flung from a guard tower or perhaps the brandishing of a rifle. This was typically enough to send folks on their way. Violence in these instances was rare, but there were some reported cases where a curious outsider was shot to death by security. An especially flummoxing case of excessive force was the story of a welder who met a tragic end on April 23, 1944. He had been called in the middle of the night to come in for an emergency. Once he arrived onsite he was informed that there was no pass waiting for him at that gate, but at a different gate that would require back-tracking to Knoxville twenty miles away to take another approach road to Oak Ridge. The welder, believing time was short for the needed task, said, "This is an emergency job. I'm going in." The guard barked back, "If you do, you're a dead man."[24] And then, tragically, he was.

The Atomic City and Mental Life

The first city of the Atomic Age was a place of orderly disorder, a mix of pleasures, stresses, and threats. In spite of all the inconveniences, many delighted in the intrigue brought about by the secrecy of the place. My grandmother and her friend Helen Schween told me that "during the war, this was the place to be." Herb Snyder chimed in: "Oak Ridge was a special place. In some ways we were isolated, but we liked it that way."[25] As the German sociologist Georg Simmel writes of the secret society, "In these cases, secrecy and mystification amount to heightening the wall toward the outside and hence to strengthening the character of the group."[26] For many, employment on the Manhattan Project provided a sense of impor-tance and pride, creating a stark division between those inside and outside the fence, regardless if workers knew the true nature of their jobs. For oth-ers the distance between life in the Atomic City and life outside of it—the pressure and pace of it all—caused disturbances to their mental life. They were neither blasé nor excited by the atomic frontier, but disturbed and agitated by it. They were the first atomic neurotics.

The secrecy measures employed by the Manhattan Project simultane-ously created realms of repression and realms of curiosity; the limiting of certain communicative behaviors gave rise to all kinds of imaginations, fantasies, and rumors. As Simmel writes, "The secret produces an immense enlargement of life. . . . The secret offers the possibility of a second world alongside the manifest world," where the manifest world is "decisively influenced" by the imagined one.[27] Even though the pressure to keep quiet was constant, most Oak Ridgers were curious or suspicious about the work they were doing. An Oak Ridge librarian reported that during the Manhat-tan Project the library's dictionary had to be replaced frequently because of wear and tear to the pages containing the words "uranium" and "fission."[28]

Even with some pretty good sleuthing, nearly all the Oak Ridgers and outsiders who had guessed correctly what was being worked on in the secret city were left with the bigger question of how.[29] Some knew the ins and outs of the atomic processing methods being pursued at the particular factory in which they worked, but they were at a loss to tell you what went on in the other plants. There were only a small number of people on the Project who knew everything, as everyone was kept on a strict diet of "need-to-know." While reports of complete ignorance until after Hiroshima were certainly exaggerated, the fact that isotopes being separated for use in an atomic bomb was a surprise to so many in Oak Ridge attests to the success of the secrecy measures.

Even after the secrets of atom splitting were revealed, a cloud of mystery and excitement remained over the city. The stress and the pressures remained there, too, like the heat lightning that frequently rides sidecar to the clouds of Tennessee summers. Relentless sloganeering, job pressures, and even the hectic social life that many workers kept up could be said to wear on the atomic residents from time to time. Yet in the beginning "there were no social workers—probably the only community organized in recent times without such services. It was assumed that everyone on the project had a job and a place to live," and therefore there would be no need, wrote the chief psychiatrist for the Manhattan Project, Dr. Eric Clarke.[30] In hindsight, it is not surprising that the pressure of the war, the intense work schedule, the separation from friends and family, and the secrecy and security measures took a toll on Oak Ridgers' mental health.

By 1944, it was determined that psychological issues were a severe enough problem to warrant placing professional counselors in some dormitories and adding psychiatric staff to the medical facilities. According to Clarke, for the mental health professional, "Oak Ridge offered the most gorgeous chance to test out in practice the theoretical philosophies in sociology, psychology, psychiatry, psychosomatic medicine, preventive public health, and community nursing that one could seek. Here was a new, highly organized city of substantial size where an ideal of community living could be introduced."[31] The patients Clarke ended up seeing were mostly from high-level positions. Of course, it was not only the bigwigs who suffered from mental strain. All workers felt pressure on the job and varying degrees of anomie, but many workers were afraid of psychiatric treatment, being stigmatized, and/or losing their job. Clarke reported many cases of emotional distress and physical exhaustion brought on by the pressures of the job, mostly "acute anxiety neurosis, comparable to battle fatigue encountered in overseas units."[32] The battlefield comes home again in Clarke's treatment notes.

Yellow Pantsuit

My parents met because of the mental life of Oak Ridgers, although it was not until years after the Manhattan Project had ended. They both worked at the Oak Ridge Mental Health Center, my father, a recent graduate of the University of Tennessee, as a clinical psychologist and my mother as a secretary. It was the 1960s, and she was the first woman to wear pants to the office. She wore a yellow pantsuit. She said it was gorgeous.

CHAPTER FIVE

From Hiroshima to Normalization

The sum of their separate labors astonished a divided world.
It was the atomic bomb.
—Philip E. Kennedy, co-sponsor
of the Youth Council on the Atomic Crisis

It was an enriching experience for me.
—Naomi Brummit, Calutron Girl

Sometime in 1945, a coworker leaned over to Shirley Woods and said, "Think of it Shirley, someday we'll drop an atom bomb and destroy a whole city!"[1] Woods was shocked at these words, which were clearly a break in the secrecy chain of Oak Ridge. She also doubted their veracity. Yet in a few months, Woods, the rest of Oak Ridge, and the entire world would learn the truth of this prediction. On August 6, 1945, the atomic bomb with the diminutive name Little Boy was dropped on Hiroshima, Japan. The bomb, containing fissionable uranium from the atomic factories of Oak Ridge, caused massive devastation to Hiroshima and its residents. It is estimated that 70,000 of Hiroshima's 76,000 buildings were destroyed upon impact and that between 70,000 and 100,000 people were killed the first day. The number of dead roughly mirrored the population of Oak Ridge, a chilling rhyme of arithmetic. These were the immediate effects; the full extent of the bomb's destructive power and its radioactive aftermath is still unfolding.

The news that Oak Ridge had been involved in a secret war project to create an atomic bomb came over the national airwaves around 10:00 AM Eastern Standard Time. The hour of the report meant that in Oak Ridge it was often housewives and shift workers who first heard the news. When they phoned their husbands or friends at work, it came as a shock to those on the other end of the receiver. Knees weakened. Hearts raced. Blood drained from faces. Although rumors of what was being produced in Oak Ridge had begun to circulate more freely, speculations were always whispered—never spoken aloud, never shouted, and certainly never telephoned. The secretaries who could field and ferry these calls, the managers who had direct lines, and the scientists who had some inkling but no explicit confirmation of their working goal were afraid security had been breached. The penalties for loose talk were well known: unemployment, eviction, arrest, and even imprisonment.

When the news finally sunk in that the mission of Oak Ridge was no longer a secret, and that it was being broadcast not only nationally but throughout the world, most were stunned to learn what they had been working toward all those fevered and secret hours in the enormous factories and labs. Some of those who knew more about the science of the Project, the chemists and the physicists, ran up and down the halls of the laboratories shouting, "Uranium! Uranium!"[2] Finally able to say the name of the silvery-gray element with atomic number 92 out loud, they gleefully yelled it with reckless abandon. The rest of the community, those without a working knowledge of the periodic table of elements or scientific backgrounds, scratched their heads and wondered just how all that dial twisting, button pressing, and slug loading was able to produce such a devastating device.

For Oak Ridgers, August 6, 1945, was a day of jubilation, of celebration, of back pats, of kissing strangers and offering congratulations. On this humid summer day, the end of the war seemed near. By mid-afternoon, hundreds of residents gathered in Jackson Square, one of the main centers of the city, giving it the appearance of "a miniature Times Square on New Year's Eve."[3] Spontaneous parties erupted all over Oak Ridge that day and lasted until the following morning; faces were turned Tennessee-mud-red from shouts of joy, whiskey, and lipstick-laden kisses. "When the bomb was dropped, we danced all night long," remembered one reveler.[4] Children, along with their parents, celebrated in the news. A famous image from the day shows a group of boys joyously hanging an effigy of Tojo, a macabre photographic postscript to the message that was written by Lieutenant Nicholas Del Genio on the hull of Little Boy: "From us in Oak Ridge to Tojo."[5] The journalist Jay Searcy remembers banging pots and pans with other neighborhood kids until a neighbor, a scientist at one of the labs, asked the boys to stop, saying, "We still have to get up and go to work tomorrow."[6]

The day of the Hiroshima bombing, newspapers from nearby Knoxville sold at a blistering pace, even though the prices were jacked up for the occasion from the usual five cents to a dollar.[7] When the local paper, the *Oak Ridge Journal*, reported the story, it ran a bold shouting headline that took up most of the real estate above the fold: "Oak Ridge Attacks Japanese." Also posted on the front page was a message from the top Army official in

Oak Ridge, Colonel Kenneth D. Nichols, district engineer of the Manhattan District, quoted here in full in order to give a sense of the mood of the day:

> To Contractors, Workers, Residents of Oak Ridge: Congratulations to all the workers at the Clinton Engineer Works and to the people of Oak Ridge! You have done the impossible. This project has been, from the start, a cooperative enterprise, based on mutual faith—faith of the scientist that engineers could translate his discoveries—yes, and his world stirring dreams—into practical process designs; faith of the engineer that material and construction men could turn those designs into brick and mortar and process equipment; faith of the operating contractor that local non-technical workers would be trained to perform new and strange tasks so exacting that they would normally be entrusted only to skilled scientific experimenters; faith of the construction workers and operators that their supervisors knew their business; and faith of all groups—management and employee—scientific and service—that somehow ways and means would be found to house, feed and transport them. This faith has been justified by the successful use of your product against the Japs. The success of the project was made possible only because everyone did his or her part and "stayed on the job" from the Nobel Prize winners whose scientific theories and experiments mushroomed into huge production plants to the sweating construction worker and the cafeteria girl with her tray of dishes. . . . History will record the full significance of your fabulous achievements in unlocking the stupendous energy of the atom. May it be used not only as an effective weapon but in the future may it play a major part in humanity's service.[8]

Colonel Nichols's congratulatory letter in the newspaper addressed key themes that would come to define Oak Ridge in the coming years: atoms for peace, the necessity of a nuclear America, and atomic utopianism.

Just three days later, on August 9, another atomic bomb was dropped on the port city of Nagasaki. The second bomb contained fissionable plutonium produced at the Hanford site and was given the more corporeal nickname Fat Man. An estimated 70,000 people were killed in the bombing of Nagasaki, another ghastly numerical echo with the population of Oak Ridge; in addition, the number was five times the population of Richland, the bedroom community of Hanford. Japan surrendered on August 15, less than a week later, bringing an end to the fighting. Mass radiation poisoning and slow deaths continued to ravage the targeted landscapes, but Oak Ridgers and Hanford workers were not aware of this. The propaganda around the atomic bombs created clouds of confusion, and most Manhattan Project workers had no idea of the actual effects of the bombs. They were just thrilled that the fighting had ended and that their loved ones would come home.

The close of the war was an immense relief for the nation as a whole, and Oak Ridge was no exception, but there were some unique anxieties that plagued the community now that the secret was out. Residents began to wonder what would become of their clandestine wartime utopia. Would all those homes built in just thirty minutes be disassembled in equal time? Would all workers lose their jobs? Would the land be returned to its previous owners? Would they tear down the gates and let just anyone in? Would Oak Ridge cease to be the privileged and cultured island in the middle of Appalachia that many residents felt it to be? Would the Atomic City be *normal*?

The Battle for Control over Atomic Energy and Atomic Image

The conclusion of the war created an environment of uncertainty behind the fence. The city's raison d'être had disappeared in a mushroom cloud, and residents were unsure how to organize their lives after the fallout. Similar worries vibrated throughout all the Manhattan Project sites. For Oak Ridge, these fears were partially alleviated when on September 6, 1945, Colonel Nichols announced that the site would continue to operate, although it was not entirely clear in what capacity and on what scale. This would depend on a decision by Congress regarding who would control the nation's atomic weapons and nuclear energy industries.

As for Oak Ridge's western plutonium producing counterpart, "Hanford remained something of a stepchild within the atomic complex."[9] Unlike Los Alamos and Oak Ridge, Hanford did not achieve national laboratory status immediately after the war—that took until 1965—but like the other two sites, it remained an important node in the postnuclear landscape. The communities around Hanford that wished the new nuclear industry would keep ticking, keep scattering jobs and paychecks in the cheatgrass and sagebrush that huddled in the sere landscape, could also breathe a sigh of relief when the federal government decided that plutonium-239 should be the primary fuel for nuclear weapons in the post–World War II era, eventually providing the bulk of the nuclear nectar for the thirsty Cold War arsenal.

While American citizens, both inside and outside the no-longer-secret locations of Oak Ridge, Hanford, and Los Alamos, celebrated the end of the war, many scientists had grown ambivalent or even entirely against the idea of atomic weapons. Some felt the bombs should not have been used at all after Germany surrendered. Others worried about the precedent set by the bombing of Japan and what the future of atomic weaponry and atomic warfare could bring. Oak Ridge physicist J. H. Rush reacted to the atomic bombings with trepidation:

> I would like to be able to say that I felt only a terrible elation, only the electrifying realization that the war was over. . . . We all felt pride of achievement. We had helped do a bold and difficult job, and had stopped a war in its tracks. That was enough for the moment. Second thoughts came later. . . . For me, they came when I picked up a paper and saw in block letters: TERROR BOMB HITS NAGASAKI. I felt suddenly sick. Hiroshima had been the climax both for us and for the Japanese, and I realized that I had not expected a repetition of its horror. *Why hadn't we given them more time?*[10]

The uncertainty and unease reflected in Rush's response was indicative of the thinking of many of those involved in the Manhattan Project, especially those in the scientific fields.

Ordinary workers who contributed to the atomic bomb project were also subject to soul-searching over the weapons used on Hiroshima and Nagasaki, but they could more easily plead ignorance to their creation. Writing about Hanford (although the same could be applied to Oak Ridge), Paul Loeb suggests that Project security created an environment where lower-level workers could trust that "their efforts were necessary to win the war, they could immerse themselves in details. They could take pride in having overcome the harsh environment, the pressure and awkward restrictions to meet an unprecedented technical challenge. They had the satisfaction of carrying out a job they were asked to do."[11] Meanwhile, many of the scientists in Oak Ridge and Los Alamos who were equipped with greater knowledge from the start bore the weight of atomic responsibility more fully.

Beginning in 1946, the question over who should control nuclear weapons, civilians or the military, was a hot-button issue in Washington and throughout the new postnuclear landscape. A historian of the early Cold War period, Jessica Wang, describes the moment as "a brief, exciting, tumultuous period, [when] the atomic scientists moved to the center of American politics as the leaders of a fledgling political movement, launched at a turbulent time."[12] Scores of concerned scientists, including Rush, formed the Federation of Atomic Scientists (FAS) to discuss the emerging issues of atomic weapons and nuclear energy. The most pressing concerns according to FAS were the need to control fear and the need to cement arguments for a world governing body to control atomic power.[13] FAS's first priority was to exert pressure on Congress to defeat the May-Johnson Bill, which would have kept atomic weapons under the provenance of the military. As an alternative, FAS lobbied for the McMahon Act, known officially as the Atomic Energy Act, which would place atomic weapons under civilian control.[14] The scientists prevailed, and the McMahon Act passed both houses of Congress, creating the Atomic Energy Commission. President Harry S. Truman made it official with his loping signature on August 1, 1946.

The national and international FAS could count several Oak Ridge scientists among their ranks, but there were also local groups concerned with the ethical issues around the new atomic industries. Two of the most active were the Association of Oak Ridge Engineers and Scientists (AORES) and the Youth Council on the Atomic Crisis. AORES was the combined effort of several previous grouplets situated in the separate labs of K-25, X-10, and Y-12. AORES was not an anti-nuclear organization by any means—it did not try to interfere with operations at the Oak Ridge labs or seek a halt to nuclear industries—rather, it advocated for policy makers, scientists, and politicians to be aware of potential issues and dangers that could emerge from nuclear energy. These risks included radiation, accidents, environmental contamination, espionage, and theft.

Like the FAS, AORES members also advocated for international control of nuclear industries and for some say in the new atomic world they had helped to create. Millicent Dillon, a young physicist working on a secret project for nuclear-powered airplanes called Nuclear Energy for the Propulsion of Aircraft, recalled the group: "The committee members . . . had experienced the war in Oak Ridge in a secret facility. Before them was a potentially terrifying future, which they felt they had to make some effort to affect. They were, on the whole, self-controlled and intelligent, not given to wild outbursts of emotion. Though imagination had a place in their work— for scientific work demands a particular kind of imagination—they were not given to flights of fancy."[15] She goes on to say, "Would the word *mythic* ever have been voiced in that room? Never. Not by them, certainly not by me. And yet the effect of being in a living myth was there in that room, week after week, while those controlled discussions went on."[16]

While not anti-nuclear, and in Dillon's words "self-controlled," the Oak Ridge scientists were no shrinking violets; they were outspoken critics of what they saw as the tendency toward militarization of all atomic science. Yet they were living in myth, all the myths of the Atomic Age that they created and hoped to control and contain. In light of these views they came under scrutiny from the House Un-American Activities Committee, which found their positioning in the atomic debates to be a little too "Red." Scientists who were suspicious or resistant of military control were deemed naive at best and at risk of falling for communist plots at worst.

In order to interrupt atomic secrets from getting out, the FBI organized elaborate personnel security programs that tracked scientists and other workers with access to classified information. They attempted to identify individuals ahead of time who might become ideological threats or those whose character or personal flaws (according to the FBI) could put them at risk for betraying state secrets: communist sympathizers, homosexuals, drunks, addicts, adulterers, gamblers, and so on. From this system sprang countless erroneous charges, as well as an anxious and pressure-filled environment, producing the fear of plots even in the best adjusted. Eugene Wigner, the former director of the Oak Ridge labs, was shocked at the atmosphere that emerged and responded with outrage: "It is almost fantastic to hear people, who have been with the project since its inception and whose work is part of its foundation, get to wondering lest they be considered untrustworthy in the future."[17]

In June 1947, AORES received an investigatory visit from Congressman J. Parnell Thomas, chairman of the House Un-American Activities Committee. Thomas issued his findings in a sensational article in *Liberty* magazine entitled "Reds in Our Atom-Bomb Plants," where he warned, "The Atomic Energy Commission must come to grips shortly with pro-Soviet infiltration of its own organization. Fellow travelers, if not actual members of the Communist Party, have, for instance, ensconced themselves in the great plants at Oak Ridge, Tennessee, where U-235 is separated for use in the atomic bomb. . . . The laboratories are the most heavily infested."[18] Thomas found Oak Ridge scientists to be loaded with rouge-tinged ideas and was appalled that they could continue to hold their laboratory jobs. As a result of pressure from Thomas and others in Congress, in May 1948 the AEC conducted "loyalty" investigations of 30 percent of their employees. The former editor of the *Oak Ridge Journal*, Dick Gehman, wrote a critical response published a few months later in the *New Republic*, calling the whole operation a "witch hunt."[19] A great number of former Manhattan Project scientists who were still working in Oak Ridge lost their jobs on anonymous charges of communist sympathies or connections to communists. FAS and AORES actively protested these allegations but had little success in reinstating the scientists. Careers were ruined, lives derailed.[20]

Meanwhile, in 1948, a series of articles by the science journalist Stephen White assessing the anxious situation in Oak Ridge appeared in the *New York Herald Tribune*. The articles described "a new and staggering blow to morale that was already scraping the ground" and hinted at the possible demise of Oak Ridge as a powerful science center if conditions were not improved. White reported that a third of the senior physicists had already flown the coop and more could be on their way, headed for universities or industry work that would require less suspicion of their private lives and ideas.[21]

Meanwhile, another type of senior Oak Ridger was busy considering the atmosphere of the city and heading off to university—the seniors of Oak Ridge High School who were active in the nuclear awareness group the Youth Council on the Atomic Crisis. The group emerged from concerned students at the school in December 1945, just four months after the atomic bombing of Hiroshima and Nagasaki.[22] The initial idea for the group was sparked after a student discussion of *Modern Man Is Obsolete*, a harrowing account penned by Norman Cousins, warning of a global apocalypse unless a world government could be formed to hem in the power of the atom.[23] The need for more discussion and activism was further stoked by a visit from the atomic chemist Charles Coryell, who told the students, "Unless the atom bomb is controlled for peace, one out of three persons in this auditorium will probably die of the effects of atomic energy."[24] Coryell's assessment of this risk was based on his work as the chief of the Fission Products Section for the Manhattan Project.

Coryell was apprehensive about the use of the atomic bomb even before the close of the war. He was among the concerned scientists who signed the Szilárd Petition in the summer of 1945, urging President Truman not to use the atomic bomb "without restriction," suggesting instead that the bomb be "described and demonstrated" to the Japanese first, giving them ample time to consider its effects and hopefully to surrender before the bomb would be used.[25] The students, shocked and afraid after hearing the warnings of Cousins, Coryell, and others, crafted the council with urgency; as the president of the group, sixteen-year-old Richard Glasglow, stated, "We may be children, but if atomic war should come, we'd be just as dead as other people."[26] In September 1946, *American Magazine* ran a profile of the group in order to explain its motivation and, like most news outlets of the time, it took great pains to present Oak Ridgers as both normal Americans and citizens with special knowledge of the dangers of the new age: "Typical of kids in Oak Ridge, Joe himself is an average high school boy. Knowing how too potent is the power packed in the parcel no larger than a football, which destroyed a city as large as Buffalo, has sobered Joe up a lot. While he still likes jitterbugging, Dick Haynes, football, and amateur dramatics, Joe wants to make sure that he can keep right on living and enjoying these things without fear of atomic bombs."[27] Oak Ridgers were the canaries in the mine of the Atomic Age, and these young council members had begun to sing. The council, nicknamed "Yak-Ac," created an atomic energy library at the school, held local meetings, invited prominent scientists to speak to the community, encouraged letter writing, and traveled across the country for speaking engagements. The group functioned as a kind of consciousness-raising project, although the members of the group did not always completely agree with one another. *Time* magazine reported that the sharpest disagreement among Yak-Acs was over whether the United States was justified in the atomic bombings of Japan. The magazine reported that most girls thought the bombings were unjust, while most boys felt they were necessary to end the war.[28]

In the midst of these debates, on January 1, 1947, the civilian-run AEC officially took the reins of the U.S. atomic energy program from the Army and General Groves. David Lilienthal, the former director of the TVA, became the first chairman of the AEC. Once known as Mr. TVA, Lilienthal later became known as Mr. Atom because of the reassuring public face he gave to atomic energy, although his diaries betray a deeper ambivalence over the utopian potential of the atom.[29] While it felt celebratory at the time to its backers, in many ways the passage of the Atomic Energy Act was a hollow victory. Even though the military officially lost exclusive control over atomic energy, they succeeded in getting almost everything else they wanted, including a powerful military liaison committee, which would be able to wield considerable decision-making power within the AEC. From the very start, the "peaceful atom" danced on marionette strings that were at least partially controlled by the Department of Defense.

While the military had muscled into the AEC and could be said to be pulling strings in the background, atomic scientists were a visible presence in the public sphere and in public culture. Never before and never since had scientists commanded as much national attention as they did in the 1940s. Nuclear physicists could be seen and heard everywhere through all the major media outlets. Robert Oppenheimer's intense gaze stared out from *Time* and *Life* magazine covers, innumerable atomic scientists could be heard on countless special radio reports, and in 1947 Hollywood got into nuclear science with the Metro-Goldwyn-Mayer (MGM) film *The Beginning or the End*, a docudrama that focused on the Manhattan Project and even listed General Groves and several top scientists as consultants.[30]

The Beginning or the End had an unusual provenance. It originated not from Manhattan Project scientists or movie studio executives, but from the correspondence between the young Hollywood actress Donna Reed and her high school science teacher, Edward R. Tompkins, who worked at Oak Ridge during the Manhattan Project.[31] Tompkins told the members of the local scientists' interest group AORES about the potential project, and they indicated that they were on board. Several scientists worked as technical advisers: Albert Einstein and Leó Szilárd begrudgingly allowed their names to be used, but other prominent European scientists, such as Lise Meitner and Niels Bohr, flat-out refused to be associated with the film. Oppenheimer's approval was aggressively courted, and although he finally relented, he was not altogether pleased with the end product. Ever the aesthete as well as the scientist, Oppenheimer had more negative things to say about the creative aspects of the film than the historical or scientific. Perhaps this was because his character was idealized and portrayed as pleasant, with both his irritating and charming qualities sanded off, making him appear smooth but wooden. More oddly, General Groves gave permission for his role to be fictionalized and was awarded the title of "primary consultant." For his trouble, MGM paid the general $10,000.

The film, which turned out to be a box office flop (although it did win an Oscar for special effects), was originally seen as an exciting prospect for many of the Manhattan Project scientists who felt that a movie might help "to get across a message to a segment of the population which cannot be effectively reached in any other manner."[32] The scientists seemed to have in mind a kind of date night at the movies, with buttered popcorn, soda pop, and a plotline advocating that in the postwar era atomic bombs should rest under the care of a worldwide coalition of scientists. If this could have been achieved, they might have been able to live with the contrived romantic subplots that are obligatory in most Hollywood movies. Instead, the main theme of the film was to reassure American viewers that the atomic attacks were not only justifiable but absolutely necessary, and thank God the atomic bombs are in the hands of American scientists (and their international helpers) and not those other guys!

In the Atomic City, *The Beginning or the End* was much more popular than in other places in the postnuclear landscape. For many Oak Ridgers, the film screen reflected their ideas about themselves and their role in the war effort. The MGM nuclear drama played to packed crowds at the Grove Theater, where the marquee proudly listed its own subtitle: "Story of the Atomic Bomb and Oak Ridge." When the end credits rolled, the theater filled with raucous handclaps, drowning out the leaving squeak of shoes treading on spilled soda and flattened puffed kernels of dropped popcorn.

In the late 1940s, the majority of the American public was celebratory of the Manhattan Project's success and willing to gawk at the atomic scientists as new celebrities. But not everyone was thrilled by the attempts to

"The Beginning or the End," Grove Theater, Oak Ridge, 1947
(photo by Ed Westcott, courtesy of U.S. Department of Energy Photo Archives)

heroize the Project's scientists. One of the most prominent skeptics was the physicist Leó Szilárd. He scoffed that the scientists had made "a circus of themselves." More harshly he noted, "It is remarkable that all these scientists . . . should be listened to. But mass murders have always commanded the attention of the public, and atomic scientists are no exception to this rule."[33]

Einstein, for his part, saw the increased attention on the figure of the scientist as an opportunity to produce critical dialogue. During his tenure as chair of the Emergency Committee of Atomic Scientists, an organization where Szilárd also played a key part, Einstein sought to warn the public that there was no scientific defense against atomic bombs, that world government was the key to controlling this new weaponry, and that this realization must come from the people, from "the village square." Einstein appealed to the public to get involved; he felt that the panic and urgency of World War II had lulled the populace into behaving as sheep, "out of the habit of doing their own thinking." Instead, Einstein argued for "a new type of thinking" that would change the hearts and minds of folks against further secrecy and nuclear armament. From his perch at the Institute for

Advanced Study in Princeton, New Jersey, the scientist urged the public to "realize we cannot simultaneously plan for war and peace."[34]

Meanwhile, in Oak Ridge the nuclear laboratories were nearly as busy as they were during wartime doing just that: planning simultaneously for war and for peace. The attitude toward the atomic bombing of Japan, the atomic weapons program, and atomic energy was largely positive in the Secret City (and still is). Those who chose to stay in the city after the war accepted that Oak Ridge was the birthplace of the atomic bomb, whether they were enthusiastic boosters of the new nuclear industries or not. Still, along with the rest of the nation, they had to deal with some harsh realities of the Atomic Age. By 1946, it was clear that now that the formula and method for developing atomic weapons had been devised, (1) atomic bombs could be manufactured rather quickly and relatively cheaply by an organized nation-state, (2) there is no military defense against atomic bombs, and (3) the U.S. monopoly on nuclear weapons would be fleeting. After World War II, despite or perhaps because of the global fear of atomic warfare, Oak Ridge simply went about its business—the business of separating isotopes and enriching uranium for nuclear weapons. And the hum and the buzz of the factories continued. And it was discovered that a temporary community born from the emergency of war could be made to last if that spirit of emergency could be extended indefinitely, as Walter Benjamin wrote, to be "not the exception but the rule."[35]

The Atomic City in Technicolor

From 1943 to 1945, everything in the Atomic City was uniform but the leaves blazing in the autumnal Appalachian hilltops. By 1946, the physical and social landscape of Oak Ridge had undergone many changes: the trailer camps were removed, plans were drawn up for more permanent housing, the city had a radio station with the popular morning show *Up 'n' Atom*, Southern Bell had taken over the phone lines from the military, a civilian newspaper (the *Oak Ridge Journal*) was in circulation, and residents were able to paint their houses any color they wished. In the 1946 Oak Ridge High School yearbook, *The Oak Twig*, Joan Gilliam described the newly hued postnuclear house in rhyme: "Square shaped box / Flat on top / Painted the color / Of a lollypop." Like a soldier home on leave, Oak Ridge began to slip out of its olive drab and into something more colorful and comfortable, transforming the town's aesthetic. Despite all these changes toward a more typical American community, the future of the city and its relationship to the emerging nuclear industries hung in the balance.

The year spent waiting for the federal government to decide the fate of nuclear energy and the nuclear weapons industries was a tense one for Oak Ridgers, marked by uncertainty, rumors, and the mass exodus of many friends and neighbors. After World War II, the population of Oak Ridge rapidly dropped from 75,000 to 52,000 in only three months. And by June 1946, the population had fallen to just 43,000. Workers left for a variety of reasons; many had come only "for the duration." Some left on their own accord, either because they could not handle the job insecurity or simply because they desired to be somewhere else, whether for employment opportunities, familial reasons, or romantic possibilities, any of the common reasons why people leave one place for another. Others were subject to the massive layoffs that occurred when the city's needs changed. And some left because they disagreed with the decision to use the atomic bomb against Japan and regretted their role in killing innocent civilians. In a display of Oak Ridgidness, my grandparents stayed on, hoping for permanence. They never left.

While it is difficult to determine the exact numbers of those who vacated for each of these reasons—exit interviews were not often given or recorded, especially for those in lower-skilled jobs—what is certain is that after the war, what was left was a leaner, more elite, and more civically and scientifically dedicated population. The community that remained was proud of its cosmopolitan background, of its members being from someplace else, and equally proud of deciding to create a new space, a new type of community dedicated to science and nuclear industries. At the dawn of the Atomic Age, Oak Ridgers vocally celebrated their role in the Manhattan Project. They looked toward the future of atomic energy with a utopian optimism and the future of atomic weaponry with a sober belief in the necessity of an atomic bomb program for global security and freedom. As they faced the world outside the fence, they wore the mantle of the Atomic City with pride.

When the size of the city went into decline, there was less need for new homes and other community buildings. For this reason, it is not surprising that construction workers were the group that initially received the most pink slips. The second hardest hit were the operators of Y-12, many of them young female workers—the Calutron Girls among them. Toward the end of the war it became clear that the method employed at K-25 was the far more efficient process for separating uranium isotopes. As a result, Y-12 moved out of the nuclear weapons production business and into other national security services, eliminating the need for thousands of workers. By 1947, the number of workers at Y-12 was reduced from 22,000 to 1,450. This was known as the "Big Crash." In the postwar years, the process of isotope separation became more streamlined and efficient, requiring fewer workers to operate the machines. In the span of just three years the area that contained Oak Ridge had undergone swift industrialization, only to abruptly give way to the first steps toward deindustrialization.

The rapid rise and decline of Oak Ridge led to a curious situation where a city that had existed for only three years contained within its borders a ghost town. The Happy Valley trailer camp area, which housed the construction workers for the K-25 plant, was abandoned as early as October 1946. During the war, Happy Valley functioned almost like a separate secret city within the Secret City. To get into the community you had to have an additional resident pass, and, conversely, Happy Valley residents had to have a separate pass to travel into Oak Ridge proper. Once a vibrant, raucous community, Happy Valley became an abandoned site. Thelma Present penned a note to Margaret Mead describing "row upon row of empty trailers, hutments, barracks, empty stores, a cafeteria, a post office with not a soul around . . . structures already starting to decay and sag."[36] Nearly seventy years later, some traces and ruins of the community still exist, although the forest has mostly consumed what was left. If you wander through the woods and you know where to look, you can find lonely fire hydrants and evidence of the pathways that worked as streets of the former community. These fixtures constitute forgetting. The disappeared streets once named after birds are now home to many varieties of fowl, but to no people.

By contrast, those who lived in the townsite and remained after the war were surprised to find that not much about their lives had changed. "Meanwhile, our work went along pretty much the same as usual, as did our strange life."[37] Besides the uncertainty of the nuclear industries, many Oak Ridgers' daily lives stayed the same or even improved. As my grandmother remembered, "To keep us happy after the war everything was still nearly free—bus service and movies and everything."[38] The sharp drop in population increased the efficiency of city services, overcrowding ceased to be a problem, and bonds of friendships were cemented between those who chose to stay. A new civic spirit had also emerged, which could be seen in the postcards and souvenir pennants for sale in the local drug store, proclaiming "Oak Ridge—Atomic Capital of the World." The same message was a popular feature on the metal tags that residents affixed to their license plates, which carried the town's motto through thoroughfares and back roads writing the atomic highway with their spinning wheels.[39]

Once the secret of the Atomic City was known, workers had to make a choice: either to rally behind Truman's decision to drop the bomb and their role in producing the weapon or to reject the decision and question their wartime service. Those who were in stark opposition to the use of nuclear weapons tended to leave Oak Ridge once knowledge of the damage in Japan became known. In the late 1940s, the city was still very much a government-company town in the sense that nuclear industries were the main employment opportunities and the federal government the main employer. The nuclear scientists who disagreed with either the decision to use the atomic bomb against Japan or with the further development of nuclear weapons programs typically left the government-controlled laboratories in Oak Ridge and Los Alamos (either by choice or by firing). Many of these scientists became politically active in advocating for more international and civilian control over nuclear science industries; they joined the FAS, the One World or None Movement, the Union of Concerned Scientists, the Committee for Nuclear Responsibility, or one of the many anti-nuclear local and grassroots movements that formed in the wake of Hiroshima and Nagasaki.

Most workers on the Manhattan Project who stayed in Oak Ridge after the war enjoyed their work and still speak with pride about the job they did and the grit they exhibited under the tough and anxious conditions of wartime. In a 1946 article for the *American Journal of Psychiatry*, Oak Ridge's head psychiatrist Eric Clarke wrote, "Living behind a barb wire barricade had its advantages."[40] Expressing a common sentiment, another resident said, "It was terrible, but we loved every minute of it."[41] My grandmother told me "it was a step up" for our family.

The decision to stay put was sometimes called "Oak Ridgidness," an extenuation of the "can do, make do" wartime ethos. This sensibility also carried with it the belief that Oak Ridgers knew what was best for Oak Ridge and for the world concerning nuclear industries and nuclear technologies. Individual workers in Oak Ridge came to think of the success of the Manhattan Project as contingent upon their role; each worker a necessary and essential component to the sprawling apparatuses of atomic fordism. They saw the success of the Project as not merely the result of Oppenheimer and his team of scientific geniuses in the desert of New Mexico, but rather as the combined result of all those who stuck it out when the rubber met the road.

Folks who stayed in Oak Ridge became, in E. L. Doctorow's words, "people of the bomb," and their Oak Ridgidness grew with their renewed commitment to the possibilities of nuclear science in the immediate postwar moment and became even stronger as the community stepped up to the challenges of the Cold War.[42] This banding together created a new type of connectedness, a new type of social cohesion among those who worked on the atomic bomb project and lived in the community it created. In her memoir, Joanne Gailar wrote of Oak Ridgers, "First and foremost, we were all a part of the A-Bomb, of the tension of the deep secrecy that prevailed."[43]

By 1947, the Cold War defense industries kicked into high gear and Oak Ridge was right there swinging its legs. X-10 became the Oak Ridge National Laboratory (ORNL), and the X-10 graphite reactor became a piece of atomic heritage when it was declared a National Historic Landmark in 1966. Meanwhile, Y-12 and K-25 retained their original names, sounding like the beginning of a locker combination. X-10's transformation into a national laboratory helped secure Oak Ridge's place in the postnuclear landscape. Alvin Weinberg, the director of ORNL, described the significance of this time period:

> When the Atomic Energy Commission inherited from the Manhattan District the two scientific children of the Chicago Metallurgical Laboratory—the facilities at Oak Ridge and Argonne . . . no one really knew what a national laboratory was. In a general way, these institutions were supposed to explore the peaceful uses of nuclear fission. But in choosing to call them "national" rather than "atomic energy" laboratories, the commission displayed extraordinary foresight, or perhaps luck. An atomic energy laboratory, in principal, goes out of business when the problems of atomic energy are solved, are taken over by commercial enterprises, or are regarded (as at present) as unimportant. A national laboratory, by contrast, is more or less ensured immortality by virtue of its name. The designation "national" implies that no problem of national importance—whether in energy, environment, defense, industrial competitiveness, or basic science—is necessarily off-limits.[44]

With its new national laboratory status, the immediate anxiety over the town's longevity was allayed. Factories went into a twenty-four-hour production schedule and the atomic beehive buzzed again. "It's a funny thing. In the old days they used to have a poster around here that said, 'YOU CAN LICK JAPAN!' Now they've got one that says, 'YOU HOLD THE KEY TO WORLD PEACE.' And we're working the same way with the new poster as we did with the old one," wrote Y-12 worker Edward Jackson in his description of the postwar environment.[45] The city of Oak Ridge became a life-sized working model of Oppenheimer's statement: "The development of atomic energy for peace cannot be separated from its development for war."[46]

In the late 1940s, as X-10 was transformed into the Oak Ridge National Laboratory, K-25 and Y-12 continued to produce uranium-235 in order to increase America's stockpile of nuclear weapons and to "keep the world safe." As work at the atomic factories picked up again, so did the rhetoric of the civilian soldier, but this time workers would serve in the war against communism rather than the Axis powers. Fear of the Red Menace had invaded Oak Ridge, like the rest of the United States, and security concerns became paramount for the AEC. To root out secret communists, the AEC engaged in "loyalty investigations" of anyone suspected of red tendencies. Paranoia was rampant. Even the first mayor, A. K. Bissell, reportedly worked as a spy—or a creep, as they were known in Oak Ridge—for the federal government. A couple of examples, chosen out of hundreds, of the extreme measures taken by the AEC should illustrate the environment of fear and suspicion. An Oak Ridger, who wrote columns for the K-25 atomic plant's paper, the *Carbide Courier*, was followed by the police and ultimately questioned and threatened because of a book review she wrote of *The Yogi and the Commissar*, by the former communist Arthur Koestler.[47] And an Oak Ridge scientist was nearly fired when it was "discovered" that a distant relative by marriage was possibly a communist and that a copy of the *New Masses* was found in his garbage can.[48] Ultimately, this strategy employed by the AEC caused many scientists to lose their jobs and many other highly qualified scientists and technicians to leave government work out of disgust.

Normalization

In the immediate postwar years, the government tired of managing the cities of the Manhattan Project and decided that Oak Ridge should undergo the process of normalization. Two major plans were discussed: the first would be a federal district, along the lines of Washington, D.C.; the second was to transform the city into an incorporated municipality in the state of Tennessee. The latter plan was the one eventually accepted, although it faced a major roadblock early on because Tennessee law stated that municipal incorporation could only be put into motion following the request of at least 100 landowning residents. But there was no private property in Oak Ridge since the federal government owned all the land, so full incorporation would not be reached until 1959. Despite this challenge, by 1948 the AEC had outlined three major steps in order to transform Oak Ridge into a self-governing, self-supporting municipality, including the removal of the gates surrounding the perimeter of the city, the opening of the community to the general public along with increased security for the production and research facilities, the introduction of private property, and finally the incorporation of the city into the state of Tennessee.

Through the process of normalization, the intention was not only to normalize the town, but also the Bomb and nuclear industries in general. Taming the atom bomb and its legacies had its challenges. The Project retained a mythic quality; a kind of halo of magic hung about the word "atomic," conjuring utopian images of flying cars, superheroes, and all sorts of glowing objects resplendent with energy and power. Dangerous? Yes. Powerful? Definitely, but controllable in capable hands, if only barely so. Then, beginning with the Cold War, as atomic conversations slowly transformed into nukespeak, nuclear power entered into a new sobriety, where the industries that trucked in fissionable materials had to fill three contradictory roles: menacing threat, protecting force, and provider of "clean," abundant energy.[49]

Atomic vs. Nuclear

From the late 1940s into the 1960s (and arguably even today), "atomic" was an adjective that carried a certain sparkle and shake. People sipped atomic-themed cocktails, entered and were entertained by Miss Atomic beauty pageants, and drove to Las Vegas to watch aboveground tests from the rooftops of trendy hotels. Of course, atomic had a dark side, too, made manifest in such things as duck-and-cover drills and fallout shelter architecture. And by the 1970s and into the 1980s, the frosty stare down between the United States and the Soviet Union became scarier, a catastrophic nuclear event felt more possible, and all things atomic became a little bit less fun.

Atomic's heir in the grammar of new weapons technology—nuclear— did not carry the same charm: nuclear winter, nuclear meltdown, nuclear arms race, the nuclear option. Atomic, which now seems quaint, was crazy but exciting; nuclear was just plain mad—or MAD, as in Mutual Assured Destruction, the Cold War military strategy of national security employed by the U.S. and the USSR that used as a rhetoric of deterrence the threat of retaliation, wherein if one side attacked the other, the stricken nation would immediately answer, leaving both sides completely obliterated in an act of "awful arithmetic."[50]

After the atomic bombings of Japan, it was no longer possible to think of a pre-nuclear world. In the aftermath of the mushroom cloud, new occupations, new social types, and new cities were created—proving once again the concept of "normal" to be a moving target. Oak Ridge was ahead of the curve, pioneering two characteristic features of the Atomic Age: a new kind of American community planning that would spread across the country in the 1950s and the new science of nuclear physics that would shape military and energy policies for decades to come. Even after the federal government's forced process of normalization—and perhaps partially in response to it—Oak Ridgers never cop to being normal; they cling to their

Oak Ridgidness, still different from those outside the now invisible fence, still special, still scientific, still dedicated to Brahms and bombs.

A Separate City, Over There

Even as Oak Ridge was celebrated as the first wholesome all-American city of the atom, it maintained a landscape of racial segregation. By 1946, the problem of housing for black workers could have been alleviated, but the city moved slowly. Enoc Waters wrote in the *Chicago Defender*,

> If there was ever any justification in overcrowded conditions for relegating Negroes to sub-standard conditions divorcing them from the social and recreational life of the community, even that reason does not exist today. Housing at Oak Ridge today is so plentiful that the soldiers who have occupied barracks are being transferred to more commodious dormitories. Whites are abandoning hutments. It would be a simple matter to offer the families of Negro workers still employed at the reservation homes commensurate with those of similar white workers. With the general slowdown in construction work, it would be a simple matter to turn carpenters and bricklayers loose to develop educational, religious, and recreational facilities to Negroes if it were thought inadvisable for Negros to share existing facilities.

During wartime the atrocious living conditions of the black workers were not mentioned in the press, but afterward many felt the situation could no longer be ignored.[51] One journalist writing for *Mid-South Magazine* referred to the lack of quality housing for black workers as a "thorn in the Oak Ridge rose bush."[52] In 1950, after subsequent pressure from the black community, a federally built African American neighborhood was established. The neighborhood was located in the area of Gamble Valley, a hollow enclosed by two 300-foot ridges and the city dump. When the new neighborhood was built, the city's black leaders made a decision to call it Scarboro, the name of the pre-atomic community that occupied that swath of land before the Manhattan Project. As homage to its African American heritage, all the streets in Scarboro are named for historic black colleges. Tuskegee Drive is the neighborhood's main thoroughfare, with Fisk Avenue, Spellman Avenue, and Wilberforce Avenue, among other academically named arteries, spilling off in various directions.

Most white Oak Ridgers rarely traveled on Tuskegee Drive. Scarboro was isolated from the main body of the city; two miles and a four-lane highway separated the neighborhood from the nearest white homes. It was so set off from the rest of Oak Ridge that it was sometimes referred to as "a separate city" or simply "over there." Journalist Joan Wallace suggested that "it may have been the most deliberately isolated black community in the country."[53] As she explained, "For while in most southern cities there was and still is some pattern of racial separation in housing—white concentrations, black concentrations of residence—in virtually no other city was the separation so pronounced—so meticulously planned—as it was in Oak Ridge, a city planned and built by, of all people, the federal, not the state and local government."[54]

It is sad to say that even considering its isolation and its malodorous position next to the dump, Scarboro was a step up for black workers in Oak Ridge. As Wallace argued, "Relatively speaking, black citizens were likely pleased . . . as they had formerly been housed in small, ramshackle 'hutments'—buildings without plumbing, constructed during World War II."[55] Understandably, some Oak Ridgers found it hard not to be bitter that while Oak Ridge was being touted as a model city of the future, the federal government had created a ghetto for black workers during and even after the war. This kind of segregated landscape grew more prevalent across America in the following years and decades, when suburban living really began to take off. Oak Ridge was simply ahead of the curve.

The Opening Swing of the Gates

One of the first steps toward normalization was to allow greater access into and out of the city. From 1943 to 1949, entry to Oak Ridge was controlled and monitored by rifled patrolmen nested in guard towers like exotic, agitated birds while their hand-gunned compatriots pecked and squawked at each passing car below. After 1949, only the entrances to the atomic plants and other still-secret facilities were so closely patrolled.

The plan to open the gates, drafted by John C. Franklin, the Oak Ridge Operations Manager of the AEC, had been in the works since 1948. In the city this was not a popular initiative. Across the country in Los Alamos, the atomic city on the mesa, they also wanted to keep their fences. Like Oak Ridgers, Los Alamosians worried their community would become a spot for sightseeing and that bringing the fences down would create a more dangerous and uncertain environment, one that would make them think twice about letting their daughters ride the bus at night.[56] To discuss the matter, an Oak Ridge Town Council meeting was called and 200 people filled the room; when a vote was taken on whether to open the city, only 17 voted in favor of removing the gates, and many of these folks were pressured by their bosses to vote in that direction. The vote turned out to be an exercise in futility, and the AEC continued with its plan, much to the displeasure of the large majority of Oak Ridgers.

The outspoken and bespectacled cultural critic and urban activist Jane Jacobs was not surprised by the reaction of Oak Ridgers. In graduate school, quite by accident, I discovered her screed against my first city, making Oak Ridge again seem like a special place to me. In *The Death and Life of Great American Cities*, Jacobs's treatment of the Atomic City was rough, quite the opposite of her loving passages devoted to the great ballet of urban life she found in the West Village of Manhattan. Still, I loved that Oak Ridge was in the text; it felt like seeing my own name, and I excitedly underlined this passage while sitting on a bench in Washington Square Park where the ghost of Jane Jacobs would be, if she were anywhere: "But, on the whole, people seem to get used very quickly to living . . . with either a figurative or a literal fence, and to wonder how they got on without it formerly. . . . It seems that when Oak Ridge, Tennessee, was demilitarized after the war, the prospect of losing the fence that went with the militarization drew frightened and impassioned protests from many residents and occasioned town meeting of high excitement. Everyone in Oak Ridge had come, not many years before, from unfenced towns or cities, yet stockade life had become normal and they feared for their safety without the fence."[57] Jacobs was right in that some members of the Oak Ridge community, like those in Los Alamos, feared that the opening of the city would bring an influx of crime and endanger their children.[58] But Oak Ridgers' desires to keep their city closed encompassed more than security concerns: residents also wanted to preserve their atomic utopia. In the words of Jay Searcy, Oak Ridge was "a beautiful enclave that we didn't want to share."[59] One element of this attitude has to do with elitism and a sense of entitlement. During the war an enormous amount of federal and corporate allowances flowed into the city, giving it a school system head and shoulders above those in surrounding communities, advanced medical care, technological superiority, and a plethora of cultural opportunities, including a symphony orchestra, that no other city of comparable size in the region could boast. These perks were dispensed by the federal government as compensation for relocation and for the importance of the work done in Oak Ridge. Other reasons for their resistance were more practical: Oak Ridgers did not pay taxes, were given free coal, and enjoyed free or very inexpensive medical care and incredibly cheap rents, and all maintenance services were provided free of charge.

The closed city also gave Oak Ridgers a shared sense of specialness that went beyond the gated community's fear of crime, looky-lous, and declining property values. The powerful social bond shared between Oak Ridgers, mainly that they were once a secret people doing secret work, helped to erect a barrier separating themselves from those living outside the fence, even from family members or close friends. As Simmel writes, "The sociological significance of the secret is external, namely, the relationship between the one who has the secret and another who does not. But as soon as a whole group uses secrecy as its form of existence, the significance becomes internal: the secret determines the reciprocal relations among those who share it in common."[60] Insulation from the outside strengthened the social bonds between Project workers, as they internalized the importance of their secret work. The shared bond of secrecy made Oak Ridgers qualitatively different from those who did not participate in the Manhattan Project experience. Afraid of losing their specialness, of becoming more like their neighbors, of becoming *normal*, Oak Ridgers protested.

Despite all protest, the gate opening went on as planned.

Operation Open Sesame

On March 19, 1949, the Atomic City was opened with a tiny mushroom cloud. A standard ribbon-cutting ceremony executed with a snip of scissor blades would have been far too gauche for this science city of the future. In its place, a mini-simulacrum of an atomic bomb blast was ignited, setting ablaze the scarlet ribbon that stretched across the city's main gate. The tiny mushroom of smoke was the result of an electrical impulse generated from a uranium chain reaction initiated from the graphite pile of the Oak Ridge National Laboratory (x-10 during the Manhattan Project). This charge caused the ribbon, which had been treated with potassium chlorate and magnesium, to catch fire in order to make a loud pop. Many of those in attendance were visibly startled, as can be seen in the photographs taken on that day; many believed they were witnessing a live atomic explosion.[61] Others, without waiting for the smoke to clear, scrambled for bits of singed ribbon for their scrapbooks. Margaret Truman, the daughter of the president, was initially invited to sever the ribbon (the method was not specified), but she had declined due to a scheduling conflict. My grandmother cleared her schedule and was there that day and recalled being frightened, but also in awe. My grandfather, never one for crowds, opted to stay home and tinker with an old truck he was working on, a spark plug that refused to spark.

As part of the AEC's Operation Open Sesame, the ribbon-burning helped to usher in a new phase of visibility for the former secret city of the Manhattan Project. This spirit of openness marked a drastic change

Gate-opening celebration, Elza Gate, 1949 (photo by Ed Westcott,
courtesy of U.S. Department of Energy Photo Archives)

for Oak Ridge; the city would no longer function as a completely closed federal military reservation, unmapped and invisible to the Rand-McNally universe. Although the AEC referred to Oak Ridge's transition as part of its process of normalization, Operation Open Sesame was not a normal day; it was a spectacular event with thousands of people in attendance, including numerous celebrities and politicians.

The gate-opening ceremony was followed by an elaborate parade consisting of thirty floats, elaborately decorated vehicles, motorcades of dignitaries (both local and national), twenty-three marching bands, several National Guard units, multiple horse cavalcades, and a few Hollywood stars tossed in for good measure. As the floats meandered through the town, autograph seekers would swarm the cars, sometimes requiring the parade to come to a full stop. The cowboy actor Rod Cameron, who rode a Tennessee Walking Horse named Mr. Fox, was perhaps the day's most celebrated guest. He was reported as being very genial, and also perhaps a little drunk, nearly falling off his horse at various points.[62]

Throughout the day, national celebrities mingled with representatives from local communities. Neighboring cities sent what they called

Opening-day float, 1949 (photo by Ed Westcott, courtesy of U.S. Department of Energy Photo Archives)

"invasion forces," who marched under large banners marking where each group was from. Each city also had a main float that was meant to evoke the spirit of the residents' place of origin. For example, the nearby community of Lenoir City had a banner that declared "home of the hopeless," while Gatlinburg's float coasted with the more celebratory statement, "Headquarters of the Smoky Mountains National Park." The Gatlinburg float was one of the most popular; it included mountain flora, a working waterfall, and a fly fisherman outfitted in full regalia. The float dedicated to the city of Oak Ridge carried Parade Queen Pat Sutton and her court, decked out in flowing white gowns; they looked like Appalachian vestal virgins keeping the sacred atomic flame alive. Suspended on the float was also a large globe meant to symbolize the world, a dove to signify peace, and, just under the name of the town, a mushroom cloud created out of what looked to be aluminum foil.

The mood of the day was jovial and festive. With the new spirit of openness, adjacent communities flocked to the town; they were curious and excited to see what it looked like on the other side of the fence. For so long, Oak Ridgers had been seen by their neighbors at best as outsiders or "foreigners" and at worst as invaders in this corner of East Tennessee. Suspicion and even animosity had marked the relationships between Oak Ridge and other cities in the area. This antagonism stemmed from the trivial to the more substantial. For example, a great number of Knoxvillians were reportedly perturbed by the amount of red clay mud that Oak Ridgers tracked everywhere they went. It was also reported that neighboring towns were annoyed that many Oak Ridge women wore trousers to town. In fact, if ladies from Oak Ridge wore khakis or dungarees, they often did so for reasons of modesty, because they had to travel on overcrowded buses and regularly had to sit on the floor with their packages, not to mention that nylons were tough to come by during the war.

Outsiders interpreted Oak Ridge ladies' trouser habits as stemming more from liberal or progressive political ideas than practical reasons and were more critical than they might have been had they ridden on the buses themselves and attempted to balance their purchases and their modesty, as the rickety machines jostled and jerked. Still, Oak Ridge was a much more cosmopolitan and liberal place than the surrounding counties of Tennessee. So, political pants-wearing might have occurred alongside practicality.

Oak Ridge was also an important place for the federal government and was given preferential treatment. This favoritism sparked the more serious side of the grievances against the Atomic City. Oak Ridge sucked up a vast amount of resources, often at the expense of neighboring communities, from electricity to rationed goods to able-bodied workers to talented educators. Lafitte Howard, the head of the Associated Press bureau in Knoxville, described a situation where "almost any worker—from technician to household domestic—was gobbled into the maw of the mystery city. . . . Businesses, offices and plants—already depleted by calls to military service—were crippled further by workers leaving for Oak Ridge."[63] To combat the Atomic City's consumption habits during the war, some retail clerks in Knoxville even refused to sell goods to Oak Ridgers: "We're saving them for civilians."[64]

Miss Atomic Blonde, the Nation's Best-Dressed Man, and the Specter of Communism

Even if Oak Ridge rubbed some of its neighboring communities the wrong way with its special privileges and cosmopolitan ways, scores of folks showed up to take in opening day. Ten thousand Oak Ridgers and "outsiders" attended the ceremony, lining the streets of the Secret City, sometimes five or six deep. They listened as Vice President Alben Barkley credited Oak Ridge with ending World War II a year early. President Truman had been invited to address the crowd, but he was unable to attend. Following Barkley, the community affairs director Fred W. Ford delivered the keynote speech, which was then broadcast nationally on NBC Radio's World News Round-Up program, sonically filling homes around the country with news of Oak Ridge's opening.

Later that day there was a fashion show featuring the latest designs from the style houses of New York and Paris, hosted by the Oak Ridge Woman's Club. Here Hollywood actresses, such as Marie McDonald and Adele Jergens, mingled with local ladies as they watched regional models sashay down the runway in mink stoles and swimwear. This display of feminine attire might have reassured neighbors' concerns about pants-wearing women. The process of normalization also included gender normalization.

After the fashion show a cocktail reception, gala banquet, and dance were held, with Jack Bailey, the host of the *Queen for a Day* radio program, as the evening's emcee. It was Bailey's honor to crown Marie "The Body" McDonald "Miss Atomic Blonde."[65] Also in attendance was the film actor Adolph Menjou, voted the nation's best-dressed man nine times over. Tennessee congressman Albert Gore Sr. was also there, as was Senator Brien McMahon, the main author of the Atomic Energy Act of 1946.

During a toast, the governor of Tennessee, Gordon Browning, tried to bring the focus back to safety, security, and the threat of communism. Having the floor and an audience of important politicians, he also wanted to make sure Oak Ridge kept receiving government defense contracts. To this end, he said, "The purposes for which Oak Ridge was created are still in existence, and America is the only nation standing in the way of World domination by Russia. . . . This unique but wide-awake city is now part of all of us without restrictions except where restrictions should be."[66] The grandiose and enigmatic statement illustrates the importance of Oak Ridge in the nuclear and defense apparatus at that time. The city was "part of all of us." As Americans, we had all become "people of the bomb," yet Oak Ridge stood apart, still had some secrets—secrets that outsiders should never know.

While the tone of the day was undeniably festive and celebratory, there were waves of seriousness, such as Governor Browning's speech. In addition, several groups capitalized on the mass audience to air their grievances—de Certeauian tactics biting at the ankles of city management's strategies for normalization. Dormitory residents hung protest signs from their motorcade—"Open the Gate to a Fair Rent Rate"—in demonstration against the AEC, which had just cut back on maid service and raised their rent by ten dollars. Also, the much celebrated bus service of Oak Ridge was on strike the day of the opening ceremony, so many residents carpooled or even walked to the celebration. The protests ultimately had little effect on the new policies. Normalization would lead to the end of free maid service, to higher rents, and to major cutbacks in public transportation. Even with these changes and all those that would follow in the years and decades after the razzle-dazzle of Oak Ridge's opening celebration, the stubborn Atomic City has never conceded to normalcy and perhaps never will. At least not as long as there is Oak Ridgidness and atomic nostalgia.

Los Arzamas

In the late 1940s, when Oak Ridgers were busy worrying about what would come next, Soviet scientists were hard at work in the USSR's top-secret atomic laboratories. The premier lab was housed in a former monastery called Sarov, but with its new secret status, it gained many nicknames, as secret places do. Andrei Sakharov, who invented the Russian hydrogen bomb, favored "the Installation"; others called it Base-112, Kremlev, or Arzamas-16, while the scientists with the best senses of humor called the place Los Arzamas.[67]

On August 29, 1949, just a few months after Oak Ridge's opening bash, the Soviets detonated their own nuclear gadget. The device was similar to the Fat Man bomb used on Nagasaki, which is not surprising since it was based on plans scurried out of Los Alamos by Soviet spies, including Klaus Fuchs and David Greenglass. The Soviets called their bomb The Manufacture. The United States renamed it Joe-1, after Joseph Stalin. Whatever its name, in the summer of 1949 the U.S. nuclear monopoly disappeared with a mushroom cloud over Kazakhstan.

CHAPTER SIX

Happy Memories under the Mushroom Cloud

I see now that the life I was raised to admire was entirely the
product of this isolation, infinitely romantic, but in a kind of vacuum.
—Joan Didion, *Where I Was From*

It must have been quite a red-letter day for those who were able to travel to Oak Ridge for Operation Open Sesame, the daylong celebration of the new visibility of the formerly secret Atomic City. On March 19, 1949, in addition to the symbolic opening of the gates and the festive parade, another premier event was held; the world's first museum of atomic energy tossed out its welcome mat and opened its doors. The inauguration of the American Museum of Atomic Energy was carefully planned to coincide directly with the opening of the town; in fact, only two hours separated their respective public introductions. The timing was intended to solidify a particular version of the events leading up to and following the end of World War II.

From the first news of Little Boy, Oak Ridge has sought to celebrate and legitimize its role in winning World War II, and since the very beginning the city has attempted to tell this story through its museum. The museum has been a mainstay of atomic socialization, helping residents crystallize a very recent memory, creating a story for outsiders, and instructing all visitors in what is important to know about atomic history and nuclear weapons. The Manhattan Project has always been lauded at the museum, although other nuclear projects and characters of the atomic past, such as the atomic prophet John Hendrix, come and go, depending on the changes in attitudes toward nuclear energy, local interests, federal policies, and national security.

The museum's trajectory, from its celebration of atomic utopianism to its current tone of atomic nostalgia, mirrors the arc of the city itself, and to some degree the national narrative as well. Both dispositions—atomic utopianism and atomic nostalgia—are mystifying positions that thwart critical analysis of the use of atomic bombs against Japan, as well as the problematics of the Cold War legacy such as nuclear energy and nuclear waste. While the town's nostalgic shift can be seen through many lenses and social institutions, such as histories, documentaries, and newspapers, as well as the annual Secret City Festival, the museum might provide the best vantage point to view the phenomenon, as it marks one of the first self-conscious attempts to narrate the city's past and to articulate the possibilities of the future with all things nuclear.

The Road to the Atomic Museum

Before gaining a more permanent location, the American Museum of Atomic Energy first appeared as a traveling exhibition organized by the AEC. The mobile atomic museum was composed of a collection of displays showing atomic energy in a positive light, intended to garner support for the nation's nuclear energy and weapons programs. Not unlike a whistle-stop political campaign, the exhibit traveled across the country repeating its message over and over. The exhibition was incredibly popular, attracting large numbers wherever it went. Its most substantial crowd was drawn in June 1948 at the Golden Jubilee Celebration in New York City, where it received over a million look-sees. The Oak Ridge Heritage and Preservation Association described the exhibition hyperbolically as "a cooperative effort of industry, science, government, and education that brought atomic energy from the dark regions of fear and misunderstanding into the bright light of public comprehension."[1] The language chosen by the association speaks to a kind of atomic enlightenment, a rupture from a shadowy age of ignorance that leads to the warm glow of knowledge fulfillment.

As Oak Ridge was transformed from a closed federal military reservation into an open city, part of its agenda included branding itself as the Atomic City. This was difficult in that anything overtly atomic in the city was hidden, the result of joint efforts during and after the war by the federal government and the military to maintain secrecy and security. Even as the city became more open, the AEC certainly did not want visitors trekking through the still-top-secret atomic factories that were busy readying fissionable materials for the nation's Cold War arsenal. As a trial run, the AEC allowed visitors into Oak Ridge for the first time on October 22, 1948, to tour the "Man and the Atom" exhibit. The trial was a resounding success, with over 70,000 visitors lining up to take in the displays about atomic energy and the nationalistic and pro-nuclear messages on offer.

With confidence in the appeal of an atomic museum to the public, the decision was then made to set up a permanent space for the displays. The first incarnation of the museum was located in a former wartime cafeteria, where hungry Oak Ridgers had dined on buttermilk biscuits and chicken-fried steak; there, new visitors could learn about calutrons, isotopes, and of course the successful story of the Manhattan Project. The creators of the museum organized the displays around major spheres in which they felt the atom could be useful: energy, medicine, agriculture, and international peace. The exhibits put a positive spin on the decision to use the atomic bomb against Japan, as well as the separation of isotopes of uranium for peacetime purposes and security, thus legitimizing Oak Ridge's role during World War II, the Cold War, and beyond.

Atomic Dames and Irradiated Dimes

The American Museum of Atomic Energy offered a spectacular and sexy introduction to the possibilities of atomic energy and scientific advancement. At the opening party, Hollywood stars in fur coats, such as Patricia Neal, star atom-splitters, and prominent politicians circled with the rest of the public around the displays, creating nests of excitement. The message of the museum was clear: our lives are getting better all the time thanks to science and technology. Left out of this celebration was any discussion of the destructive elements of scientific progress or the gruesome aftereffects of the atomic bombs that were dropped on Japan. The true horrors of war and the potential dangers of fissionable materials both at home and abroad were hidden behind the overt utopianism of the displays.

With the end of World War II and the beginning of the Cold War, the AEC felt a need to control the message surrounding the atomic bomb and atomic energy in general. The museum in Oak Ridge, created by the AEC along with the Oak Ridge Institute of Nuclear Studies, was a key part of this plan. The stated goal was to educate the public by providing information on all things atomic, alongside displays of some other technologies that were in vogue at the time—robotics, time-saving kitchen gadgets, futuristic automobiles.

While the museum's initial focus was "Man and the Atom," the virtues of scientific and technological knowledge in general were celebrated. For example, there was a robotics exhibit featuring a set of mechanical hands that could take care of light tasks. In the (near) future there would be no need for such exertions. The first person to demonstrate the dexterity of the robotic digits was the actress and chanteuse Marie "The Body" McDonald;

Movie stars Rod Cameron, Marie "The Body" McDonald, and Adele Jergens with mechanical hands at the American Museum of Atomic Energy, opening day, 1949 (photo by Ed Westcott, courtesy of U.S. Department of Energy Photo Archives)

she volunteered her smoke. As the Hollywood vixen gracefully leaned forward, her cigarette hanging from a handsome holder, the cut tobacco rolled in its paper shell was ignited and successfully lit, as elegantly perhaps as Clark Gable would have done.[2] During World War II, McDonald posed for GIs in the military magazine *Yank*, among other publications, and became one of Hollywood's most celebrated pin-up gals. Her appearance in the museum that day with her smoldering robot-lit cigarette would have caused a stir for many, the two-dimensional beauty unpinned and present in all three curvy dimensions.

Long after opening day the museum continued to be a curiosity for visitors, both local and from very far away, attracting those who were interested in science and energy as well as those who wanted to get closer to the power of the atom. One way that visitors were able to increase their proximity to atomic energy was through some rather odd souvenirs. For example, in the museum's early years visitors could walk away with an irradiated dime—the charge would be neutralized by the time they reached the parking lot, but for a few seconds they could possess a bit of radiation, hold it in their hands, and put it in their pockets. From 1949 to 1967, 1 million dimes were irradiated.[3] The practice of irradiating dimes was discontinued after the metal composition of the ten-cent coins was changed, which caused them to hold on to radioactivity longer.

Above my writing desk sits my own formerly radioactive dime encased in its plastic protective shell with a halo of text—American Museum of Atomic Energy Neutron Irradiated—circling FDR's stately profile. It is fitting that the president who began the Manhattan Project should be thus enshrined. I trust the scientists who tell me that it is now a regular dime, that its atomic aura is only symbolic and historical and will not make me sick, and that I am not making the same mistake as the great scientist and two-time Nobel Prize winner Marie Curie, with her glowing jars of radioactivity lovingly placed at her bedside, nightly invading her cells like biological nightmares as she slept.

Irradiated dimes were not the only souvenirs that promised owning a bit of atomic energy (even if untapped); during the 1950s and 1960s visitors could also purchase uranium ore from the gift shop. Encased in plastic and embossed with the museum's logo, tourists were able to take away as memento the raw material for producing an atomic bomb. Less radioactive, but just as domesticating of atomic energy, was the comic book *Dagwood Splits the Atom*, which could be bought for ten cents—perhaps an irradiated dime if one had been willing to part with it. "Blondie . . . oh, boy . . . I DID IT! I got th' touch—It's Splitting!" reads one comic text bubble next to a picture of uranium, colored bright red. Just as the spectacle of celebrities on opening day obscured some of the ugly truths regarding the atomic bombings of Japan, later the souvenirs worked to domesticate the dangers of radiation in general. After all, how bad could radiation really be if you could carry it around in your pocket or if even Dagwood could mess around with it?

At the AMSE, exhibits were often interactive. In addition to the dime irradiator, there was a "radiation detector," which in the words of the museum's exhibit manual was "built to meet a definite public demand." The detector was composed of a Geiger counter and probe and was used to test samples of ore and watches with luminous dials. More frightening were the exhibits aimed at children, especially the "Radioactive Turtles," an atomic shell game where young visitors would locate, with the help of a sliding Geiger counter, the radioactive reptiles as they milled about with the non-radioactive ones.[4]

The museum was utopian in its vision that atomic energy and the stockpiling of atomic weapons could provide a safer, more democratic, and better future for us all. This sentiment is echoed in the catchphrase "Atoms for Peace!" that was used by the museum in the 1950s and 1960s. The slogan was borrowed from the speech President Eisenhower gave to the United Nations General Assembly on December 8, 1953, part of the U.S. government's media propaganda campaign "Operation Candor," which sought to put into context the hopes and dangers of the nuclear future. The president gave a complicated "recital of atomic danger" in "the language of atomic warfare" in order to demonstrate the "arts of peace."[5] Eisenhower's address and the museum's message it inspired were characteristic of the difficult waltz of emotion management that typified the Cold War era. The emotions of fear and hope could be worked with, manipulated, pumped, and used to prod people into action, while terror and complacency with what had been "achieved" through nuclear projects or with what might come with future endeavors were more static emotions, less likely to produce action.

During the time of Operation Candor, the AEC also continued its outreach program and reinvigorated its traveling exhibitions. Large trucks and buses plastered with giant swirling atoms and the messages "Atoms for Peace" or "Your Stake in the Atom" jazzed up the new interstate highway system like scurrying billboards. Meanwhile, my grandfather, wearing his trademark aviator sunglasses, crisp indigo Levis, and side-zip boots, drove an inconspicuous unmarked GMC truck for the AEC, couriering whatever sorts of materials needed couriering, in secret. He told my grandmother, "Nannie, I'll be back in five days." She knew better than to ask where he was going, knew he couldn't say. My uncle Frank told me recently, "We never even thought to ask a question about where he was going, everybody's work was secret."[6] As much went unsaid in Oak Ridge, atoms for peace and atoms for the Cold War zipped past each other on Eisenhower's newly built interstates, keen with "the wisdom of broader ribbons across the land," nimble roadways constructed (at least in part) to get us all out of the cities quickly and orderly in case of nuclear attack.[7]

The American Museum of Science and Energy

In its first decades, the museum's message was future oriented and utopian: nuclear materials would not only be used for bombs, but also to heat our homes, fuel our cars, and provide clean, limitless energy, forever. Sometimes, though, forever has a brief shelf life. As early as 1978, the American Museum of Atomic Energy dropped its once-proud atomic title and changed its name to the American Museum of Science and Energy. The museum explained that the switch "reflected the expanded programs in all energy alternatives and energy research."[8] While left unstated in the museum's official response, it seems likely that this change could also reflect a growing malaise over nuclear power and nuclear weapons industries.

In the following years and decades, aided by events such as the Three Mile Island accident, the Chernobyl disaster, and the Fukushima Daiichi nuclear meltdown, as well as the fear of nuclear winter and the many health problems plaguing downwinders in the American West as a result of decades of nuclear testing, the utopian idea of nuclear energy as an unproblematic energy source has become a thing of the past. It should be noted that nuclear energy remains in the arsenal of energy solutions employed by the United States to feed the nation's ever-increasing demand for power, and that in the early twenty-first century there was some talk of a "nuclear renaissance," a new focus on nuclear energy as an alternative to fossil fuels and greenhouse gas emissions, although this idea has cooled somewhat since the disaster at Fukushima.[9]

By the 1970s, nuclear sloganeering had lost much of its original purchase. Nationally, the emotions of bewilderment, fear, dread, and ambivalence replaced, or at least confronted, the hopefulness once attached to atomic energy. It was no longer the early days of atomic hope, where "community boosters competed with each other throughout the West and elsewhere in the nation for a slice of the atomic pie," but a time in which the cries of "Not in my backyard!" drowned out those who continued to whisper "Atoms for Peace!"[10] With these changes, Oak Ridge's identity came into question; its challenge was to sell its uniqueness and importance—historically as a starting point for the Atomic Age and in the present as both a crown jewel in national security and as a global player in scientific brainpower and engineering wherewithal.

In the postnuclear landscape of the 1990s, as the Cold War slowly thawed and the fate of the labs and nuclear industries in Oak Ridge became a bit uncertain, the museum and the community as a whole directed more of their attention toward the preservation of the city's utopian moment. It was to be a celebration of the beginning of the Atomic Age rather than the shaky nuclear present or the more recent Cold War past—a legacy that carries more ambivalence.

Many Oak Ridgers, past and present, remained convinced that their unique history as a secret atomic city is akin to a technological Shangri-La. This image of an idyllic existence is perhaps no more apparent than in the series of rooms at the AMSE that detail Oak Ridge's role in the Manhattan Project. This portion of the museum was created in 1975, when the museum moved from its first location in the ramshackle 1940s cafeteria to a new, modern, two-story building that today, nearly forty years later, seems a bit dated and behind the architectural times.

Despite the regional interest, the museum's Secret City rooms are not a completely provincial affair. From 1975 to the present, there have also been displays of national newspaper headlines and various documents and images from World War II. Replete with black-and-white photographs, objects, and products from the 1940s, this wing of the museum celebrates consumerism and citizenship, along with what Tom Englehardt calls "American victory culture"—the notion that the United States is a land of freedom and ever-expanding liberties, a place that is always on the right side of things and uses force only in response to an attack.[11] Victory culture goes hand in hand with the American culture of innocence, the myth of a benevolent nation stripped of any lust for power. It is a position of denial that ignores the role the United States has played in global politics and instead presents the nation as a non-aggressive entity, only attacking when attacked, such as the use of the atomic bomb in response to the "stab-in-the-back on Sunday Morning," as Pearl Harbor was described.[12]

The Secret Telephone

As a kid I found the most disturbing part of the museum to have been a chilling call from the past. I would pick up the off-white telephone next to the glowing neon-orange-and-blood-red mushroom cloud, which seemed to emerge from Hell itself, to hear . . . THE SECRET. The secret turned out to be a very brief one-way conversation narrated by Colonel Paul Tibbets as he maneuvered the Enola Gay over Hiroshima and dropped Little Boy on an unsuspecting Japan on August 6, 1945. I remember wanting to ask the voice on the other end, What happened next? How many people were killed? How much radiation was released into the atmosphere? I knew if I asked these questions out loud, I would be met with silence; I troubled over this interrupted connection.

The philosopher Avital Ronnell writes in *The Telephone Book* that the phone is about communication and also about answerability. By picking up the phone, one signals that a call has come through, or that one is about to make a call. The secret telephone made me feel responsible, complicit, at the very least a witness to the atomic bomb. When I picked it up, I felt as if Hiroshima was just then being devastated; I was hearing it happen. Why didn't I just hang up? Holding the secret telephone, I could feel its plastic heat up. I couldn't tell if the warmth I felt was from my hand or if the phone

The Secret, 2004 (photo by Amanda McCadams)

had become radioactive. The electric speech from the past scrambled my brain and made an omelet of my emotions.

Compulsively, on each visit I always had to hear its message. Maybe this time Tibbets would say something else. Fantasies of all the Oak Ridges and Hiroshimas that never happened rested on the other side of the switchboard; the wires just needed to cross differently in the past. Ronnell warns through text and tone: "You will become sensitive to the switching on and off of interjected voices."[13] The telephone communicates a message of technology, schizophrenia, and electric speech. The secret phone seemed to be always ringing, even though it never actually rang, audibly at least.

Then, one time I went to visit the museum and it was gone. The mounted telephone had become outdated; it looked too old-timey with its corkscrew cord, manila-file color, and bulbous shape in an age of wafer-thin smart phones. Tibbets's message, by contrast, could never become outdated. It is fixed in time and oozes throughout the museum, fills the streets of Oak Ridge, suffuses atomic Appalachia, travels the atomic highway, and circles the world.

The Secret City Rooms

To enter the Secret City rooms of the museum you must snake through a curvilinear structure that begins with a mounted television screen flashing black-and-white images of the Third Reich. Once inside you are confronted with a Plexiglas display where Nazis goosestep across the visual plane, the mini-mustachioed Hitler performs his famous salute, the itinerary of the Enola Gay is mapped, and a brief description of the first atomic bomb dropped on Hiroshima is offered. To counter the villains, who are easily recognized, the museum casts the heroes of World War II: the U.S. military, "our boys overseas"; Oak Ridgers, along with other Americans who are "doing their part for the war effort"; and the international cohort of scientists—"the greatest minds in the world"—who worked on the side of the Allies.

The most famous of these minds resides in the skull of Albert Einstein, who appears more times in the museum than any other historical actor. Through the figure of Einstein, the museum's outlook toward the atomic bomb and the scientific uses of nuclear energy can be easily ascertained. Einstein's presence is reassuring; of all the physicists, he is the most recognizable, his genius the most trusted, and his corporality the most comforting. Typically pictured wild-haired and sweater-clad, he plays the comforting grandfather to Oppenheimer's rakish and slightly unsettling charms. From the entrance of the museum Einstein plays a starring role; a painting of the scientist hangs in the mezzanine directly above the information desk. He pops up again upstairs in the portion of the museum dedicated to the Y-12 National Security Complex; here Einstein is a ghostly image, a specter visible in the background of a poster that shouts, "Defending the Free World," where he looks over some papers with fellow scientist Leó Szilárd. Images of Einstein and Szilárd are used as props to bolster the U.S. Homeland Security agenda. Both Szilárd and Einstein later felt ambivalent about the use of the bomb, even though they initially encouraged research in that direction during World War II. Szilárd, especially, became an avid and vocal critic of U.S. Cold War policies. The placement of the scientists here feels a bit dishonest.

Back downstairs is the third most obvious placement of Einstein, where the scientist is rendered in wax, Madame Tussaud style, and an adjacent card states, "He laid the groundwork for splitting atoms." Next to the display there is also a copy of the famous letter that Einstein wrote with the aid of Szilárd and the scientists Eugene Wigner and Edward Teller to President Roosevelt on August 2, 1939, urging development of an atomic fission program and suggesting that Nazi Germany might be on to the same thing. Addressed to the president, the anxious letter states,

> Some recent work by E. Fermi and Szilárd . . . leads me to expect that the element uranium may be turned into a new and important source of energy in the immediate future. Certain aspects of the situation which has arisen seem to call for watchfulness, and, if necessary, quick action on the part of the administration. . . . It may become possible to set up a nuclear chain reaction in a large mass of uranium, by which vast amounts of power and large quantities of new radium like elements would be generated. Now it appears almost certain that this could be achieved in the immediate future. This new phenomenon would also lead to the construction of bombs, and it is conceivable—though much less certain—that extremely powerful bombs of a new type may thus be constructed. A single bomb of this type, carried by boat and exploded in a port, might very well destroy the whole port together with some of the surrounding territory. . . . In view of this situation you may think it desirable to have some permanent contact maintained between the Administration and the group of physicists working on chain reactions in America. . . . I understand that Germany has actually stopped the sale of uranium from the Czechoslovakian mines, which she has taken over.

Left out of the museum's display cases is Einstein's later regret. Toward the end of his life he said to his friend Linus Pauling, "I made one great mistake in my life . . . when I signed the letter to President Roosevelt recommending that atom bombs be made; but there was some justification—the danger that the Germans would make them."[14] The complexity of his feelings toward the bomb are missing, making it appear as though Einstein had given a rousing endorsement. This absence, countered by his omnipresence throughout the museum, makes it appear as though Einstein not only wholeheartedly supported the Manhattan Project but also supported all the U.S. Homeland Security measures at Y-12 in response to the "global threat of terrorism," as proclaimed by the museum's displays. As with Marie "The Body" McDonald, the celebrity spectacle of Einstein helps to distract the visitor, to distance and obscure the dangers of nuclear materials, and to mask the realities of the destructive pasts and the dangerous potentials of nuclear weapons.

Snapshots of Atomic Culture, Everyday Life, and Devastation

Positioned in the center of the first room of the museum, setting the tone for visitors, are photographs by Oak Ridge's official Manhattan Project photographer, Ed Westcott. His highly staged snapshots depict patriotic sentiments, a Protestant work ethic, and wholesome family values. The images offer an idealized version of the work that was done at the atomic factories. They feature two-dimensional Kodak teenagers in letter sweaters and knee-length skirts doing the Twist, women tending victory gardens, and swarms of smiling workers filing out of the K-25 plant during a shift change, among other evocative photographs showing patriotic sacrifice for the war effort. The term "Kodak teenagers" is used here not merely as a turn of phrase, but also in a literal sense. The Eastman Kodak Company originally managed Oak Ridge's X-10 Graphite Reactor, which delivered the first significant amounts of plutonium to Los Alamos. Perhaps more than any other object or display in the AMSE, these photographs elicit nostalgic feelings for the Manhattan Project era.

One of the most recognizable images of the bunch is that of the Calutron Girls hard at work in 1945. This photograph shows two rows of young white women working in the Y-12 plant, monitoring multiple dials embedded in tall grey metal cabinets. In addition to illuminating the role of the generic (white) worker, the photographs provide evidence that women played a part in the war effort; Rosie the Riveter lays down her rivet gun to observe an electromagnetic separation dial.[15] Row upon row of these women can be imagined in multiple rooms stretching out like so many Tiller girls across the stage.[16] The description that the German sociologist Siegfried Kracauer gives to the Tiller dancers could easily be applied to the workers in Oak Ridge: "These products of American distraction factories are no longer individual girls, but indissoluble girl clusters whose movements are demonstrations of mathematics."[17] The image conveys the enormous scope of the Manhattan Project and its labor intensity, where everyone is doing her part in atomic fordism to achieve a collective goal.

Perhaps not surprisingly, there has been no permanent counterbalancing exhibit on the destruction of the cities of Japan. Media activist and founder of Paper Tiger Television DeeDee Halleck, who grew up in Oak Ridge, remembers visiting the museum as a child in the 1950s and seeing

Calutron Girls (photo by Ed Westcott, courtesy of U.S.
Department of Energy Photo Archives)

photographs of the devastation caused by the atomic bombs. The images
were of landscapes and cityscapes lacking human figures, making her
wonder if everyone had been killed. Halleck remembers her frustration
that the museum did not spell out the number of casualties. She thought
that maybe "everyone went into the air raid shelters or under their desks,
as [she] learned to do at school."[18] Later Halleck came to the terrible realization that this was not the case. There was one image that pierced her
through, an example of Barthes's punctum, that special quality of certain
photographs to affect us—body and mind—through a detail: "One photograph showed a shadow imprint of a human being with the curious title,
'Permanent shadow on such and such bridge.' I was puzzled. A shadow
is impermanent, dependent on light for its creation. When I studied the
charred outline of a head and body etched on stone, I realized in horror
that human beings had lived in Hiroshima and Nagasaki."[19]

Years later, an image of a Japanese sufferer was added to the museum,
one lonely figurative photograph of a badly burned victim in Nagasaki that
weakly underrepresented the devastation. The man with charred skin was

alone, both in the frame of the photograph and in the museum. It is telling, too, that the image is set in Nagasaki, the second city hit, and the one crumbled by a different bomb, not Oak Ridge's. The aftereffects of Little Boy have been historically absent from the museum, left to the imagination of each individual visitor.

Yet in 2013, a special exhibit was launched that marks a distinct break in the way the AMSE has typically dealt with nuclear imagery. The exhibit "Japan 1945: Images of U.S. Marine Photographer Joe O'Donnell," organized by the Tennessee State Museum, shows stark photographs of the Japanese cities after their ruin from the violence of atomic bombs—although again here Nagasaki rather than Hiroshima dominates.

O'Donnell served as an early witness to atomic devastation. The black-and-white images of burned bodies and scorched land, of nothingness where once vibrant cities stood, that were on display in the Oak Ridge museum were not taken in his official capacity for the U.S. Marines; those stand at attention elsewhere in military archives. The photographs hanging at the AMSE were the result of de Certeauian tactics, individual operations performed while implementing the official documenting strategies of the U.S. government. O'Donnell captured these harsh images with his own camera, not the one the government provided him. Some were secreted out of Japan as negatives in a box marked "Photography paper: Do not expose to light" in order to prevent the military from seizing them. Others he developed in makeshift darkrooms fashioned in tents or in abandoned Japanese homes, as he rode his horse, Boy, around the devastated landscape where uranium and plutonium had ridden inside the bombs Little Boy and Fat Man only days before.

O'Donnell was overcome by the nuclear ruin and the human suffering he saw again and again as he developed his rogue images. After the war, he locked his personal negatives in a trunk. The black-and-white snaps of devastation stayed there for over fifty years—ghostly images collecting dust. In 1989, O'Donnell embarked on a religious retreat in Kentucky; while hiking he happened upon a nun's sculpture of Jesus nailed to a cross and ravaged by flames, a monument to the memory of the victims of Hiroshima and Nagasaki. After this encounter, O'Donnell open the trunk, five decades of repressed memories enveloped him, and he knew he must finally show the photographs to others.

Inside the frames, whole cities are made ghostly, visions of omnicide become possible, and imagining the destruction of all life by nuclear war does not seem far-fetched. We can see no birds, no weather, no evidence that bustling cities once existed. A blasé attitude is not possible when witnessing the nuclear necropoles. O'Donnell's photographs are suffused with a sense of doom, making a provocative counterpoint to the display of the cool and joyful Westcott photographs that hang catercorner. The images force the recognition of "meanwhile." It becomes clear that as Oak Ridgers danced and celebrated en masse that their gadget had worked, whole cities and their populations were ravaged and irradiated. The Manhattan Project workers did not comprehend the devastation; they had not seen what O'Donnell had.

While only a temporary juxtaposition, the scene at the AMSE in the summer of 2013 marks an example of how two visions of the historic atomic bomb project could exist face-to-face in opposition, each magnifying the effect of the other. The critical potential of atomic nostalgia emerges when discordant memories are intentionally placed side by side to work on each other.

The Future of Atomic Nostalgia in the Museum

Despite the fact that the adjective "atomic" was excised from its official name, exhibits devoted to the Manhattan Project still dominate the museum. From the 1950s onward, there have been many attempts to diversify the space, albeit within the constraints of certain historical perspectives. The AMSE is a national museum, a Smithsonian affiliate operated by the Oak Ridge Labs along with the University of Tennessee-Battelle, a Department of Energy contractor. From the Manhattan Project to Cold War politics to the Department of Homeland Security, new exhibits have steadily been added that reflect the political moods of the federal government (and the corporate entities that remain closely attached) toward nuclear energy and nuclear weapons.

The overly positive attitude toward science and technology in the AMSE, while expected, is questionable in a museum that owes its life and content to a city that was created for the sole purpose of the development of the atomic bomb. The museum's message strongly asserts that the end of World War II led to an age of nuclear deterrence and to a world that was safer for democracy. And then, just as strongly, it promotes the message that democracy is something that is always at risk, something that we must always be defending. This position is not unique to the AMSE. American nuclear museums in general have been characterized by this push-pull, what Bryan C. Taylor has called "throbbing history marked by paradox and risk."[20]

Even before visitors enter Oak Ridge's museum, they are doubly reminded of the precariousness of postnuclear life by the two sculptures that are parked at the edge of the parking lot. The first is of an atom with whirling electrons, made slightly rusty from time spent in the elements. Next to the atom at hand-holding distance sits a 9/11 sculpture, a 1/100 scale replica of the Twin Towers fashioned by Limor Steel of Nashville. These three-dimensional renderings are remarkable in how they scramble time and space, strangely connecting science, catastrophe, and unrelated historical events, encouraging thoughts of innocence and victory and the imperative to never forget. The atom is blown out of proportion, huge, magnified, person-sized, whereas the Twin Towers are miniaturized, truncated, and abbreviated, but also human-sized. The sculptures have been made to confront the visitor, standing up to us eye-to-eye, mano-a-mano. In the postnuclear landscape in which we move, the sculptures—and the events and emotions they symbolize—are connected by placement and by ideology. They work to draw us toward them, and they ask us to make sense of their appearing together at this time, in this place.

Oak Ridge's museum was the first nuclear museum in the United States; now there are many, including the Bradbury Science Museum in Los Alamos, the National Museum of Nuclear Science and History in Albuquerque, the Atomic Testing Museum in Las Vegas, the B-Reactor Museum in Hanford, and the Rocky Flats Cold War Museum in Arvada, Colorado.[21] These museums are important in that they are among the most public cultural institutions discussing nuclear weapons. They influence the American public's ideas about the history of the bomb and the nuclear present, while at the same time they seek to legitimize history and current policy for an international audience. As the sociologist Matt Wray points out, "Few museums of technology ever stray from the ideological path that equates technological advances with human progress and cultural and moral superiority."[22] The fact that these museums remain largely uncritical and nationalistic damages the possibility for debate regarding the United States' nuclear past, present, and future.

As the original creators of the Atomic City enter their eighties, nineties, and beyond, and as even their children coast into middle age, Oak Ridgers have begun to ask themselves how they want to remember their past. At present, plans are in the works to create a new museum in Oak Ridge. Former employees of the Manhattan Project, as well as local preservation groups, were hoping to save a portion of the massive tuning-fork-shaped K-25 building for this purpose, although it looks now as if none of the original building will be salvageable.

A K-25 History Center has been proposed at another location. The suggested site, although not on the original grounds, would contain a "withdrawal alley fitted with authentic World War II processing equipment" and an "interpretive center focused on the methods pursued at Oak Ridge to produce enriched uranium."[23] In addition to its didactic features, the K-25 history site would also include examples of what historian and memory scholar Alison Landsberg calls "experiential" space, where the visitor experiences elements of the past physically.[24] The goal would be to "allow visitors to delve deeply into the richness of the culture and exhibits of seeing *the real thing*, the real equipment, smelling the place, and knowing one is where it actually happened."[25] If this museum space is realized, it will introduce additional sensual layers—olfactory, optical, and tactile—in order to create the aura of being in the actual atomic factory circa 1945.

Building on the work of Walter Benjamin, the British sociologist Jon Urry argues that while older museums have relied on the aura of authentic historical objects, in postmodernism there has been a change from the auratic to the nostalgic. Urry's distinction is too sharp. In the postnuclear landscape, aura and nostalgia are not at all oppositional, but impossibly intertwined. Nuclear sites are emotionally and sensationally productive, lending themselves to all sorts of wild imaginations.[26] Proposals for the new museum space reflect these sorts of visions, the concatenation of which describes a schizophrenic distraction factory. Murals illustrating the history of Oak Ridge have been proposed, as well as an expansion of the current AMSE, the display of authentic artifacts from the 1940s, and many commercial activities, including a brew pub, roller-skating rink, squash courts, bicycle rental store, and a performing arts center. (I have to wonder if the squash court is a nod to Fermi's Chicago experiment; nobody really plays squash in East Tennessee.) As the marketability of atomic historical spaces continues to grow, it could be possible for the grandchildren and great-grandchildren of the original Oak Ridgers to receive an entirely new type of atomic socialization; they could roller-skate through the K-25, while their parents enjoy a micro-brew at the local uranium-themed pub. On offer, one would hope, would be ales of stronger stuff than the "near beer," the 3.2 percent variety that Oak Ridgers could buy during the war.

The nuclear pub concept is not without precedent. There already exists a nuclear-themed roadhouse called Rocky Flats Lounge near Boulder, Colorado, where in addition to beers and spirits, you can purchase a T-shirt emblazoned with the phrase "I got nuclear wasted." Also, in Richland, Washington, the bedroom community to the secret Manhattan Project site of Hanford, there is a lovely organic pizza and craft beer spot called Atomic Ales. Unfortunately, when I was in Colorado I never made it to the Rocky Flats Lounge, but I was lucky enough to while away an evening at Atomic

Ales drinking a pint of Oppenheimer Oatmeal Stout, a name that must have been chosen based on criteria other than the stature of the slim scientist. The building that now houses Atomic Ales was a drive-in fast-food joint in the 1950s featuring waitresses on roller skates, including the ill-fated actress and Playboy centerfold Sharon Tate. In 1959, while still a teenager, Tate was crowned Miss Richland at the annual Atomic Frontier Days festival that celebrated the region's role in the beginning of the Atomic Age. Sharon Tate was from Richland. Sharon Tate glowed in the dark.

CHAPTER SEVEN

Manhattan Project
Time Machine

The scenery of the future. Eventually the only scenery left.
The more toxic the waste, the greater the effort and expense a tourist will be willing to
tolerate in order to visit the site. Only I don't think you ought to be isolating these sites.
Isolate the most toxic waste, okay. This makes it grander, more ominous and magical. . . .
And the hot stuff, the chemical waste, the nuclear waste, this becomes a remote landscape
of nostalgia. Bus tours and postcards, I guarantee it.
—Don DeLillo, *Underworld*

After completing a bus tour of the former Manhattan Project factories in
Oak Ridge, I jotted off a few quick postcards to my friends in New York:
"Wish you were here." In his 1997 novel *Underworld*, Don DeLillo turned
a gimlet-eye to the close of the twentieth century and satirically but pre-
sciently foresaw tourism to nuclear sites. This fictional imaginary has
since become a reality and promises to grow in the future. Former sites
of the Manhattan Project, as well as its progeny—nuclear storage facilities
and aging apparatuses from Cold War nuclear complexes—are becoming
places of interest for tourists. Just as industrial tourism became popular
in areas of de-industrialization, so nuclear tourism is becoming a more
common practice in spaces of de-nuclearization; a clear example of this
practice is the tourism generated by the Secret City Festival of Oak Ridge,
which includes tours to the enormous former factories of the Manhattan
Project.[1]

Looking out onto present-day Oak Ridge from the window of a slow-
moving tour bus on the hottest of summer days, it is difficult to imagine that
this sleepy city was once teeming with world-renowned physicists and vast
scores of laborers working around the clock in order to separate and collect
enough fissionable uranium-235 for an atomic bomb. Today, Oak Ridge is a
small city of nearly 30,000 that resembles many other North American cities
with its modern subdivisions, Starbucks, and Walmart. Yet, at its core, the
community continues to be a major science center with strong ties to the

Greetings from the Atomic City, Oak Ridge, Tenn., 1960s
(photography and design by Robert E. Calonge; postcard image
courtesy of Richards & Southern Postcard Co.)

federal government, which remains the city's largest employer. Oak Ridge is the site of a national laboratory, as well as the Y-12 National Security Complex and often home to the world's fastest computer, not only in my dreams but also in reality.[2] While science is still the dominant field in Oak Ridge, the city has turned to atomic tourism as a way to make visible the community's former invisibility as a secret city—both to remind locals of their atomic past and to attract visitors to the region. The bow-tied and convivial Bill Wilcox, Oak Ridge's longtime historian who passed away in 2013, told me the mission of atomic tourism was to "get folks to turn off the interstate."[3] But more than this, tourism is a way to stoke the fires of atomic magic again, to revivify Oak Ridge's importance at the start of the Atomic Age.

For many years, the remains of the Manhattan Project, the atomic factories of the 1940s built at warp speed to produce fissile materials, had been left in ruin, their contaminated corpses exposed in plain sight. In recent decades, there have been efforts to perform the dual procedures of decommission and decontamination on these toxic bodies. Cleanup efforts, which are undisputedly necessary, are geared in three major directions: eradication (complete removal and burial of radioactive materials), resurrection (attempts to renew spaces for scientific or commercial endeavors), and most nostalgically, tourism.

Sites of atomic tourism attempt to breathe new life into these decaying bodies, to halt the erasure of the nation's nuclear past, but they do so mostly by conjuring the prelapsarian days before many of the dangers of nuclear weapons were known. These are nostalgic spaces that look backward to a time when an undisputed enemy gave meaning to the Manhattan Project and where, later, during the Cold War, the fate of democracy seemed to rest on the production of these weapons—times before the immense waste of capital, people, and land were more fully known. The entire picture will never be known, of course. Bringing new information to light is an ongoing process; some documents remain classified, and many more have been destroyed.

Atomic Tourism as Nostalgic Tourism

While tourism to former Manhattan Project factories may seem an odd choice for Americans with limited vacation days, people are drawn to these spaces, making atomic tourism a burgeoning industry. As mentioned in the previous chapter, in the last twenty years, many new sites of nuclear tourism have emerged and other long-standing spaces of nuclear heritage have been reimagined and renovated: the B-Reactor Museum at the Hanford site; the Atomic Testing Museum in Las Vegas; the Greenbrier Bunker Museum in White Sulfur Springs, West Virginia; the Rocky Flats Cold War Museum in Arvada, Colorado; the National Museum of Nuclear Science and History in Albuquerque; and the Bradbury Science Museum in Los Alamos. Congress has also debated a proposal to add the three major Manhattan Project sites to the U.S. National Park Service's roster of National Historical Parks. Another example of this trend, although perhaps less nostalgic and well outside the United States, is Ukraine's Emergency Situations Ministry, which has begun accepting tourists at Chernobyl's "zone of alienation," the area surrounding the failed reactor from the catastrophic nuclear accident that occurred in 1986.

Even as a micro-genre within the tourism industry, atomic tourism draws visitors from a wider population than one might expect, including those interested in nuclear physics and science more generally, but also history buffs, anti-nuke activists, dark tourists, patriotic tourists, post-tourists, and nostalgic tourists.[4] Visiting the immense factories and testing grounds of the Atomic Age is a type of risk, dark, or thanatourism, where part of the appeal is being close to the actual or perceived danger of the space.[5] While atomic tourism fits into the dark tourism category, it is also more specifically a form of what I call nostalgic tourism, especially when it involves visiting sites located in communities that owe their existence to the beginning of the Atomic Age, such as Oak Ridge or Los Alamos.

What such tourists are nostalgic for is a more difficult question. Nostalgia, like memory, is a diffusion of feeling, difficult to pinpoint, messy, and vague. Although compared to memory, which is viewed as noble even when confused, nostalgia often carries a negative connotation, as sickeningly sentimental, emotionally indulgent, and even tacky; nostalgia is the velvet Elvis painting to memory's Caravaggio. The architectural historian M. Christine Boyer refers to nostalgia as "a sweet sadness generated by a feeling that something is lacking in the present, a longing to experience traces of an authentic, supposedly more fulfilling past, a desire to repossess and re-experience something untouched by the ravages of time."[6] Although it is often mistaken as such, nostalgia is not only a feeling inflicted on individuals but also and perhaps primarily a social phenomenon.[7] Nostalgia not only interferes with individual psyches; it can also have a destabilizing effect and threaten the well-being of societies. Sociologist Dean MacCannell warns of the dangers of a society caught longing for the past, which leaves it "vulnerable to overthrow from within through nostalgia, sentimentality and other tendencies to regress to a previous state . . . which retrospectively always appears to have been more orderly or normal."[8] Longing for mid-century Americana and the dawn of the Atomic Age is a particular strain of the nostalgic condition; one of the side effects is the desire to visit sites where this past can be experienced. When feelings of uncertainty and malaise in the present grow, the desire to return to a time deemed more stable and meaningful escalates.

A prominent position in the sociology of tourism argues that touristic practices are the modern form of pilgrimage and a quest for authenticity in a world seen as increasingly commodified and artificial.[9] As more of the world becomes knowable through ever faster and vaster communication and transportation technologies, this search for authenticity turns more inward—toward one's own society rather than outside it. In other words, the search for authenticity becomes primarily a temporal expedition rather than a spatial one. As tourism has become more historically bent, it has become more nostalgic.

Nostalgic tourist spots conjure a desire to be there in situ, to act out, and to consume the past. This desire to "reexperience" is what makes nostalgia, performance, and tourism such good bedfellows, a logical ménage à trois. Often connected to a sense of home or homeness, nostalgic spots are places where we imagine that we fit, a community of which we are a part and from which circumstances have separated us, but to which we long to return (or to turn for the first time, if we have never been there before). Nostalgia is painful because it carries with it a sense that there is something *out there* or *back there* that is authentic, something that we belong to or something that belongs to us—a *something* that is just out of reach. If this is nostalgia, are there people who actually long for the atomic bomb, for the imagined hearth of the calutron at the uranium production plant? Absolutely. And Oak Ridge, Tennessee, is the proof.

Nostalgic tourism is a type of death tourism; it is a visit to the death of a dream slipped away, an imagined future or present just out of reach. Through nostalgic tourism we can visit collapsed dreams in a representation of their former glory. In general, nostalgic tourists want to visit another time, they want to see progress, not quite at a halt, but at a moment of past-progressing, which is not quite a frozen moment, but more of a running in place, a treadmill moment that elicits a feeling of being there. No one is completely fooled by the treadmill effect, but it does get our bodies and minds to a place of imagining and/or remembering. In other words, it can take us to a place where nostalgia can be felt and where ideas about the past can be fixed into our own memories, even if we did not experience these pasts directly.[10] In the case of atomic tourism to the former Manhattan Project sites of the 1940s, this means connecting to memories of being suspended in those heady times of working on the bomb against two formidable enemies: time and the Axis powers.

As sectors of the United States turn from industrial organizational modes to post-industrial social structures and practices, tourism emerges as a leading industry that reshapes the landscape. The very factories that used to produce material goods become tourist sites where narratives about the industrial past are transmitted and consumed; the same is true for atomic factories as it is for other industrial products. These spaces become fascinating because they no longer exist; while their form is still material, their content is ghostly and the work that was performed there has become phantasmagorical. As their usefulness as producing apparatuses fades, they become nostalgia factories, sites of reverse futurism. Exposure to atomic sites could lead to critical reflection and to the demystifying and questioning of the past. But when visits to these spaces are only celebratory, these sites become dangerous tools of nostalgic propaganda and spaces for the engineering of forgetting.

Today, Oak Ridge finds itself in a purgatorial present, where both its golden era as a key site for the Manhattan Project and its once-imagined future as a driving force toward atomic utopia can only be experienced through mnemonic practices in the present. According to St. Augustine, we can only live in the present, but this present has three registers: "a present of things past, memory; a present of things present, sight; a present of things future, expectation."[11] Life is always lived simultaneously in these tri-temporal registers, but there are times and places where their overlap and entanglement become more intense. Historic festivals are particularly good at conjuring a feeling of spatial-temporal multivalence because they are focused on action and participation in the present while simultaneously functioning as conduits to the past.

The Secret City Festival, Main Grounds

"The festival promotes the history of the city and unites its World War II heritage with the technological advancements that are ongoing within the City of Oak Ridge."[12] Through the two-day celebration the city commemorates its atomic heritage and at the same time attempts to reaffirm its status as a science city. While tours are mostly filled with nostalgic praise for the efforts of Oak Ridgers during the Manhattan Project, there is always a mention of the current nuclear medicine and techno-scientific security work being done in the laboratories and plants. Oak Ridge makes radioisotopes for research and treatments for various cancers. The imbalance of information—where the past far outweighs the present—may be attributed to several factors, including (1) a deliberate focus on heritage tourism, (2) the difficulty in explaining complex nuclear physics to a general audience, (3) the fact that much of the work being done in Oak Ridge continues to be secret and connected to national security, especially at the Y-12 National Security Complex, and (4) the powerful drama of a victorious wartime story, including the first atomic bomb, is arguably more compelling and entertaining than the current stories that can be told, such as breakthroughs in medical isotope technology.

Composed of a network of loosely connected sites, the Secret City Festival spreads through the city like kudzu. The main festival grounds are located adjacent to the library, just off Oak Ridge Boys Way, named for the country-western group most famous for their camp country hit "Elvira." In direct view across the turnpike is the recently renovated high school with an enormous atomic symbol affixed to its brick facade. The festival then spills out onto Bissell Park, located just beyond the library; here there are craft stands, food vendors, and a DJ who spins records for a handful of dancing teenagers while younger children jump around like excited electrons in oversized blow-up playground equipment. All these activities take place as the sounds of faux warfare rage in the background, the World War

II reenactment nearly drowning out the stereo spewing the latest hip-hop and pop radio hits. During the weekend there are also special events at the AMSE, as well as the bus tours to the original Manhattan Project factories, and a vintage train tour.

The festival, held every June, is an odd affair, where mid-century bobby-sock nostalgia does the Twist with nuclear physics and military machismo.[13] Strangely, one of the most popular performances of the two-day event is the restaging of World War II battle scenes. It is nearly 100 degrees outside as soldiers in period dress invade "Normandy" in the Appalachian valley. Artillery is on display, from tanks to guns to grenades. Smoke blankets the battlefield as ersatz soldiers scamper across the grounds, taking and giving orders, grunting, clutching their chests and dying with dramatic flair. The medics are there too, scooping up the injured and attending to wounded brethren. This resurrected battle carried out on home soil is peculiar for a place that was actually a haven from fighting during World War II, where neither bayonets nor grenades but microscopes and Geiger counters were wielded daily. Perhaps this spectacular display was chosen because it is hard to imagine what a reenactment of scientists working in their labs with minuscule particles would look like. But this is precisely the legacy Oak Ridgers are fighting for: the recognition that the laboratory did as much to win the war as the battlefield. The live performance illustrates how the Secret City Festival shrinks time and space—the war is brought home, and festivalgoers are transported to the 1940s.

The Secret City Festival is also a commercial undertaking. There are several food stalls, mostly dominated by fried things—funnel cakes, corn dogs, fried Oreos, fried Snickers, and so on—as well as many souvenirs, from the practical to the kitschy. The available objects include all matter of keepsakes, including water bottles, key chains, and Frisbees, each item emblazoned with the festival's theme: "From the 40s to the Future!" There are also sweatshirts and T-shirts with an image of a guard at one of the city's gates with the words "Oak Ridge, America's Original Gated Community" printed across the breast. Other items are adorned with glow-in-the-dark ink, a wink to radioactive properties. I search in vain for a retro-version of my favorite childhood T-shirt, the one that boasted, "I'm from Oak Ridge. I glow in the dark."

Thwarted in my quest, I wander over to the souvenir table receiving the most attention, which was arguably the most nostalgic. Looking over the clutch of atomic shoppers I see that the table is covered with black-and-white prints from the official Manhattan Project photographer, Ed Westcott, whom I saw just minutes ago walking around the festival grounds. During

Oak Ridge's tenure as a secret city, as pointed out earlier, civilians were not permitted to freely take photographs, so Westcott's snaps are the dominant and often solitary visual record of that time. Westcott was an employee of the federal government, and his post is reflected in the images, which have an unmistakable propagandistic quality—Oppenheimer poses as an atomic dandy, smoking; industrious women tend victory gardens; Girl Scouts march in front of the x-10 graphite reactor; and even the garbage collectors smile as they haul heavy barrels of who knows what. The commercial and nostalgic nature of the festival with its emphasis on participation and consumption reflects a change in the way societies remember beginning in the second half of the twentieth century. As the French historian Jacques Le Goff points out, "This pursuit, rescue, and celebration of collective memory . . . less in texts than in spoken word, images, gestures, rituals, and festivals, constitutes a major change in historical vision. It amounts to a conversion that is shared by the public at large, which is obsessed by the fear of losing its memory in a kind of collective amnesia—a fear that is awkwardly expressed in the taste for the fashions of earlier times, and shamelessly exploited by nostalgia-merchants; memory has thus become a best-seller in a consumer society."[14] In historic and nostalgic tourism today, the visitor more often than not becomes part of the performance of the space, actively consuming and purchasing memories, along with gift shop souvenirs.

Department of Energy Facilities Public Bus Tour

As part of the annual Secret City Festival, the city of Oak Ridge along with the Department of Energy conducts bus tours to sites of atomic heritage and current scientific research centers in order to connect the two. Bus tours have long been a staple of the modern tourism industry, particularly where security is at risk. Poverty tours, disaster tours, and gangland tours, just to name a few examples, all favor the bus with a cinematic window on the dangerous and untouchable sites outside the glass. The tourists are thus protected inside the vehicle's hulking shell and delivered to sites where they may exit and reenter. Here, the bus becomes a liminal zone between everyday life and touristic experiences—a placeless place, a timeless time.

Accompanying the revolutions of axles and wheels underneath the hull of the bus, there is steady chatter emanating from the tour guide, who is almost always attached to the community but no longer actively so. For example, the tour guide in the Gangland Tours of Los Angeles is a former gang member, the Hurricane Katrina Tours operated by Circle Line are often led by a former resident of New Orleans's ninth ward, and in Oak Ridge the guide is usually a former Manhattan Project worker or Cold Warrior. Because of their connection to the site, the tour guides are most often seen as experts imbued with local and inside knowledge, giving their narratives a gloss that seems authentic.

On June 17, 2010, I board a bus to take a tour of the Department of Energy Facilities in Oak Ridge. I show my passport to prove that I am a U.S. citizen and not a foreign national, which would make me ineligible for the tour. Having passed this test, I then climb the short steps into the body of the bus. The vehicle is modern, but the atmosphere is retro; the cabin is filled with music from the 1940s. I am a little disappointed, hoping that the bus would be a refurbished version of an original Oak Ridge work bus, some of which came from the 1933 World's Fair in Chicago—"From a Century of Progress." Now on the bus, having overcome this minor letdown, I see that I am the youngest person by at least three decades, so I settle in the penultimate row, letting those with canes and walkers take the anterior seats. As the last of the passengers settle in, the tour guide takes the microphone and informs us that we will visit three of the eight signature facilities of the Manhattan Project: the tour will make stops at Y-12's New Hope Center, the Oak Ridge National Laboratory, and finally the historic X-10 Graphite Reactor. We will not be visiting the Y-12 National Security Center because the work that is being done there is top secret, but we will make a stop at their new history center. There is some grumbling at this news. I can't help but wonder if this forbidden site also connects with the past history of the place, making the tour more exciting—there are still secret things that cannot be seen!

As our tires edge out of the parking lot, one of the first things we are told is that in 1942 it was "proved that science can be moved from the laboratory to the battlefield" and that this is "the one thing to take away from the tour." Next, the guide suggests that a pseudonym for the Manhattan Project could be "miracle": "The science was a miracle. The city of Oak Ridge itself was a miracle." I write MIRACLE in large capital letters in my field notebook and circle the word with violence. I wonder at first if this is a peculiarity of the tour guide, this thing about miracles, but as I take part in the two-day festival, I will hear magic, science, luck, and miracles all held responsible for the "success" of the Manhattan Project.

Writing about the culture of religiosity around the nuclear weapons assembly and disassembly complex corporation, Pantex, in Amarillo, Texas, A. G. Mojtabai refers to this theme as blessed assurance—"the promise, for true believers of exemption and safety" from the suffering caused by nuclear weapons.[15] The rhetorics of science, security, and religion tangle and turn over on themselves as Oak Ridgers attempt to tell the story of their past, a story told as if the outcome were inevitable and/or divinely ordained. The myth of John Hendrix, as always, is mentioned.

Our first stop is the new Y-12 History Center, which was created, according to our tour guide, to "improve the lab's ability to communicate with the community." Here we watch a propagandistic video and are able for a few minutes to walk around and look at some artifacts—including my favorite, an "Atoms for Peace o' Mary" medal given to Catholic airmen during the Cold War. I spend some time looking at this amazing artifact. There is a globe engraved with the word PAX resting prominently across the waist of the equator like a Texas rodeo rider's belt buckle; moving upward a mushroom cloud bursts out from the top of the earth with Mary hovering above the explosion, hands clasped, looking serene and nonplussed as always. I'm not quite ready to stop looking at the medal, but soon we are instructed that it is time to go, and we are on the move again, given plastic bags to "fill up on goodies," which includes promotional DVDs (seven in total), Y-12 logo pencils, and not much else. The DVDs cover the history of Oak Ridge and of Y-12 from its beginning—*Our Hidden Past: Y-12's First Mission*—to the more contemporary—*This Is Y-12: America's Uranium Center of Excellence.*

Next stop is the Oak Ridge National Laboratory, formerly the X-10 Graphite Reactor, where now the major focus is no longer on fissionable materials for atomic weapons but on something called the Spallation Neutron Source. We are told that this is the largest industrial project in the world and that it contributes to research in the field of medical isotopes. This is the part of the tour that is focused on promoting current research and painting a picture of Oak Ridge as the future of nuclear science for medical research in addition to its famous Manhattan Project past. Not quite out of the secrecy and security game, we also learn that ORNL is the residence of the Headquarters for Homeland Security Technology Section. Not much can be said about what goes on there because, like many things in Oak Ridge, this is still top-secret.

With our heads filled with current facts about isotopes and wild imaginings of the past and present secret life of Oak Ridge, we coast down Reactor Road to the historic X-10 Graphite Reactor. We stare at the reactor's gigantic loading face, full of cylindrical holes where mannequins dressed in protective suits stand in halted action, looking like believers at the foot of a holy temple. The place is all metal knobs, levers, and lights. Upstairs in the observation deck, large cutouts of workers illustrate what the protective clothing would have looked like. Like the mannequins on the lower level, they are paused but somehow more lifelike even though they are only two-dimensional, because they are actual photographs of real workers blown up to life-size.

We are encouraged to place ourselves back in time when the reactor was in operation, 1943–63. I comply with a daydream of sneaking in the cardboard cutout of Miss Atomic from the Atomic Testing Museum, adding her to the scene, making a kind of imaginary party of the past. This is a daydream, but also something I feel could happen on a special day at the lab, marking some important atomic anniversary or a day with a particularly good yield. Soon, I'm snapped out of my mid-century atomic fantasy as another group arrives, a tour made up entirely of members of the armed forces. My group is shooed out as they are hustled in. I can hear a snippet of their tour guide's spiel, and from two minutes I can tell that it has an even more patriotic tone than the one we heard.

Back on the bus the colorful tour guide reminds the passengers that there were "many miracles in the Manhattan Project." The guide launches into an explanation—he says one day he realized that science and miracles were not contradictory, and that in fact "Jesus demolecularized himself, just like 'Beam me up Scotty.'"[16] He continues talking about science fiction from the twentieth century; trying to add some mystique to Oak Ridge, he says, "You get into *The Twilight Zone* with Oak Ridge—seven gates, seven bridges."[17] Next we are told that in addition to the Manhattan Project, the site has another claim to fame: the former atomic factory is in the *Guinness Book of World Records* for the most raccoons in a dumpster at one time—twenty-one. While I know this is an attempt at levity, it makes me think of the radioactive bunnies recently found in Hanford and the damage done to the environment at these sites.[18] After some more comedic attempts and efforts to connect with the group through pop culture, the tour guide turns nostalgic and posits "the success of the Project in World War II was not something this nation could do today—the country has become too individualistic." This narrative of a selfish nation in decline is the most repeated theme during the festival, thirteen times according to my field notes. Later in a classroom in Buffalo, New York, during a conversation about the Atomic City, I ask if what happened in Oak Ridge in the 1940s could happen today. Thirty-five of forty students raise their hands to say "yes."

Secret City Scenic Excursion Train

On June 19, 2010, progress in Oak Ridge was derailed. The Secret City Scenic Excursion train, carrying a slew of atomic tourists, hopped the tracks and ended up with the caboose nearly topsy-turvy.[19] No one was physically injured in the accident, although we can imagine that local pride was bruised. As the unruly locomotive lay on its side, the seventy-five to eighty passengers were herded onto a bus that would take them back to the center of the city. This interruption of progress draws attention to other stalled technological fantasies of the twentieth century. Perhaps more than any other part of the festival, the train tour contains multiple levels of industrial history.

Tickets for the tour are purchased from a converted Manhattan Project guard station. The small structure wears a sign that says "Wheat," a nod to the pre-atomic community. My mother and I have our pictures taken in front of it. I show the picture to my grandmother later and she says, "Oh, Wheat! You know that's where my friend Moneymaker was from." I wonder what Dorathy Moneymaker, the chronicler of Wheat, would think about this gesture toward her erased community. I wonder if the ghost of Wheat ever rides the rails, or if he puts pennies or irradiated dimes on the tracks to be flattened. I wonder if John Hendrix imagined the future rolling out and then rolling back to the same railroad spur, or if his visions ended with the ground shaking in 1945.

De Certeau writes of the rumbling music of the train, its "orchestra" that "makes history, and, like a rumor guarantees that there is still some history."[20] The Secret City Scenic Excursion Train wears old clothes, fancier than we wear today, and tells stories of the past, more grandiose than how we talk now, but does so in order to continue the history it knows and wants others to know, to continually produce it, not only to communicate it from bygone days. But in train rides, as in the historiographic operation, "there is also an accidental element . . . jolts, brakings, surprises."[21] The train ends up on its back and we have a moment to think about how all time is dumped from the past and poured in from the future into the same pool of right now. The tour guide says, "Oak Ridge could never happen today." My students say, "Oak Ridge could absolutely happen today."

The train tours are run by self-proclaimed train geeks who have some knowledge of the atomic history of Oak Ridge, although the narrative focus of the tour is centered on glorious technological pasts largely writ: triumphs of the railroad engineers and of the atom splitters ride side by side as first-class passengers.[22] My mother and I ride farther back. We are taking it all in while sipping sodas. I am writing notes. My mother is staring out the window wearing the gigantic sunglasses she prefers.

The locomotive begins to lumber. An armed guard unlocks the gates to allow the train to enter the former Manhattan Project and Cold War facility grounds to see "where history was made." The train runs on a rail line that was built by the U.S. Army Corps of Engineers specifically to move materials into and out of K-25. Despite the celebratory rhetoric of the Secret City Excursion Train, ghosts of expired technological utopias haunt the space both inside and outside the locomotive. Outside, a post-utopian landscape is visible. Its most obvious feature, at least until 2013, was the massive ruin of the K-25 atomic production plant with its mammoth walls and girders partially exposed, protruding like defiant fists in the air. These have since come down and rest softly alongside the ghostly skeleton of the plant. I can see their absence punching the empty space above the hills.

Shuttered in 1985, the K-25 factory has been reduced to a relic of the Atomic Age, a Superfund site, and a ruin to gaze upon outside the window of a tourist train car.[23] At one time, the U-shaped K-25 plant was a modern architectural marvel, one mile around and four stories high. Now a highly toxic ruin, K-25 illustrates the failure of the Atomic Age to create efficient clean energy and global peace. Its sepulchral shell is a reminder of the failure to plan for the wastes that these factories would produce. Executives from the Bechtel Jacobs Company, the Department of Energy's major cleanup contractor in Oak Ridge, described the dire situation, where the plant has been idle for "years with little or no maintenance, and has caved-in roofs, unsafe floors and cracked columns."[24] The extremely contaminated materials will remain for millennia with no chance for recycling or renovation.

The train scoots past the remains of K-25, past an old gray train car with large letters tattooed into its side: L&N. I think of standing beside it with my grandmother and taking a picture, but the train is in motion and my grandmother is at home today preparing her Sunday school lesson. The lazy train yawns and stretches along Poplar Creek and Highway 327, following the gentle contours of the hills and valleys of East Tennessee. We cross a latticed bridge with peeling paint. The scenery yields water towers with their spindle legs, small houses with neatly stacked woodpiles, yarded dogs of various sizes, and at least one trainspotter holding two cameras—one for still photography, one for capturing motion. The sounds of the train whistle fill the car as we pass the jutting arm of Watts Bar Lake. The northern edge of the route was featured in the film *October Sky*, starring Jake Gyllenhaal and Laura Dern. The film, set in 1957, is a story of the Cold War dipping into Appalachia. The protagonist is expected to work in the mines, like the generations of men before him there, but after hearing about the USSR's launch of the rocket *Sputnik-1*, he can't bring himself to go underground. Instead, he dreams of outer space. Technological utopian dreams consume him.

Inside, the train functions as a rolling museum of railroads and industrialization. Promotional materials for the tour wax nostalgic with promises to "turn the clock back to yesteryear" with a "return to the heyday of passenger railroading."[25] For my tour, I ride in car no. 2164, built by the Pullman Company in 1926 for the Southern Railway system.[26] This particular train worked both the *Carolina Special* route as well as the *Tennessean*, which ran back and forth between Knoxville and Washington, D.C. Today, the train rolls again, but now only at fourteen-mile stretches at a time—seven miles out to Blair, Tennessee, and seven miles back to the K-25 Heritage Center. De Certeau says, "The windowpane is what allows us to *see*, and the rail, what allows us to *move through*."[27] But we don't seem to be moving past this history in Oak Ridge, only a little distance away and then right back to where we began the story.

In the 1880s, George Pullman, an industrialist from Illinois and the manufacturer of my tourist train car, attempted to create a model factory town outside Chicago. In 1894, increasing tensions between the workers and the managers led to a wildcat strike, which brought down his utopian vision. The fighting was sparked by the heavy-handed paternalism and excessive restrictions that Pullman had placed on his workers, as well as a steep reduction in wages.[28] If you know the story of Pullman, the workers' revolt comes to mind. If not, the train car exists alone, as a beautiful object from which a more complicated past has been whittled, leaving only "the heyday of passenger railroading." On my tour, there was no mention by the tour guide of the connection between industrial strife and Pullman train cars. I knew the story, but I did not expect to hear it.

Although the age of the railroads and the age of the atom seem disconnected, proximity to rail lines was a key component in choosing locations for the secret sites of the Manhattan Project. Even in the age of airplanes, the railways were deemed more important for transporting materials for the production of the atomic bombs. The rails, laid out like enormous zippers, crisscrossing the country, were thought to be less conspicuous and less dangerous than the skies. Materials from Oak Ridge, Hanford, and other sites would travel to Los Alamos mostly by train, sometimes by road, often with atomic couriers dressed as salesmen with uranium encased in small canisters of nickel and gold strapped to their wrists or tucked inside briefcases.[29] My grandfather, as part of this secret cadre, might have done this, although imagining him with a briefcase, even as a prop, is difficult.

It is not hard to imagine the writer Walter Benjamin carrying his own precious briefcase stuffed with texts, as he fled the Nazis from Paris to the Franco-Spanish border, just a few years earlier. Frank McLemore was not at all like Walter Benjamin, not in the least. But these two men were burdened by the same historical emergency of World War II, although in vastly different ways: a briefcase of words and a briefcase of fissionable uranium, both set to blast out the continuum of history, one over Europe, one over Japan. Theodor Adorno wrote of his friend Benjamin, "Everything which fell under the scrutiny of his words was transformed, as though it had become radioactive."[30] My grandmother said, "I still don't know what all Frank drove around, but I think most of it was radioactive." The Tarheel truck driver and the German Jewish intellectual would never have met except inside this text, or inside my own briefcase, which contains fallout from both.

Can You Identify the Culprit?

While my train tour was the standard trip, there are also thematic ones: an excursion focused on fall foliage, a "Santa Train," a Valentine's day jaunt, and most fantastical, a "Mystery Dinner Train" at the intersection of atomic and railway history.

> Secret City mysteries exposed!!! The Southern Appalachia Railway Museum and the Oak Ridge High School Masquers drama club present an evening of mystery and intrigue set against the background of one of World War II's most secret facilities. Breathtaking drama ensues. Can *you* identify the culprit and save the free world? . . . Menu selections include beef tenderloin with mushrooms and garlic butter, chicken breast with wine sauce, and a vegetable medley. Each dinner includes a tossed salad, specially prepared vegetables, fresh bread, dessert, and tea or coffee.[31]

This performance fits into the living history genre of historical tourism, where the intention is to transport the visitor to the time in question through interaction with the past in the present. In this case the tourist is transported back to the Cold War and patriotically called into the service of the nation—to spot the atomic spy, all the while nibbling on a hot meal.

It has been a long time since Manhattan Project workers were confused by the trains coming into the Secret City full of materials, leaving with nearly empty loads. Today, trains transport much of the "hot" waste from nuclear production facilities and decommissioned reactors to storage locations. In fact, trains carrying toxic materials from the rusting K-25 building run parallel to the refurbished throwback trains from the early twentieth century, carrying atomic tourists. Henri Bergson describes memory on a continuum from the past to the present, where in the middle lies "the memory-image," whereas Jacques Le Goff describes memory as "an intersection."[32]

Forgetting, then, travels on parallel tracks that never meet. For Bergson and Le Goff, memory is called upon to make sense of present perceptions, to fill in the gaps, and to provide context, so that the body (individual for Bergson, social for Le Goff) can be induced to act. If radioactive waste is kept out of sight and narratives about its dangers are silenced, if we are kept on the other tracks hearing only the triumphant stories, it is possible that the more complicated history of the Atomic Age will be forgotten. At present, the toxicity of the ruins of K-25 cannot be as easily ignored, but there are questions as to what will happen years down the line when the processes of decommission and decontamination are declared finished. Will we build tourist sites that feature our nuclear waste, as DeLillo mused, or as Ukraine has done in Chernobyl? Or will we move on, as if this never happened?

The Future of Atomic Tourism

The atomic history of the United States is the history of the American twentieth century, in which the building of the bomb and the victory of World War II elicit emotional responses—nostalgic longing for some, feelings of horror for others, or perhaps some combination of the two. The mid-twentieth century is widely portrayed through museums, media, and popular culture as a time when America was on top, or at least felt like it was. This kind of nostalgia lines the casket of atomic history, and with it is buried the stillborn dreams of a nuclear paradise. The story of the bomb was supposed to end with "atoms for peace," the nuclear equivalent of happily ever after, yet we never quite got there. Alongside current fears of Iranian and North Korean nuclear pursuits lies the stalled dream of nuclear ease: fantasies of atomic cars are now on blocks in the yard of our collective imaginations, and visions of entire cities populated with nuclear-heated homes have grown cold, frozen into collective memories of what was once thought possible.

While we no longer imagine a happy atomic future on the horizon under the comfortable glow of completely controllable nuclear energy, we still fear the darker side of the nuclear age. Nightmares of terrorists from the breakout countries of the former USSR with smuggled warheads haunt our imaginations, as do our fears of unstable nations full of power-lust with working reactors, and accidents and leakages of all sorts, prompted by natural disasters or political catastrophes worry our collective heads. Yet in places like Oak Ridge, dreams of an atomic utopia are being reexperienced and performed through atomic tourism and nostalgic storytelling.

Before the gates to the city were opened in 1949, one of the major reasons voiced against this move by residents was the fear that "Oak Ridge will be overrun with tourists and curiosity seekers."[33] Now this is something that is actually hoped for. The Secret City Festival is a self-conscious effort to jog local, regional, and national collective memories of the victory of World War II and the end of the Cold War by calling attention to the role the city played in those undertakings.

Interest in atomic tourism continues to grow; the latest push is to create a Manhattan Project National Park, which would connect Oak Ridge with sites in Hanford and Los Alamos to form the first multi-sited national park in the nation's history. These three sites are to be thought of together, even though it would be nearly impossible to visit them all in one day—thousands and thousands of miles separate them. Reminding us of Niels Bohr's claim, "The Manhattan Project is only possible if you turn the entire United States into one huge factory."[34]

Typically, when we think of national parks, we tend to think of Yellowstone and Yosemite, not nuclear laboratories and atomic bomb factories with complicated and controversial histories. This may be changing though, with sites like the Manzanar National Historic Site, which marks and documents the difficult history of an internment camp for Japanese Americans and Japanese nationals that operated during World War II, a site that is ironically located in Independence, California.[35] Still, it is odd to think that in the shadow of the Great Smoky Mountains—the most visited national park—there could be this sort of park, populated with vacationers and brown-shirted rangers. Though in a backhanded way, if the Manhattan Project park is built, it will fit with the ethos of the national park project as originally conceived by Teddy Roosevelt. Roosevelt, concerned that rapid industrialization would destroy the landscape, and bothered by the fact that all the buffalo could be gone before he had a chance to shoot one, created the National Park Service as a way to conserve a wild American past that was not quite gone but slipping away. The same logic goes for our national nuclear projects: atomic bombs are the new buffalo. The herd is thinning.

If the Manhattan Project National Park is built, there will likely be more discussion about the message it will convey.[36] Historically, national projects, as we have seen, are not the most critical of spaces. It is encouraging that the park will include some kind of interpretative center with a historical focus, instead of billing itself as a nature park. This approach has been taken by Congress before, when in 2001 it passed the National Rocky Flats Wildlife Refuge Act, with the intent of turning the area around the former Rocky Flats nuclear weapons facility into a nature preserve. Over ten years later and after some massive cleanup efforts, the site is still deemed too toxic for human visitation.

Something similar is being done in Oak Ridge. The National Wildlife Federation has recently declared a Wildlife Habitat in what the local press refers to as the "front yard" of the former K-25 plant. What a gentle name for the space along the perimeter of the factory that produced vital materials for the bombs of the nation's Cold War arsenal! Spaces like these are doubly dangerous—threats to health and threats to history—as attempts to erase the messiness of the Manhattan Project and the Cold War past. These not-yet-natural preserves lying in the ghost spaces of former weapons plants emit a dark shadow around the hiker's creed: leave no trace.

As the temporal distance from the Manhattan Project grows, there is a danger of forgetting, either through an imagined return to a natural landscape or through nostalgia. If the Secret City Festival is any indication of the story that the original Oak Ridgers intend to impart to future generations—and I believe it is—then the legacy penned will most likely be a morality tale of good versus evil, in which the United States is always cast as the good guy, with Oak Ridgers starring as atomic cowboys riding tall in the saddle and wearing white hats and lab coats. Plans for new memory projects of the Manhattan Project can look like pantheons to the myths of the Atomic Age, reinvigorating old myths, ghosting the present with the past. John Hendrix, the atomic prophet, has perhaps never been so alive. If these myths are not met with counter-stories, the more complicated cultural history of the Manhattan Project could be lost forever. If these spaces are built, the hope is that critical tourists will come armed with skepticism, carrying counter-narratives and a secret knowledge of the hidden atomic past.

CHAPTER EIGHT

Atomic Snapshots

History decays into images, not stories.
—Walter Benjamin, *The Arcades Project*

Thumbtacked to the wall above my desk is a photograph of Oppenheimer taken in Oak Ridge by Ed Westcott. The image shows Oppenheimer sitting cross-legged in the Oak Ridge Guest House, smoking. Just moments before the shot was snapped, the famous physicist was feeling frustrated because he desperately wanted a cigarette but lacked the change to purchase a pack. The young photographer, intent on making his subject at ease, handed over the necessary coinage. Oppenheimer then slipped the coins in the slot of a vending machine, and a box of Chesterfields appeared—one of the four or five packs he would smoke that day. The photograph was taken on Valentine's Day in 1946; a little more than five months had passed since the atomic bombings of Hiroshima and Nagasaki.[1] Oppenheimer had put on a little weight; he looked healthier than he had at the end of the war, when he weighed only 115 pounds. Westcott directed Oppenheimer to sit "slightly askance" and then took the photograph from a low vantage point. The angle makes Oppenheimer appear larger than life with a knowing, troubled expression on his face. He does not seem like a nervous scientist recently calmed by nicotine; he seems almost sphinx-like. What is captured is more than a moment of a man sitting for a photograph; the whole of the Manhattan Project, the Bomb, the aftermath of Hiroshima, the uncertainty of what lies ahead shows on his face; as Barthes writes, "This is why the great portrait photographers are great mythologists."[2]

Behind my desk chair, hovering above a metal table stacked with papers to grade, articles to read, and projects in various states of completion, is another photograph that I suspect was taken by Westcott, given its aesthetic and the time period in which it was taken, but I have not been able to confirm this. The image captures an experiment in progress in a science class at Oak Ridge High School in the late 1950s. A young woman is pushing her breath through a long tube igniting an explosion—the mimesis of

J. Robert Oppenheimer at the Oak Ridge Guest House, 1946
(photo by Ed Westcott, courtesy of U.S. Department of Energy Photo Archives)

a mushroom cloud. Rapt students look on, one woman with a confused expression nearly as large as the giant bow on her dress. She scratches her head as a clean-cut young man stands seriously in the back, hands on his hips, elbows out. In addition to the fiery experiment, there is another figure at the focal point of this image: my mother, Bobbie Freeman. She is seated in the front row, fingers at her temple. She is sixteen. My mother doesn't remember the photograph being taken, but my grandmother does

Oak Ridge High School science class, 1950s (photo by Ed Westcott, courtesy of U.S. Department of Energy Photo Archives)

(even in her nineties she remembers everything from the old days). The image evokes the continuation of the Atomic City: the next generation, those with "the atomic bomb as their birthmark"; all-American kids in gingham and plaid with atomic hearts and keen minds continuing in the path of their parents; the great brain trust of Oak Ridge on display for the world to see.[3]

To my left, another snapshot taken by Westcott occupies wall space; in it three gentlemen stand with their hands crossed. The two on the left in jackets and ties wear Oak Ridge identity badges pinned to their lapels, whereas the man on the right wears a badge and a gun. He is an atomic courier who hauls "hot" materials and sensitive documents from AEC operations in Oak Ridge to other atomic facilities around the country. He is also my grandfather, Frank McLemore, who drove an unmarked white GMC truck on the transportation routes that connect various atomic laboratories, processing facilities, and mining operations on what Peter C. van Wyck calls "the highway of the atom."[4]

Oppenheimer. My mother. My grandfather. These are but three photographs out of the thousands of images that capture the beginning of the Atomic Age in the top-secret city of Oak Ridge. The photograph of my

The author's grandfather (*far right*) in uniform (photo by Ed Westcott, courtesy of U.S. Atomic Energy Commission, Oak Ridge Operations Office Photographic Services Section, File No. ORD-64-0106)

grandfather, who passed away many years ago, was recently given to me by my grandmother, Nan McLemore, which explains the creasing; she is not the best archivist. This was a generous gift because personal cameras were not allowed near the atomic factories during this time in Oak Ridge, so this is one of the only visual documents of my grandfather all suited up in his uniform finery.

At the height of productivity during the Manhattan Project, the city was filled with innumerable engineers, construction workers, dial monitors, scientists, soldiers, pipe-fitters, policemen, firemen, mechanics, reporters, bakers, shop workers, tailors, doctors, nurses, and teachers, but only one photographer: Ed Westcott.[5] In the years since, Westcott's images have become one of the main sources documenting the beginning of the Atomic Age, nationally and globally as well for Oak Ridge.[6] Westcott's photographs are ubiquitous but until recently have always been displayed anonymously with only institutional taglines, such as "courtesy of the U.S. Army Corps of Engineers" (1942–46), "the Atomic Energy Commission" (1947–74), or "the Department of Energy" (1974–present).

Westcott's photographs stare out from history books about the bomb, they rest on the walls of the AMSE and inside the neatly labeled binders in the Oak Ridge Room of the city's public library, and they also lay nestled in the National Archives: over 5,000 images. The subject matter ranges from aerial shots of the land to depictions of the immaculate workspaces of the atomic factories, from workers loading slugs into the face of a reactor to housewives with ration tickets in line at the butcher shop. They are idealized and contrived, depictions of an atomic utopia of order, efficiency, and the wholesome pleasures of mid-twentieth-century Americana on Kodak paper. The images are so prevalent it is hard to think of the Manhattan Project without a Westcott photograph coming into view in my mind's eye. It works the opposite way as well: just as thinking of the Manhattan Project conjures Westcott images, seeing his photographs triggers thoughts of the Manhattan Project. I suspect this is the same for many others with or without their being conscious of it. This situation makes for a perfect moment to turn the sociological imagination toward these images to "work out . . . the problems of history, the problems of biography, and the problems of social structure in which biography and history intersect," as C. Wright Mills writes.[7]

The trick here is to locate these intersections. The official atomic archive is built on secret information; it is incomplete, redacted, coded, and covert. By contrast, the unofficial atomic archive is storied, rich beyond belief, and hiding in attics, desk drawers, and the minds of those who lived it; in other words, it is slipping away. Of course, the unofficial archive is also incomplete and built on shaky remembrances, exaggerations, and a variety of haphazardly archived materials—contracts, certificates, diaries, love letters, ticket stubs, snapshots—ephemera of the lived atomic life. The task is to draw lines and make connections between the official photographs and the official and unofficial narratives of the beginning of Oak Ridge, to attempt to understand how the images of atomic utopianism have become the symbols of atomic nostalgia and how an anonymous government photographer became a visual artist and an invaluable documentarian of a particular socio-techno vision of the Atomic Age.

In the oft-quoted *Camera Lucida*, Barthes writes, "Cameras, in short, were clocks for seeing"; during the Manhattan Project the federal government wanted to control visual time.[8] Those in charge of the Oak Ridge operations were afraid that photographic images would leak and that enemies would see the size and scope of the city and know something was up. Now, when we crack open the archive, these same images attest and act as a witness to what was up, at least to the activities that the government wanted to document. We see what Susan Sontag calls "the tangibleness of their vanished world. How touching and good-natured the pictures are."[9] It leaves me wondering what is missing, so I ask people about their lives and try to compare the stories I hear to the images I see. Sometimes they match up and sometimes they don't. As Benjamin writes, "History decays into images, not stories."[10] We need storytelling and we need memories to slow the decomposition.

Official Oak Ridge Photographer

In 1941, James Edward Westcott joined the U.S. Army Corps of Engineers as a photographer in the Corps' Nashville District. This post included traveling around the region to document sites of interest to the military. With this appointment, the self-taught lensman also had opportunity to document his first secret site, an area outside Crossville, Tennessee, that later became an Axis prisoner of war camp.[11] After proving himself with these earlier tasks, in 1942 the twenty-year-old Westcott was assigned to the Clinton Engineer Works. We can assume that the role of photographer was quite important to the Project, as Westcott was the twenty-ninth person appointed to the brand-new secret city.[12] From 1942 to 1946, Oak Ridge was meticulously documented through one of two visual clocks wielded by the young photographer, a Speed Graphic or 8 x 10 Deardorff view camera.

From the outset, the Manhattan Project sought documentation. The kind of documentation is what is surprising. In Oak Ridge, Westcott had a dual assignment—to produce visual proof of the construction and operation of the community for the Army Corps of Engineers, and to record the daily life of the atomic citizens for the *Oak Ridge Journal*, the weekly newspaper, which, during secret times, was overseen by the military like everything else. The photographs were meant to serve as proof of Oak Ridgers' patriotism and social prosperity, as well as of engineering feats, scientific achievement, and a new way of living. The images were also meant to normalize the atomic citizens and the community that produced the bomb, to show them as exceptional but also recognizable to the American public, residents of the model Atomic City of the future.

For the most part the photographs did just that—here we have the Oak Ridge Symphony Orchestra, here a man tends a victory garden, here teenage Oak Ridgers spill out of a car with "Atom Smasher" painted on its side, and here stands the K-25 gaseous diffusion uranium processing plant.[13] There is some slippage with respect to social niceties when looking through the lens of history: among these images of cheerful work, play, and sacrifice we find evidence of farms that were removed for the Project, segregated water fountains, and, behind the smiling shots of African American workers, evidence of racial segregation and underemployment.

In *Through the Lens of Ed Westcott*, a collection of photographs representative of Westcott's oeuvre published in 2005, African Americans are depicted in only a few areas of employment, including hauling trash or coal and washing dirty laundry. An image of a laundry worker employs an offensive caption: "No Tickie, No Washie."[14] Other images show rows of outhouses, the signs on the doors reading "white" and "colored." Oak Ridge, like the rest of the American South at that time, was practicing segregation; the atomic photographic record offers a stark reminder of Jim Crow on the atomic frontier. The photograph, as Barthes writes, "immediately yields up those 'details,' which constitute the very raw material of ethnological knowledge."[15] The discrimination and inequality that was overlooked or accepted at the time comes into view in the present.

Manhattan Project Photography

As Baldwin Lee, professor of art at the University of Tennessee, notes, "Westcott's photographs can be roughly divided into two categories: first are those photographs that describe the efforts involved in the developing of the atomic bomb, and second are those photographs that describe the normal social, domestic, and recreational aspects of living within the fences that surrounded the secretive project."[16] The fact is that these images cannot be separated, even "roughly." It is not "normal," for instance, to be living behind fences of a secret project. Furthermore, it is the aura of the Manhattan Project that makes Westcott's photographs interesting sociologically. Whether the image is of workers in the uranium processing plants or teenagers roller-skating, it is the fact that these activities, and many others of everyday and not-so-everyday life, were happening simultaneously that makes them noteworthy. The images, when viewed in the present day, are equally haunted on one side by nostalgia for a bygone America and on the other by the specters of war, radiation, and secrecy.

The juxtaposition of everyday activities and the work of the Manhattan Project in Westcott's photographs provides a puzzle for the sociological imagination. The sociologist Carol Wolkowitz, whose own parents were early Oak Ridgers, sketches one aspect of this puzzle: "Some of these images must have been intended as a historical record, or for publication only after the war, but others were used for advertising or internal consumption. The Project faced a number of problems in this regard. For instance, the sites needed to advertise for civilian workers without telling them anything about the project itself, and they also had to provide images for people on the sites, perhaps to discourage people from trying to produce their own."[17]

Recruitment of civilian workers was difficult during the war years with much of the workforce overseas and with other competing war industries at home looking for employees. To compete in this labor market, the public relations offices of the Manhattan Project worked hard to present Oak Ridge as an ideal community, full of young, vigorous workers and ample social activities.[18] It must be remembered that Westcott's photographs were carefully selected and censored by the U.S. government. This was not an exercise in photojournalism, but something closer to propaganda, as Emily Honeycutt, member of the Oak Ridge Heritage and Preservation Association and Ed Westcott's daughter, confirms: "The photographs were taken to show that living in Oak Ridge, around the plants, was not hazardous to your health. [Westcott] did not create the need for the photos. He was given a weekly assignment of what the government wanted and he went about his business of capturing that idea. Due to the shortage of film, he had to make every shot work. He did stage many photos to make the best use of film. Also, he had an 'eye' for what he wanted to accomplish."[19] There was a lack of film in part because the Tennessee Eastman Kodak Corporation had turned to other endeavors during World War II, including the management of the x-10 atomic plant in Oak Ridge.

The government-sanctioned images produced during the Manhattan Project not only were employed to recruit workers but also were used after Hiroshima to soften the image of the atomic factories and the work that was done there. They contributed to the public relations campaigns for the nuclear weapons and nuclear energy industries that were launched immediately following the war. When Westcott's images were first circulated in 1945, after the atomic bomb attacks on Hiroshima and Nagasaki, the photographs of the Manhattan Project workers and the atomic laboratories of Oak Ridge served as a usable present. They were visual advertisements intended to present the Project as scientifically clean, orderly, and no different from other industrial or technological workplaces. In *Atomic Spaces*, Peter Bacon Hales describes the mood of those photographs: "Everything's under control in the control room."[20] More recently, Westcott's images construct a usable past; they serve as ready-mades for any nostalgic scrapbook of atomic utopia. As the only images of that time, they have come to define the Atomic City's Brahms-and-bombs aesthetic, washed in hues white, gray, and black.

Public Relations

Immediately after the atomic bombing of Hiroshima, Westcott's photographs reached their largest audience to date. In the summer of 1945, eighteen images were selected to accompany prewritten stories focusing on the production of the atomic bomb and the secret locations where the atomic facilities were located. These selected images played a key role in the government's public relations campaign to garner support for the justification of the use of the atomic bomb. One of these photographs, taken in the summer of 1945, depicts General Groves, well fed and pinched tight in his government-issue khakis, focusing intently on a map of Japan, as if bombing the target with his stare. Westcott, who was unaware of the plans for the atomic bomb, asked Groves to focus his significant gaze on Tokyo; in his characteristically gruff way Groves said he would look elsewhere. Later, Westcott realized Groves was staring straight at Hiroshima.[21] In hindsight, some intentions come into clear view; "the historian is a prophet facing backward."[22]

The journalist William Laurence was tasked by General Groves to write the press releases that would appear immediately after the bombings; they would relay the "official" story of the creation of the atomic bomb. Laurence had written a couple of articles on the possibilities of atomic power for the *New York Times* and the *Saturday Evening Post* in the early 1940s and therefore was considered knowledgeable enough to do the job. An intensely patriotic man, Laurence was thoroughly vetted by General Groves, proving through interviews that he was "the man for the job."[23] While working on this secret assignment, Laurence continued on the *New York Times* payroll, but with all his additional expenses paid by the U.S. government.

For two months, the reporter banged away on his typewriter in the special office in Oak Ridge that he was given to work on the press releases. To throw off suspicion, the *New York Times* published an article by Laurence on August 1, 1945, with a London dateline, giving him an editorial alibi.[24] During this time, he produced fourteen distinct press releases full of purple prose detailing the nuclear physics behind the bomb's development, the construction of the atomic plants, the social and cultural life of Oak Ridge, and stories about the military's top brass. Lieutenant George Robinson, the public relations officer for the Manhattan District, selected twelve members of the Women's Army Corps (WACs) to do the job of readying the thousands of pages of press releases for distribution. By July 27, 1945, the packets were completed and sent off with intelligence and security agents from Oak Ridge to cities around the country.

At 11:00 AM on August 6, assistant press secretary Eben Ayers released the news.[25] The story of the atomic bomb, the place that made it, and the devastation of Hiroshima was picked up by newswires across the world. Just three days later, there was more news, when the United States dropped Fat Man on Nagasaki. Laurence observed the blast from a plane in the fleet of the attack, scribbling like mad. The article he wrote chronicling the experience won him a Pulitzer Prize in 1946 for the best news story of the year.[26] Following this award, to distinguish Laurence from the reporter William H. Lawrence, a political journalist also at the *New York Times*, he was given the nickname "Atomic Bill."

Laurence's Pulitzer Prize is now extremely controversial. Detractors argue that because he was on the payroll of the government, his journalistic integrity was severely compromised. Critics also take issue with the fact that Laurence insisted that radioactive fallout was relatively benign. Peter Hales writes that through Laurence's prose "the atom bomb became a man-made marvel of nature," reducing the human responsibility of the explosion and its fallout.[27] This naturalizing tone was common in the early days of the Atomic Age; it was a rhetorical style that blurred the boundaries between acts of "science" and acts of "nature."

Westcott's pictures of Oak Ridge serve as photographic accomplices to Laurence's original narrative of the Manhattan Project. Following the atomic bombing of Japan, Westcott's images and Laurence's text appeared linked arm-in-arm in newspapers across the country. This all-out media campaign initiated by the government can be read as an attempt to "get ahead of the story" and to humanize the production of atomic bombs, as well as to celebrate the organizational and scientific prowess of the United States and the can-do attitude of its populace. Look! the images seem to shout—the people who made the atomic bombs aren't all mad scientists. While there were plenty of scientific geniuses on board, the rest are just like you and me; it's only that when they went to work, they unlocked the key to the atom.

In a bizarre feedback loop, the first photographs taken by the U.S. damage assessment team in Hiroshima and Nagasaki were processed by Westcott in his Oak Ridge photography laboratory. The rolls of film containing pictorial evidence of the aftermath of the atomic bomb were developed alongside images of everyday life in Oak Ridge: the daily workings of the labs, weddings, anniversaries, high school football games, and other run-of-the-mill events.[28] Once again, Westcott, who had remained stateside during the war, became among the first people to witness the beginning of the Atomic Age, except in this case instead of massive construction and community building, he was a silent witness to the atomic bomb's horrible destructive power. In Westcott's darkroom these two places—Oak Ridge and Hiroshima—were visibly linked. While the story of Oak Ridge and the Manhattan Project cannot be told without Hiroshima and its devastation, visual representations of the two cities are almost never seen side by side.

Myth, Memory, and Postmemory

Michel de Certeau defines myth as "a story jerry-built out of elements taken from common sayings, an allusive and fragmentary story whose gaps mesh with the social practices it symbolizes."[29] Westcott's images are built on these "common sayings." The gestures and social practices captured in the snap of his flashbulb speak for the dawn of the Atomic Age. They say—this is what we were doing during the Manhattan Project: buying war bonds, planting victory gardens, standing in line, hauling coal, watching dials, welding, roller-skating, playing Chinese checkers with the WACs, dancing, drinking soda, playing the oboe in the symphony orchestra, displaying resident badges, and checking for spies at one of the city's seven gates. Westcott's photographs do not say everything, of course, and a lot is left out, including the hazardous nature of much of the work and the damage that was done to the atomic-bombed cities of Japan. This is precisely what is "dangerous" about photographs: their ability to function as "alibis" for the past.[30]

When details are forgotten, when the past becomes either myth or history and loses its "citability," memory is in danger.[31] Myths of the Atomic Age creep in to fill the gaps of lost memory. Strangely, the myths that are used to tell the story of Oak Ridge—a place that owes its existence to the atomic bomb—are appealing: the myth of the atomic prophet who predicted a city that would help to bring an end to a great war; the myth of alchemy, where a dark power is transformed and then used for good to vanquish a powerful enemy; the myth of magic geography, where an atomic-technological utopia rises up at just the right moment, bringing cosmopolitanism and power to an impoverished forgotten valley in Appalachia, practically overnight.[32]

In Oak Ridge, the passing on of atomic myths is a social practice. The hyperbolic narratives created by the first generation of Oak Ridgers are communicated to the next generation, who will then decide how to shape the narrative for the next, and so on. It is a challenge to younger Oak Ridgers to compete with the storied past of their forerunners, to overcome the triumphant myths of the Manhattan Project, to avoid, as Marianne Hirsch writes, the difficult task of the "postmemory" generation, "having one's own stories and experiences displaced, even evacuated, by those of a previous generation."[33]

For Oak Ridge's postmemory generation—those who did not live through the Manhattan Project and know only the postnuclear landscape—stories about the dawn of the Atomic Age are discovered through connections to atomic communities and encounters with historical texts, which are almost always accompanied by Westcott's snapshots.[34] It is an odd phenomenon that Westcott's pictures even function as family photographs, like those hanging in my office. The pairing of Westcott's images and Manhattan Project stories have led to what the novelist Dana Spiotta has called "a shared over-memory," a version of the past that has gained historical weight through (over)telling.[35]

Atomic Nostalgia in Black and White

The historian Peter Bacon Hales argues that in Westcott's photographs, "there were no people . . . only virtuous types," and that the lighting "give[s] the faces that washed-out generality that allows the specific people to become Everyman and Everywoman." He goes on to say, "It's doubtful you would be able to pick them out in a lineup."[36] The fact of the matter is that positioned inside the frames were real people, not models, but actual Oak Ridgers. Certainly, the shots were orchestrated and posed, but these were not the mannequins used to determine the effects of nuclear weapons during the Cold War Apple II tests—they were everyday workers in the Atomic City.[37] And for the time being it is still possible to pick them out of the photographs. Sometimes they even recognize themselves, as was the case with Gladys Owens, one of the famed Calutron Girls. On a visit to the AMSE she looked closely at a photograph on the wall and said, "That's me," which led to her recording a valuable oral history, now available alongside her photo in the same museum. In this way Gladys becomes Gladys again, no longer just a symbol of national sacrifice, but a full person in all her complexity. Erasing the personhood of those captured on film is dangerous and threatens to turn them into mythic props for propaganda, not real people who lived actual lives and created communities.

After all, who knows anything about Rosie the Riveter? When looking at photographs from the past, we are not only searching for "facts," for information, but also for an "affective connection" with the figures represented.[38] This affective connection becomes problematic in the case of the Manhattan Project photographs of Oak Ridge, where the only images from that time come from one source: the U.S. Army Corps shutterbug. Like images from the darkroom, Westcott's photographs show the development of the early Atomic Age. Idealistically posed and shot in black and white, they emit a nostalgic aura, an atomic reenchantment of a disenchanted postnuclear world. This process of reenchantment can be seen in Westcott's recent transformation from Army photographer to twentieth-century artist of iconic atomic imagery.

Westcott as "Insider" Artist

Nearly all of Ed Westcott's photographs were classified when they were first snapped, and they remained so for many years; but now access is mostly unrestricted. They even reside in the public domain, although most are displayed without any reference to the photographer; this has led to Westcott being named by some as an "artistic talent" and "the unsung hero of Oak Ridge."[39] This shift is sociologically interesting on two levels: the first is the lifting of Westcott's anonymity from behind institutional lines, and the second is the relabeling of Westcott, decades later, as an artist, rather than as an Army photo-documentarian, an "insider" artist from the city behind the fence. As the official historian of the Y-12 Nuclear Security Complex, D. Ray Smith, argues, "Ed's photographs are more than a documentary of our history. They are an artistic statement by a rare artist who has created a body of work that can be increasingly meaningful to future generations. Without Ed's photographs we would be hard pressed to comprehend the magnitude of the Manhattan Project, much less tell the stories of the workers who lived here."[40] Westcott's photographs have been conduits and accomplices to the stories of Oak Ridge from the city's inception.

In 2005, Westcott's biggest show, "Through the Lens of Ed Westcott: A Photographic History of World War II's Secret City," took place in the Ewing Gallery of Art and Architecture at the University of Tennessee. A catalog of the same name was published with the intention of showcasing Westcott's "artistic excellence," introducing him to a national audience, and linking the photographer with those familiar images whose authorship for so long has been unknown.[41] When asked about the attention from the art world his work has started to see, Westcott replied, "It is an honor, but I was just doing my job."[42]

Westcott's official career as an atomic photographer spanned from 1941 to 1977, although even in his nineties he still works occasionally as a consultant for the Department of Energy and the AMSE on matters related to his photography. Throughout his career, Westcott photographed countless nuclear reactors, storage centers, and factories, but most importantly he captured on film one of the first communities that cropped up in the Atomic Age. While the Laurence press releases of the atomic bombing campaigns have been the source of much controversy, including efforts to strip the author and the *New York Times* of the Pulitzer Prize, the Westcott images draw very little comment, critical or otherwise. As images they seem benign, which has contributed to the coffee-table-book aesthetic of Atomic Age storytelling.

Despite a stroke several years ago that made it more difficult for him to speak, Westcott can still be considered one of the main atomic memory brokers of the city. Without carrying the metaphor too far, Westcott's inability to speak draws attention to the problems of communication between the past and the present. While he can field and answer questions through an intermediary, usually his daughter or son-in-law, there is an understandable delay in the process.

Leaving the present aside for a moment, what will happen when Westcott and the dwindling population of his generation, those who ushered in the Atomic Age, are gone? Who will become the atomic memory brokers in the future? In the case of Westcott and the stories of his Manhattan Project images, the narrative authority will most likely pass to his children, who, as noted, are already speaking for him. What will be lost in this baton passing? At this point it is hard to say, but as the sociologist of memory Maurice Halbwachs writes, "Since social memory erodes at the edges as individual members, especially older ones, become isolated or die, it is constantly transformed along with the group itself."[43] As members of the previous generations disappear, collective memory of the Manhattan Project will undoubtedly be transformed. And as it does, new perceptions of the Manhattan Project will likely emerge, and the national memory of nuclear weapons, nuclear energy, and nuclear waste will be altered as well.

When the first generation of Oak Ridgers is gone and a new generation of atomic citizens become stewards of atomic memory, is it possible that temporal distance could lend analytical distance, allowing critical thought to cut through the fog of atomic nostalgia that lies over the city? Right now those leading the charge for new memory projects commemorating Oak Ridge's role in the Atomic Age are mainly those who participated in the Manhattan Project and who view this past as overwhelmingly positive—an effort that brought an end to World War II and saved lives on both sides. While it is possible for new attitudes and social practices to emerge with the changing of the guard, I am skeptical about the next generation, "generation 1.5," my mother's cohort.[44] Those who were children at the start of the Atomic Age often exhibit more nostalgia for a lost atomic utopia than even the early atomic practitioners, those employed by the Manhattan Project and early nuclear industries. As Emily Heistand from generation 1.5 writes in her memoir, "How we like that word 'physicist,' because it began in delight with 'fizz' and had a buzzy, hissy sound, and because to be a physicist then in Oak Ridge was to be a local god. In such a town, the school science fairs were the *festas* of our culture. By junior high, a good science project was a route to popularity."[45] Perhaps a critical eye toward Oak Ridge must come from outside city limits, or from the following generation (mine), the grandchildren of the Bomb.

The German cultural theorist Siegfried Kracauer writes, "Compared to photography, memory's records are full of gaps."[46] And yet in the case of Westcott's photographs, the records are also full of gaps. Like the city of Oak Ridge itself, the image archive of the Manhattan Project was carefully produced and tightly controlled. Michel Foucault was right to describe the archive as "the first law of what can be said."[47] The problem is that after this "law" was set, the same conversations about the atomic past have been repeated on loop.

In a time when many of the Manhattan Project's secret documents have been declassified and when Westcott's photographs have (re)entered the public domain, sometimes even with artistic credit attached, it is necessary to reexamine the early images of Oak Ridge. Through his lens, Westcott captured and helped to create local fantasies of "making do," specialness, Oak Ridgidness, and victory, alongside "state fantasies" of sacrifice, security, and citizenship.[48] Care should be taken in treating these Rockwellian images as realistic depictions of the past; instead, they should be viewed as potentially problematic spaces of inquiry. As Walter Benjamin writes, "There is no document of culture which is not at the same time a document of barbarism."[49] Westcott's photographs reveal the dreams of an atomic utopia that never materialized and the distance between these past dreams and current realities. By refocusing, we can capture more of the story beyond the frame before the images and the people depicted therein become only mythic symbols of a lost atomic utopian dream.

CHAPTER NINE

Longing for the Bomb

Because if it's not love. Then it's the Bomb, the Bomb, the Bomb,
the Bomb, the Bomb, the Bomb, the Bomb that will bring us together.
—Morrissey, The Smiths, "Ask"

There is a French-sounding phrase, *nostalgie de la boue*, or "yearning for the mud," which means to long for the leaner, more hardscrabble days of one's youth.[1] In Oak Ridge, this phrase works quite literally. Many longtime residents yearn for the days when Oak Ridge was a muddy frontier at the beginning of the Atomic Age, when they trekked through the unfinished townsite to work at the uranium processing factories or trudged in boots through the viscous southern mud carrying high heels or wingtips in paper sacks to put on upon arrival. The mud-free shoes were symbols of their urbanity and cosmopolitanism on the atomic frontier; they would slip them on as they attended symphony concerts and dances on the tennis courts that were kept lit twenty-four hours a day to cater to shift workers. A longing for this past is shaped by positive memories of working for a secret atomic bomb project, but it is also colored with nostalgia for an imagined golden age of mid-twentieth-century America. In Oak Ridge, as elsewhere, this sentiment not only describes an opinion about the past; it also betrays a vision of contemporary America as a nation divided and in decline, a depraved nation characterized by selfishness, strife, and ambivalence—a nation that has lost or is in the act of losing its purpose and character.

Stories of Oak Ridge in the 1940s can sound as if they were ripped from the pages of a comic book, where at Site X, as the city was first known, mysterious buzzing factories were filled with thousands of workers who labored around the clock in order to churn out minuscule amounts of a mysterious substance, gram by gram. At other times, stories of Oak Ridge's early days are reminiscent of frontier tales peppered with anecdotes of mud, dust, and "making do." Other narratives describe a bucolic utopian community bursting at the seams with cultural and intellectual capital. These accounts have been shaped by government documents, official institutional histories, memoirs, oral histories, and a tradition of southern storytelling—they are shot through with memory, myth, and local color. All these stories are partially true and, of course, partially exaggeration. This multifaceted tangle of narrative expression writes the overall relationship of the city to the bomb. And beyond this, stories of Oak Ridge contribute to a way of seeing and thinking about the atomic past, present, and future that stretches outward from this one dog-eared corner of Appalachia throughout the entire United States.

The atomic culture of Oak Ridge was nurtured through the race for the bomb, extended through the Cold War, and extends even now, shaping our current American notions of the postnuclear landscape. The culture of the place, its Oak Ridgidness, its hidebound dedication to a nuclear-fueled future, was born from this secrecy, creating a shared sense of kinship and responsibility, both during the war and after. Even though it is sometimes written that once the bomb was dropped, "the secret was out," this was hardly the case. Many of those in the dark about the inner workings of the Project during the war remained in the dark afterward.

Most of the first generation of Oak Ridgers died without knowing what hazardous materials they may have been exposed to or even who may have been spying on them. Even for those still alive, the full picture of their service to the Manhattan Project is unknown. The secrecy and security apparatus of Oak Ridge prevented workers from knowing about the possible health risks associated with their work. This was especially true for maintenance and construction workers, who had the least amount of knowledge about the Project. Workers were not told about the dangers because of concerns that there would be an even higher turnover rate if they knew the true hazards of their employment. Many nuclear workers died early because of the jobs they held during the hot war of World War II and the Cold War that followed. The Department of Labor has awarded nearly $6 billion to former nuclear workers. Lawsuits are still being waged. In spite of all this, most Oak Ridgers take immense pride in their role in the Manhattan Project and carry enthusiasm for the nuclear and security projects that followed.

After turning out the viscera of nuclear bombs for decades, the plants produced not a spotless atomic Shangri-La, but mountains of hazardous and radioactive waste, much of it disposed of willy-nilly. Department of Energy signs warning "no fishing" and "no water contact" line the city's creeks. The reservations surrounding the former atomic factories contain forests of radioactive trees, radioactive frogs, and even "hot" deer that can be hunted in season with a permit, although some are too contaminated to be taken off the grounds.

Mapping Atomic Nostalgia

Today, Oak Ridge can sometimes feel like an aged copy of itself.[2] Like the Borges story where a society beset with cartographic mania produces a map of the empire that is the exact size and shape of the empire, Oak Ridge is nearly consumed by the ground it has already covered. The question is whether this map of the past will completely smother the city's present and future, allowing Oak Ridgers to live in their self-created map, in Baudrillard's words, "the map that precedes the territory,"[3] or if Oak Ridgers and the rest of us can summon up a new magic geography—drawing on all the Oak Ridges that never happened and all the Oak Ridges that still could— and begin to think of a possible future where, again as Borges writes, "those unconscionable maps no longer satisfied."[4]

The original maps, the city's loosely gridded designs commissioned by the federal government, blueprinted and brought to fruition by Skidmore, Owings, and Merrill, were cartographic notions of order superimposed on an unruly natural landscape of ridges and valleys. Today, on these undulating hills and roadways, many of the community's residents still reside in original homes from the forties. Longtime residents of the more elite sections of Oak Ridge who are afflicted with atomic nostalgia love to talk about their early assignments, where they worked, what dormitory they lived in, or where their home sat in the housing alphabet. As de Certeau writes, "What the map cuts up, the story cuts across."[5]

The early Cemestos still dot the landscape, even as late-twentieth-century and twenty-first-century architecture makes inroads. At one time there were as many as 3,050 Cemesto houses. While no official count is available today, it is estimated that 500 or so still exist. My mother lives in one. Most have been remodeled so as to be barely recognizable from their Manhattan Project days, a process a local journalist refers to as removing the "evidence of Cemestoism."[6] Remodeling began as soon as the homes were available for private purchase from the government, beginning in 1956. Yet the homes endure, even gracing the contemporary real estate pages, where one can find "a super D," an "enlarged A," or an "extensively remodeled B."[7] Recently, as atomic nostalgia has increased, there has been a desire for the original Oak Ridge homes stripped of remodeling, marking a return to Cemestoism, or perhaps a neo-Cemestoism.[8] My mother just ripped up the carpeting in hers, revealing the beautiful original wood flooring underneath. It was time to peel back the layers of living to examine the beginnings, she told me, more or less. It was my grandmother's house. Things had been let go; it was time to go to the past in order to change the future.

Whether they dwell in new housing or old, Oak Ridgers continue to go about their everyday life under the atomic symbol, both literally and symbolically. Ubiquitous in the visual plane, Oak Ridge's atom, customized with an acorn as its nucleus, is a symbol of civic pride. The symbol hangs jauntily on the side of the high school, stares back from municipal signposts, winks from the stained glass of the library, and beckons customers to Atomic City Tattoo, Atomic Pawn, Atomic City Computers, and many other similarly named businesses. I see it today as I type these lines on a sun-cracked bench at the site of the abandoned Secret City Mini Golf. It is telling that Oak Ridge uses the atomic symbol, and not the bomb or the mushroom cloud, as its totem of collective representation. The atomic emblem of the city is an ellipsis, not an exclamation point.

Elsewhere in the postnuclear landscape, different visions of the past appear. In Richland, Washington, the bedroom community of the Hanford production site, where plutonium was produced for the Trinity test and the Nagasaki bomb, teenagers attend Richland High, where a bomber is the mascot. The iconography on display at the school is an enormous mushroom cloud with an R for Richland floating above the imagined destruction beneath. Before basketball games Richland cheerleaders form an enormous bomb shape made of their bodies in an outrageous display of plutonium pep. For each outstanding play, football players are given tiny bomb decals with which to adorn their helmets. And local boosters drive around town and on the atomic highways with bumper stickers shouting, "Go Bombers, Nuke 'em!"

In Richland, overt nuclearphilia is on display, a step not taken in Oak Ridge, where the mushroom cloud and its effects remain mostly hidden behind a scientific gloss, and where under the glow of the Friday night lights fans cheer not for the Bombers, but for the Wildcats, representing animals that roamed the region before the Atomic Age. Even though Oak Ridgers hoot and holler for the Wildcats, the days when they walked into Oak Ridge High School, heads held high, looking up at the symbol of the atom that was their past, present, and imagined future, are not forgotten. A couple of Halloweens ago, my mother (class of 1960) called up her alma mater with a rather odd request. She wanted to borrow a cheerleading outfit to wear to a party she had coming up. In high school she was a majorette; this time she felt like doing things a little differently. The school enthusiastically granted her request, and my mother sauntered into her party as both a product of and prompt for atomic nostalgia. We borrow from the past, but with each new borrowing we get the chance to change it a bit.

Atomic Gerontology

On August 3, 1944, in the *Oak Ridge Journal*, an anonymous author wrote, "The youth of the town gives us a big advantage, for we are not cluttered with the debris of old age." When she visited twenty years later in 1964, Margaret Mead was puzzled by Oak Ridge's uncluttered population; she criticized its isolationism and its youth—she worried about what she called "a city without grandmothers." Now the population of Oak Ridge is aging with plenty of grandmothers, including my own.

It is not only my grandmother and those who were on the scene at the beginning of the Atomic Age who are entering twilight years; their products—their bombs—are also aging. In addition to housing contemporary industries devoted to the nation's safety, especially at the Y-12 National Security Complex, Oak Ridge is currently involved in a massive "modernization" project of the nation's nuclear arsenal, which is part atomic chop-shop, part atomic gerontology.[9] Here, massive amounts of non-proliferated nuclear fuel are stored, and old weapons are inspected, refurbished, tested, and housed. These are mostly America's own nuclear products, but weapons smuggled out of Kazakhstan and Libya, among other places, have also landed here. Y-12 currently holds the largest stockpile of enriched uranium in the world—enough for approximately 16,000 nuclear weapons. In order to process and store these aging nuclear materials, a new facility with the hyperbolic name the Uranium Center of Excellence is being built. This center created by the Nuclear Security Administration signaled a renewed commitment to Oak Ridge as an important node in the national nuclear apparatus. Atomic fordism lumbers on, but its conveyor belts now move in reverse.

In July 2012, an event occurred that rattled this confidence and questioned the excellence of Y-12.[10] An octogenarian nun, a Vietnam veteran, and a housepainter broke into the space, a space thought to be so secure it was often referred to as the Fort Knox of uranium. On the very site predicted by the atomic prophet John Hendrix, Sister Megan Gillespie Rice, Michael Robin Walli, and Gregory Irwin Boertje-Obed began their mission. Propelled by God and guided by Google maps and a verse from the Prophet Isaiah plucked from the Christian Bible that predicts the end of war and the transformation of weapons into tools of cultivation (Isaiah 2:4), they moved toward the aging bombs under the symbolic banner of the peace activist collective known as Plowshares. The group is historically linked to this kind of action: Plowshares dates back to a 1980 operation led by the Berrigen brothers and six other anti-nuke activists who attacked Minutemen missiles with hammers and human blood at the General Electric Nuclear Missile facility in King of Prussia, Pennsylvania. But Sister Megan and her co-conspirators grabbed even more headlines by piercing the inner sanctum of the nation's nuclear holdings at Y-12.

On the night in question, the trio shuffled toward Bear Creak Valley through four fences and a humid Tennessee summer night, along the way exposing huge flaws in a $150 million security system. They carried twine, bolt cutters, flashlights, spray paint, cucumber seeds to symbolize sustenance, a loaf of bread with a cross on the top for actual sustenance, and human blood in baby bottles that sloshed as they walked. After penetrating the perimeter, they got to work delivering their own prophecy, which was the opposite of Hendrix's: the end of nuclear weapons, the end of worshipping nuclear weapons as false idols, as gods.

As I write this chapter, the three await sentencing, having been declared guilty of trespassing and intending to harm national security, which falls under the "sabotage" chapter of United States code, a charge rarely directed at civilians. The break-in has forced a new look at the nuts and bolts of the nuclear security apparatus in the United States, but it also presses on something more existential: new questions about what it means to feel safe with respect to nuclear weapons. Inside the facility there was enough nuclear material to fuel thousands and thousands of nuclear bombs. "What if they had been terrorists?" echoed throughout the next day's inky newspaper columns and the linky hypertext of online articles. And for Oak Ridgers, the bold action forces something else as well: new confrontations with the older prophecy on which the city bases its beginnings.

The Future of Atomic Nostalgia

While the Uranium Center of Excellence is meant only to refer to the storage and processing site located at the Y-12 National Security Complex, the moniker could be extended to describe the way the community sees itself. The Manhattan Project swiftly and permanently altered the culture of the area, ushering in a culture of Brahms and bombs, nuclear science, and techno-security. The question is what will happen next for the first city of the Atomic Age. Oak Ridge is caught in a purgatorial state: no longer what it was historically, yet not quite anything else so easily defined as beyond that, either. Today, in the senescence of the Atomic Age, in the aftermath of Chernobyl and the more recent Fukushima disaster, we are painfully aware of the failure of the type of atomic utopia once envisioned in the more optimistic 1950s.

With this knowledge, we must look to Oak Ridge and places like it to remember that massive national nuclear projects create real communities with real people—that the Manhattan Project built bombs, but also cities. There was Oppenheimer and his team of geniuses, but there were also Calutron Girls, Chauffeurettes, Computers, couriers, construction workers, electricians, garbage collectors, librarians, nurses, prostitutes, typists—and all manner of human characters who make up any community. It is in these cities and with these folks that a richer history of the Manhattan Project resides. Beneath the layers of celebration and justification there is more to be said. The challenge is that the material reminders of the early Atomic Age are dematerializing; huge factories and mammoth facilities are undergoing decommission and decontamination. The past is becoming more invisible, more secret. But, far more crucial, as the buildings are coming down, the atomic pioneers are also disappearing, their stories fading and being buried along with them. This moment of passing makes it possible for the critical nostalgic to see, as Walter Benjamin writes in "The Storyteller," "a new beauty in what is vanishing."[11] The present is haunted with the not-yet past, reminding us that there is so much betwixt and between John Hendrix, the so-called atomic prophet, and the trim and trig J. Robert Oppenheimer, who became "Death, destroyer of worlds."

Notes

PROLOGUE

1. Benjamin, "The Storyteller," 84.
2. Welty, "Place in Fiction," 792.

INTRODUCTION

1. The concept of "magic geography" is borrowed from the title of a 1941 article from the German sociologist Hans Speier examining how cartography is used as propaganda. Speier illustrates how maps can be manipulated not only to represent the geographical present but also to forecast a desired future, as if it were inevitable. I extend Speier's concept to apply to the product as well as the process of this kind of cartographic maneuver. See Speier, "Magic Geography," 310–30.

2. A few of the best examples from a very large field include Rhodes, *The Making of the Atomic Bomb*; Norris, *Racing for the Bomb*; Fermi, *Atoms in the Family*; Goodchild, *Edward Teller*; Herken, *Brotherhood of the Bomb*; Bird and Sherwin, *American Prometheus*; Monk, *Oppenheimer, His Life and Mind*; and Thorpe, *Oppenheimer: The Tragic Intellectual*.

3. This has actually been done. In 1959, French social theorist Guy Debord and Danish artist Asger Jorn, members of the avant-garde collective the Situationist International, published *Mémoires*, a work of art and social criticism with a sandpaper cover. Sticky asphalt and glass wool were briefly considered before heavy-grade sandpaper was chosen for its abrasive qualities. The cover illustrated that the book was meant as total critical theory, not just in its content but also in its form. It was designed to damage not only nearby books on the bookshelf but the hands of readers as well. *Mémoires* was printed in Copenhagen in 1959 by Éditions Situationist International.

4. While Present's sociological study was never written, her letters to Margaret Mead along with some additional commentary were published decades later. See Present, *Dear Margaret*. The quote appears on page 68 of that volume. The original letters are now ensconced, along with other Mead memorabilia, in the archives of the Library of Congress.

5. Hunner makes a similar argument for Los Alamos in *Inventing Los Alamos*, 3.
6. Benjamin, "On the Concept of History," 390.
7. Jameson, "Walter Benjamin, or Nostalgia," 68.
8. Nora, "Between Memory and History," 7.
9. Park, *The City*, 1.
10. Boym, *Future of Nostalgia*, 351.

11. Radstone, "Nostalgia: Home-comings and Departures," 187.

12. Hofer, "Medical Dissertation on Nostalgia [1688]," 376–91.

13. In *The Eighteenth Brumaire of Louis Bonaparte*, Karl Marx writes, "Men make their own history, but they do not make it just as they please; they do not make it under circumstances chosen by themselves, but under circumstances directly encountered, given and transmitted from the past. The tradition of all the dead generations weighs like a nightmare on the brain of the living" (15). In an alternate version of the text, the weight of tradition that Marx describes is not just a nightmare, but an alp, a creature from German folklore that invades dreams producing nightmares, among other mischievous acts. The alp sometimes sits on the chest of the sleeper, cutting off air to the lungs and suffocating him. In Marx's *Brumaire*, the nightmare (alp) "weighs on the brains of the living," interfering with thought.

14. The quote is from Radstone, "Nostalgia: Home-comings and Departures," 187. See also Boym, *Future of Nostalgia*; Davis, *Yearning For Yesterday*; and Nadkarni and Shevcheko, "The Politics of Nostalgia."

15. Didion, *Slouching towards Bethlehem*, 139.

16. Kathleen Stewart, "Nostalgia—A Polemic," 227.

17. Smith, "Historically Speaking."

18. See, for example, de Certeau, *Practice of Everyday Life* and *The Writing of History*.

19. Benjamin, "On the Concept of History," 389–400.

20. Benjamin, *Arcades Project*, 458.

21. Adorno, *Minima Moralia*, 50.

22. Adorno described his friend Benjamin's intellectual abilities as "mental atomic fission" in "A Portrait of Walter Benjamin," 230.

23. Calvino, *Invisible Cities*, 19.

24. Benjamin, "The Storyteller," 98, 92; emphasis in original.

CHAPTER 1

1. Oakes, "John Hendrix, Prophet of Oak Ridge, Predicted Project and Railroad More than 40 Years Ago!," 3; Robinson, *Oak Ridge Story*, 17–19.

2. Hendrix soon escaped and prophesized, so the story goes, that God would destroy the county farm where he was held. Months later a lightning storm burned the institution to the ground. See Smith, *John Hendrix Story*, 10.

3. Bataille, *Absence of Myth*.

4. Quoted in Sennett, *The Craftsman*, 2.

5. Hewlett and Anderson, *New World*, 76–77.

6. This story was told to me by Y-12 historian D. Ray Smith. He insists "thang" is how the senator would have pronounced "thing" (interview with the author, January 9, 2011).

7. Fine and Remington, *Corps of Engineers*, 655; Jackson and Johnson, *City behind a Fence*, 41.

8. Robinson, *Oak Ridge Story*, 37–38.

9. The power of eminent domain is outlined in the Fifth Amendment to the United States Constitution. The practice is an action taken by the state to seize private property for "public use." Under the "Takings Clause" "just compensation" must be paid to the

owners, although their consent is not required. For more on the evacuation of local residents, see Irwin, "New Places, Strange People," 20; Jackson and Johnson, *City behind a Fence*, 41; Davis, "Evacuation Area Residents All Ready to Leave 'If It Will Help to Win This War,'" 10.

10. See Irwin, "New Places, Strange People," 20, and War Department Letter to Parlee Raby, November 11, 1942, Oak Ridge Archives, Oak Ridge Public Library.

11. Seaborg was originally from Ishpeming, in the Upper Peninsula of Michigan, but moved to California as a boy, where later he would be the principal co-discoverer of not only plutonium, but also elements named for people and places that influenced his life and thinking: californium, berkelium, americium, curium, einsteinium, fermium, mendelevium, and nobelium. Later the element seaborgium, 106 on the periodic table, was named in his honor.

12. Rhodes, *Making of the Atomic Bomb*, 486, 449–51, 496; Goldberg, "General Groves and the Atomic West," 49.

13. For more on the development of the Hanford site, see Ficken, "Grand Coulee and Hanford."

14. Robinson, *Oak Ridge Story*, 29.

15. Ibid., 28.

16. Fine and Remington, *Corps of Engineers*, 663; Jackson and Johnson, *City behind a Fence*, 43.

17. Moneymaker, *We'll Call It Wheat*, iv.

18. The *Wunderblock* was a toy made of a thin sheet of clear plastic which covers a thick board made of wax. The user draws or writes on the surface with a pointed stylus, which makes an impression on the wax below the surface. When the sheet is lifted the image disappears from the surface and a new design can be made. Traces of the previous design still remain in the wax. Freud uses the *Wunderblock* as a metaphor for how memories are stored in the unconscious. See Freud, "Mystic Writing Pad *der Wunderblock*."

The Etch A Sketch is a mechanical drawing toy manufactured by the Ohio Art Company, first released in 1960. The toy is rectangular and made of molded plastic with a glass screen placed over aluminum powder. Two knobs are situated at the bottom right and left. By manipulating these knobs a dark line is created on the light gray screen. To erase the image the toy can be either turned upside down or shaken.

Here I do not mean to suggest all is completely lost. The previous design can of course be redrawn from memory if the person or persons who have control of the screen chooses to do so.

19. Dogpatch was the fictional community in the comic strip *Li'l Abner* (1934–77), by Al Capp. The community, in Capp's words, was "an average stone-age community nestled in a bleak valley, between two cheap and uninteresting hills somewhere." Capp's comic was awash with stereotypical imagery of Appalachian life—hillbillies who were too lazy to work; hog wallows; sex-crazed women; backward officials; an anti-technology, gun-toting populace; and hermits with long, scraggly beards who lived in caves. See *Li'l Abner* official site, http://lil-abner.com/dogpatch-and-dogpatch-u-s-a/ (accessed August 27, 2014).

20. Groves, *Now It Can Be Told*, 94.

21. There is disagreement on the topic. Local historian D. Ray Smith argues, "Very few moved farther than a fifty-mile radius," whereas architectural historian Peter Bacon Hales

writes, "Most farmers were forced far away, off the land to cities like Chicago." See Smith, *John Hendrix Story*, 49, and Hales, "Topographies of Power," 263.

22. Johnson and Schaffer, *Oak Ridge National Laboratory*, 17; Kaufman, "A House Stronger than Time," 38.

23. Hales, *Atomic Spaces*, 121–22; Jackson and Johnson, *City behind a Fence*, 49; Groves, *Now It Can Be Told*, 26–27.

24. Hales, *Atomic Spaces*, 122.

25. Groves, *Now It Can Be Told*, 26–27.

26. David Lilienthal would go on to head the Atomic Energy Commission from 1947 to 1950.

27. Quoted in Johnson and Schaffer, *Oak Ridge National Laboratory*, 16.

28. For more on TVA's regional improvement strategies versus the Manhattan Project's national and international focus, see Creese, *TVA's Public Planning*, 304–15.

29. Hales, *Atomic Spaces*, 125.

30. Bascom, "The Forms of Folklore: Prose Narrative," 4.

31. Ibid.

32. Barthes, *Mythologies*, 122.

33. Jackson and Johnson, *City behind a Fence*, 41.

34. Roane College was in operation from 1886 to 1908.

35. See, for example, Westcott, *Oak Ridge*, 8; Wickware, "The Manhattan Project," 94; Robinson, *Oak Ridge Story*, 8–9.

36. Quoted in Smith, *John Hendrix Story*, 31. See also Crawford "Back of Oak Ridge."

37. Irwin, "New Places, Strange People," 21.

38. Curtis Allen Hendrix's poem appears in Smith, *John Hendrix Story*, 55–56. D. Ray Smith procured the poem from Evorie Loe, a descendent of John Hendrix. Curtis Allen Hendrix died in 1944; the poem was written in 1943 or 1944.

39. Dorathy Moneymaker, interviewed by Patricia Clark, the American Museum of Science and Energy, Oak Ridge, Tennessee, July 10, 2000.

40. Benjamin, "On the Concept of History," 390.

41. See Moneymaker, *We'll Call It Wheat*.

42. Benjamin, "Paralipomena to 'On the Concept of History,'" 401.

43. Stewart, *Space on the Side of the Road*, 3.

44. Barthes, *Mythologies*, 109.

45. Davis, "Evacuation Area Residents All Ready to Leave 'If It Will Help to Win This War,'" 10.

46. *We the People*, script of a radio broadcast sponsored by Gulf Oil Corporation.

47. The *Oak Ridge Journal*, a weekly newspaper, first appeared on mimeographed sheets of typed copy on September 4, 1943. The *Journal* was originally civilian-run and published by the Recreation and Welfare Association. Citing security concerns, the military took over control of the paper in 1944. After World War II, the *Journal* was run by the AEC until 1948, when it was dissolved and commercial newspapers took its place. See Jackson and Johnson, "The Urbane Frontier," 10, and Adamson, *From Bulletin to Broadside*.

48. Quoted in Smith, *John Hendrix Story*, 13.

49. Censorship of the newspapers was a common practice during wartime, with most commercial press following the *Code of Wartime Practices for the American Press* (issued January 15, 1942). General Groves did allow for some mention of the happenings in Oak

Ridge, as he wrote in his memoir: "The Knoxville papers were permitted to carry items—mostly in the nature of social notes—about employees and events at Oak Ridge, though nothing, of course that would help the average reader determine the purpose of the project or its importance." See *Now It Can be Told*, 147-48.

50. Oakes, "John Hendrix, Prophet of Oak Ridge, Predicted Project and Railroad More than 40 Years Ago!," 3.

51. Ibid.

52. Barthes, *Mythologies*, 135.

53. Robinson, *Oak Ridge Story*, 20.

54. Ibid.

55. The U.S. Atomic Energy Commission and the Oak Ridge Institute of Nuclear Studies operated the American Museum of Atomic Energy, the first museum in the world of its kind. The museum, which changed its name in 1978, is now owned by the Department of Energy and managed under the Oak Ridge National Laboratory by UT-Battelle, LLC. A major portion of the AMSE funding is provided by UT-Battelle, LLC, in partnership with B&W Y-12 and Bechtel Jacobs Company, LLC.

56. Awiakta, *Abiding Appalachia*, 43.

57. Smith, *John Hendrix Story*, 10.

58. Jim Comish, email correspondence with the author, June 10, 2011.

59. The exhibit ran from November 9, 2010, to January 30, 2011.

60. D. Ray Smith, email correspondence with the author, March 25, 2011.

61. Keith McDaniel is the foremost documentary filmmaker of Oak Ridge; see also *Secret City: The Oak Ridge Story* and *Operation Open Sesame*.

62. Jack Mansfield in *John Hendrix*, directed and produced by Keith McDaniel.

63. Loeb notices the same sentiment in his research on Hanford, where the more religious workers perceived the bomb as a gift from God. See *Nuclear Culture*, 33.

64. D. Ray Smith, interviewed by the author, Oak Ridge, Tennessee, January 9, 2011.

65. Smith, *Ethnic Origins of Nations*, 212-13.

66. Douglas, *How Institutions Think*, 112.

67. Margalit, *Ethics of Memory*, 52.

68. De Certeau, *Practice of Everyday Life*, 109.

69. Stewart, *Space on the Side of the Road*, 3.

70. Calvino, *Invisible Cities*, 60.

71. The concept "nostalgic bridging" is influenced by the work of Eviatar Zerubavel and his concept of "mnemonic bridging," and by Michel de Certeau, who sees in every place the necessity of the "frontier" and the "bridge" for storytelling and articulating spaces. See Zerubavel, *Time Maps*, 7-8, 10, 40-55, and de Certeau, *Practice of Everyday Life*, 123-29.

72. De Certeau, *Practice of Everyday Life*, 122-23.

73. Bataille, *Absence of Myth*, 48.

74. Crane is quoted in Huotari, "Oak Ridge Council OKs Home Near Grave of 'Prophet.'"

CHAPTER 2

1. Hales writes about Oak Ridge as a precursor to Levittown in "Levittown: Documents of an Ideal Suburb." In *Inventing Los Alamos*, Jon Hunner also describes Los Alamos as a

kind of atomic Levittown, although, as he points out, in New Mexico this move happened in the postwar era, several years after Oak Ridge.

2. Abbott takes on these tropes when looking at the atomic cities of the West in "Building the Atomic Cities," 90–118.

3. Groves, *Now It Can Be Told*, 415.

4. See Benjamin, "On the Concept of History."

5. Yael Zerubavel, *Recovered Roots*.

6. Roosevelt, *Winning of the West*.

7. Marx, *Machine in the Garden*.

8. Sparrow, *Oak Ridgers*, 24; emphasis mine.

9. During the Manhattan Project, the area was full of folks with Scots-Irish ancestors (and still is), so many, in fact, that the telephone book in Oak Ridge, instead of having the standard twenty-six tabs, one for each letter of the alphabet, has twenty-seven, with Mc resting between M and N. There you would look to call my grandparents, Nan and Frank McLemore.

10. Bush, *Science*.

11. Miller, "Frontier Experience," 7–8.

12. Burgess, *Romance of the Commonplace*, 91.

13. Rockwell, "Frontier Life among the Atom Splitters," 44.

14. Jackson and Johnson, *City behind a Fence*, 19.

15. The city of Oak Ridge was not universally considered utopian. For example, the historians Johnson and Jackson argue that the goal of Oak Ridge was simply uranium production, and that if there were any gestures toward civic comfort, they were secondary. Johnson and Jackson go on to argue that the community was originally intended to be temporary, which in their opinion precludes it from being utopian. There is a mountain of evidence with respect to the effort to create an ideal town, including the architects' plans. In addition, I see no contradiction between an (initially) short-range project and a utopian agenda, although it cannot be contested that the war effort was the primary focus. For more of the opposing position, see Johnson and Jackson, "The Urbane Frontier."

16. Baxter, "A Letter from the Town Manager," 1.

17. Shangri-La was described in the novel *Lost Horizon* by James Hilton, published in 1933. Shangri-La was also the name President Franklin D. Roosevelt chose for the new presidential retreat in the Catoctin Mountain Park in 1942. The retreat was renamed Camp David by President Dwight Eisenhower in 1953.

18. Van Wyck, *Signs of Danger*, v.

19. The Oneida Community was founded in 1848 in Oneida, New York, by John Humphrey Noyes. The community believed that Jesus had already returned to earth in the year 70, and therefore it was possible to be free of sin and to create a perfect kingdom in this world. Brook Farm was a Transcendental utopian community founded by the former Unitarian minister George Ripley and his wife Sophia Ripley. Inspired at least in part by Charles Fourier, the community was dedicated to communal living and the balance of passions through work and leisure. Drop City was an artists' community located in Colorado from 1965–70. Community members were inspired by the designs and ideas of Buckminster Fuller, who argued that because of our advanced stage of industrialization our options for the future were limited to only two: utopia or oblivion.

20. Searcy, *Last Reunion*, back matter.

21. Mead, "The Crucial Role of the Small City in Meeting the Urban Crisis," 188. Margaret Mead spoke at Oak Ridge High School on May 18, 1964, where she encouraged students to join the Youth Council for Atomic Crisis, among other things. See Adamson, "Woman with a Big Stick," and Dings, "A Teenage Remembrance of 'Monumental Maggie.'"

22. Hannigan, *Fantasy City*, 189.

23. Searcy, "My Nuclear Childhood," 10.

24. Despite losing their contract to plan the city of Oak Ridge, Stone and Webster retained their contract to build the Y-12 uranium processing plant.

25. Olwell, "Help Wanted for Secret City," 52–69.

26. Kargon and Moella, *Invented Edens*, 79.

27. Ibid., 80.

28. Ibid.

29. Marx, *Machine in the Garden*.

30. Similarly, Hevly and Findlay, in *The Atomic West*, stress the idea of the relative emptiness of the Western atomic landscape that was intrinsic to federal thinking and implementation of twentieth-century atomic projects.

31. Skidmore, Owings, and Merrill, "Oak Ridge Report."

32. Even before 1942, Skidmore, Owings, and Merrill had collaborated with the John B. Pierce Foundation, creating low-cost prefabricated housing made from Cemesto board. These homes were first assembled en masse at the Glenn Martin airplane plant outside Baltimore, Maryland. See Groueff, *Manhattan Project*, 182.

33. Present, *Dear Margaret*, 12.

34. Ibid., 23.

35. Hales, *Atomic Space*, 90.

36. Wende, "Building a City From Scratch," 149.

37. Gailar, *Oak Ridge and Me*, 77.

38. Wilcox, "Oak Ridge's Dormitories," 6.

39. Originally only numbers distinguished dormitories, but on February 22, 1945, a memorandum was sent to all dorm residents that numbers would be changed to names. It has been speculated that this move was made to avoid tipping off the enemy to how many people were flooding into Oak Ridge; the number of dorms had risen to ninety. After 1945, dormitories were given the names of cities, and all dorms in the same area would be given names that started with the same letter. See Wilcox, "Oak Ridge's Dormitories," 2–3.

40. Bettie Levy, interviewed by Present. See Present, *Dear Margaret*, 25–26.

41. Clarke, "Psychiatric Problems at Oak Ridge," 437.

42. Earline Banic, phone interview with the author, May 10, 2013.

43. For a detailed neighborhood-by-neighborhood account, see Sanderson, "America's No. 1. Defense Community," 63–84. For a close look at Scarboro, Oak Ridge's neighborhood for the early black population, see Smyser, "City's Most Unique Neighborhood," 1.

44. "Atom Town," 7.

45. "Mystery Town Cradled Bomb" 94.

46. Keely, "You Rose above the Ugliness."

47. Helen Jernigan, interviewed by Present in *Dear Margaret*, 75.

48. Colleen Black, interviewed by Jim Kolb, Center for Oak Ridge Oral History, Oak Ridge, Tennessee, February 20, 2002.

49. Helen Jernigan, interviewed by Jim Kolb, Center for Oak Ridge Oral History. May 27, 2002.

50. See Overholt, *These Are Our Voices*, 94–99

51. Shirley Brooks, interviewed by Present, *Dear Margaret*, 93–95.

52. Gailar, *Oak Ridge and Me*, 19.

53. Nan McLemore, Herb Snyder, and Helen Schween, interviewed by the author, March 15, 2005.

54. Dick Smyser, interviewed by Patrick Kerry Moore in *Federal Enclaves*, 30. Dick Smyser led the *Oak Ridger* for forty-five years. He was also the president of the Associated Press Managing Editors Association from 1973 to 1974. During this time, he asked President Nixon about the huge demands that came with being chief executive of the United States of America: "To what extent do you think this explains possibly how something like Watergate can occur?" This led to Nixon's rambling answer about his busy schedule, ending on perhaps the most famous quip ever uttered by a president: "People have got to know whether or not their president is a crook. Well, I am not a crook."

55. Present, *Dear Margaret*, 8.

56. Ibid., 14.

57. Gailar, *Oak Ridge and Me*, 40.

58. Present, *Dear Margaret*, 81.

59. Ibid., 23.

60. Present, *Dear Margaret*, 14; 93.

61. Phillips, "Oak Ridge Ponders Its Clouded Future," 42.

62. Bissell, "A Reminiscence of Oak Ridge," 75; Orwell, *Animal Farm*.

63. Lang, *Early Tales of the Atomic Age*, 52.

64. Joseph, *Historic Photographs of the Manhattan Project*, 135.

65. The-Chapel-on-the-Hill was a bit of a play on words—the administrative headquarters of the Project was known as The-Castle-on-the-Hill.

66. Edwards, "Notes for Bookworms."

67. The phrase "bombs and Brahms" comes from a presentation given by early Oak Ridgers Jane Randolph, Waldo Cohn, and June Adamson at the Children's Museum in Oak Ridge in 1985. See Miller, "Frontier Experience," 5.

68. Washington, unpublished manuscript; interview with Frank McLemore; interview with Bill Wilcox.

69. Halleck, "Perpetual Shadows," 71.

70. Morse, "A Need for Me to Stay," 1.

71. Ibid. See also *Girls of Atomic City*, where Denise Kiernan profiles Kattie Strickland, an early Oak Ridger who experienced the additional difficulties of being a black worker on the segregated Manhattan Project site.

72. Waters, "Negroes Live in Modern 'Hoovervilles' at Atom City," 1.

73. Peelle, "History of Segregation in Oak Ridge," 5.

74. Waters, "Atomic City Birthplace of Paradoxes," 1.

75. Named for Herbert Hoover, the president at the time, "Hooverville" refers to the shantytowns built by the homeless during the Great Depression.

76. Waters, "Negroes Live in Modern 'Hoovervilles' At Atom City," 1.

77. Here, I refer only to heterosexual couples. Even perceived homosexuality was grounds for losing one's job in the Manhattan Project and getting kicked out of Oak Ridge.

78. Steele, "New Hope," 2.

79. Ibid., 3.

80. R. L. Ayers, interviewed by Mitch Jerald, Center for Oak Ridge Oral History, Oak Ridge, Tennessee, September 21, 2005.

81. Waters, "Negroes Live in Modern 'Hoovervilles' at Atom City," 1.

82. De Certeau, *Practice of Everyday Life*, 97.

83. Steele, "Black History in the Ridge," 6; Project worker R. L. Ayers also mentions this practice in an interview with reporter Libby Morse, "A Need for Me to Stay," 1.

84. Larson shows that the situation for white women was completely opposite in "Women Also Served,"194.

85. Waters, "Negroes Live in Modern 'Hoovervilles' at Atom City," 1.

86. Peelle, "History of Segregation in Oak Ridge," 1.

87. Jefferson Bass is the composite pen name of mystery writer Jon Jefferson and Dr. Bill Bass, forensic anthropologist and founder of the University of Tennessee's Anthropology Research Facility, better known as the "Body Farm."

88. Anecdotal evidence reveals that there was a bustling sex trade during the Manhattan Project in Oak Ridge. Because all persons living in Oak Ridge had to be employed, many prostitutes took jobs as waitresses and clerks. See Searcy, *Last Reunion*, 36.

89. Rationales for this and other planning decisions can be found in the "Construction Progress Reports" presented monthly by the architectural firm Skidmore, Owings, and Merrill to the Manhattan Project managers.

90. Steele, "New Hope," 3.

91. Searcy, "My Nuclear Childhood."

92. Emphasis mine. Marilyn Galloway, interviewed by Keith McDaniel, Center for Oak Ridge Oral History, Oak Ridge, Tennessee, June 21, 2001.

93. Quoted in Searcy, *Last Reunion*, 42.

94. Porteous, "The Nature of the Company Town."

95. Findlay and Hevly make a similar argument about Richland, Washington, in *Atomic Frontier Days*, 95.

96. Johnson and Jackson, "The Urbane Frontier," 9.

97. "Spreading the Know-How," 65.

98. See, for example, Creese, *TVA's Public Planning*, 304–5.

CHAPTER 3

1. Quoted in Rhodes, *Making of the Atomic Bomb*, 294.

2. Ibid., 605.

3. Quoted in Buck-Morss, *Dreamworld and Catastrophe*, 103.

4. For more on the similarities between the design of the atomic factories and that of other industrial factories, see Hales, *Atomic Spaces*, 91–92.

5. For a criticism of the design of the atomic factories, particularly as "undemocratic" structures, see Creese, *TVA's Public Planning: The Vision, the Reality*.

6. Kuletz, *Tainted Desert*, 9; Speier, "Magic Geography," 310–30.

7. Groves, *Now It Can Be Told*, 140; For more analysis on the issue of compartmentalization in the Manhattan Project, see Goldberg, "Groves and the Scientists," 38–43.

8. Bollings, "Work at Y-12, 1944," 80.

9. Ibid.

10. *We the People*, script of a radio broadcast sponsored by Gulf Oil Corporation.

11. Nichols, *Oak Ridge Journal*, 1.

12. Graydon Whitman, interviewed by Jim Kolb, Center for Oak Ridge Oral History, Oak Ridge, Tennessee, November 12, 2001.

13. *We the People*, script of a radio broadcast sponsored by Gulf Oil Corporation.

14. Earline Banic, phone interview with the author, May 10, 2013.

15. Compton, *Atomic Quest*, 144.

16. Johnson and Schaffer, *Oak Ridge National Laboratory*, 23.

17. Bollings, "Work at Y-12," 94.

18. Céline, *Journey to the End of the Night*, 193–94.

19. Ibid., 194.

20. Theodore Rockwell, interviewed by D. Ray Smith, Center for Oak Ridge Oral History, Oak Ridge, Tennessee, April 29, 2011. See also Groueff, *Manhattan Project*.

21. Graydon Whitman, interviewed by Jim Kolb, Center for Oak Ridge Oral History, Oak Ridge, Tennessee, December 11, 2001.

22. Gailar, *Oak Ridge and Me*, 36.

23. Colleen Black, interviewed by Stanley Goldberg, video recording, Oak Ridge, Tennessee, Manhattan Project Session 5, Smithsonian Video History Program; Olwell, *At Work in the Atomic City*, 48.

24. Green, *Company Town*, 164.

25. The Manhattan Project officers did not keep substantial records of the geographical origins of their employees. The reason for this is undocumented. It could have been a security measure or simply outside of Project concerns. In Robinson's *Oak Ridge Story*, an early history of the atomic bomb project, the chief public relations officer for the Manhattan Project in Oak Ridge suggests that workers came from specific locations where special skills were honed. See *The Oak Ridge Story*, 47.

26. Agee, *A Death in the Family*, 17.

27. Olwell, *At Work in the Atomic City*, 31.

28. For more on the roles of women in the Manhattan Project, see Howes and Herzenberg, *Their Day in the Sun*, and Kiernan, *Girls of Atomic City*.

29. Taylor, "G2: Let's Build a Bomb," 14.

30. Groves, *Now It Can Be Told*.

31. Quoted in Taylor, "G2: Let's Build a Bomb," 14.

32. Howes and Herzenberg, *Their Day in the Sun*, 169.

33. Ibid.; Olwell, *At Work in the Atomic City*, 16.

34. D. Ray Smith, interview with the author, Oak Ridge, Tennessee, January 9, 2011; Howes and Herzenberg, *Their Day in the Sun*, 169; Groueff, *Manhattan Project*.

35. Taylor, "G2: Let's Build a Bomb," 14.

36. Sennett, *The Craftsman*, 88.

37. Haraway, "A Cyborg Manifesto," 181.

38. The "Computers" have been less celebrated in Oak Ridge, and thus harder to track than the Calutron Girls, but anecdotal evidence points to the fact that lots of women held this position, with Grace Estabrook perhaps the most well known. For more on the Computers, see Howes and Herzenberg, *Their Day in the Sun*, 93-110.

39. Quoted in Howes and Herzenberg, *Their Day in the Sun*, 99.

40. Kean, *Disappearing Spoon*, 108; Dyson quoted in Kean, 108.

41. Shirley Woods, interviewed by Joan Craig, Oral Histories of World War II, Morse Institute Library, Natick, Massachusetts, October 30, 2007.

42. Quoted in Searcy, *Last Reunion*, 40.

43. Céline, *Journey to the End of the Night*, 192.

44. For more on black workers in Oak Ridge during the Manhattan Project, see Olwell, *At Work in the Atomic City*, 20-24. And for a more national perspective, see Kersten, *Race, Jobs, and the War*.

45. Olwell, *At Work in the Atomic City*, 49.

46. See ibid., 56; Karl Z. Morgan, interviewed by Michael Yuffee and Marissa Caputo, Indian Springs, Florida, January 7, 1995.

47. R. L. Ayers, interviewed by Mitch Jerald, Center for Oak Ridge Oral History, Oak Ridge, Tennessee, September 21, 2005.

48. Kattie Harris, interviewed by Valerie Smith, Center for Oak Ridge Oral History, Oak Ridge, Tennessee, September 20, 2005.

49. Leroy White, interviewed by Bart Callan, Center for Oak Ridge Oral History, Oak Ridge, Tennessee, April 16, 2005.

50. "Neutron Dance" appeared on the Pointer Sisters' 1984 album *Break Out* and in the Eddie Murphy movie *Beverly Hills Cop*. Songwriting credit goes to Allee Willis and Danny Sembello. The song was released during the height of the Cold War; the Soviet government, which had mistranslated the song as "Neutron Bomb," put Willis on a list of the most dangerous people in the United States.

51. Munger, "Oak Ridge Reveals World's Fastest Supercomputer, Titan," 1.

CHAPTER 4

1. Barbara Lyon, interviewed by Jim Kolb, Center for Oak Ridge Oral History, Oak Ridge, Tennessee, July 22, 2004.

2. Searcy, *Last Reunion*, 34.

3. Present, *Dear Margaret*, 113.

4. Gates, "Silence Means Security."

5. Here, I gesture toward Foucault's "repressive hypothesis" from *The History of Sexuality*, where he shows the productive role repression can sometimes play in the formation of identities (particularly 15-50).

6. See, for example, Gusterson's Foucauldian analysis of the internalized surveillance practiced by the Livermore Laboratory scientists in *Nuclear Rites*, particularly 68-87; and Masco's expansive analysis of how the nation-state itself practices large-scale secret keeping, which allows for creating new realities in " 'Sensitive but Unclassified,' " 433-63.

7. Rush, "Prometheus in Tennessee," 11.

8. Keim, "A Scientist and His Secrets," 69.

9. Ibid., 73.

10. Robinson, *Oak Ridge Story*, 69.

11. While there is no record of just how many Oak Ridgers worked as secret agents in this capacity, qualitative evidence gleaned from interviews indicates the numbers to be quite high. See, for example, Colleen Black, interviewed by Jim Kolb, and Reba Holmberg, interviewed by Jim Kolb and Anne Garland, Center for Oak Ridge Oral History, Oak Ridge, Tennessee, February 20 and April 30, 2002, respectively.

12. Colleen Black, interviewed by Jim Kolb, Center for Oak Ridge Oral History, Oak Ridge, Tennessee, February 20, 2002.

13. Witherup, "Mother Witherup's Top-Secret Cherry Pie," 54–57.

14. See Johnson and Jackson, *City behind a Fence*, 148.

15. Kanon, *Los Alamos*, 22. Bass, *Bones of Betrayal*, 151.

16. Foucault, *The Archeology of Knowledge*, 129.

17. One day when I was working on this book, my thoughts kept being interrupted by the desire to own a dachshund called Mary Lou Retton. Then I saw the photograph of Santa getting the once-over at the gates of Oak Ridge, an image I've looked at countless times before, only this time I noticed that he is holding a dachshund. I didn't consciously remember the little dog in the photo. But there it is, clear as day. Was that Mary Lou Retton signaling me from the past? I told my editor, Joseph Parsons, about my interrupting thoughts, and he promptly sent me a link for "Radioactive Dachshund," a glowing green creature with X-ed out eyes and an elongated body. I subsequently ordered a coffee mug with her image wrapped around it.

18. Dorathy Moneymaker, interviewed by Patricia Clark, American Museum of Science and Energy in Oak Ridge, Tennessee, July 10, 2000.

19. De Certeau, *Practice of Everyday Life*, xiv.

20. Lois Van Wie, conversation with the author, Oak Ridge Tennessee, June 22, 2013.

21. Oak Ridge Heritage and Preservation Association, *Oak Ridge, Tennessee*, 5.

22. Ibid., 9.

23. Gailar, *Oak Ridge and Me*, 20.

24. Quoted in Rockwell, *Creating the New World*, 26–27.

25. Nan McLemore, Helen Schween, and Herb Snyder, interviews with the author, Oak Ridge, Tennessee, March 15, 2005.

26. Simmel, "The Secret Society," 365.

27. Simmel, "Secrecy."

28. Wolkowitz as well as Johnson and Jackson had similar experiences when conducting their separate fieldwork in Oak Ridge. See Wolkowitz, *Bodies at Work*, 48, and Johnson and Jackson, *City behind a Fence*, 153.

29. Bill Wilcox, interview with the author January 6, 2011. See also Present, *Dear Margaret*, 49–51.

30. Dr. Clarke was the head psychiatrist for the entire Manhattan Project. Throughout the war, he traveled to all the secret cities and was present at the first atomic bomb test in Alamogordo, New Mexico, but he was stationed in Oak Ridge. See Clarke, "Psychiatric Problems at Oak Ridge," 437–44; See also Clarke, "Psychiatry on a Shoestring," 179.

31. Clarke, "Psychiatry on a Shoestring," 180–81.

32. Ibid., 438.

CHAPTER 5

1. Shirley Woods, interviewed by Joan Craig, Oral Histories of World War II, Morse Institute Library, Natick, Massachusetts, October 30, 2007.

2. Bill Wilcox, interview with the author, January 6, 2011.

3. Nash and Persechini, "The First Thousand Days," 7.

4. Margene Lyon, interviewed by Jim Kolb, Center for Oak Ridge Oral History, Oak Ridge, Tennessee, August 23, 2002.

5. See Best, "I Worked at Oak Ridge," 73.

6. Jay Searcy, interview with the author, Oak Ridge, Tennessee, January 3, 2011.

7. Colleen Black, interviewed by Jim Kolb, Center for Oak Ridge Oral History, Oak Ridge, Tennessee, February 20, 2002.

8. Nichols, *Oak Ridge Journal*, 1.

9. Findlay and Hevly, *Atomic Frontier Days*, 42.

10. Rush, "Prometheus in Tennessee," 50.

11. Loeb, *Nuclear Culture*, 26–27.

12. Wang, *American Science in an Age of Anxiety*, 9.

13. See Smith, *A Peril and a Hope*; Kevles, *The Physicists*; and Masters and Way, *One World or None*.

14. The legislation was named after Senator Brien McMahon of Connecticut, chairman of the Senate-House Joint Atomic Energy Committee.

15. Millicent Dillon went on to become a leading expert on the literary power couple Jane and Paul Bowles. For more of Dillon's experiences in Oak Ridge, see her "In the Atomic City."

16. Ibid.

17. Quoted in Wang, *American Science in an Age of Anxiety*, 155.

18. Thomas, "Reds in Our Atom-Bomb Plants," 15.

19. Gehman, "Oak Ridge Witch Hunt," 12–13.

20. For more extensive treatment of FAS, the Oak Ridge Scientists, and the House Un-American Activities Committee, see Wang, *American Science in an Age of Anxiety*, esp. 44–84 and 150–51.

21. Wang, *American Science in an Age of Anxiety*, 170; White, "2 Atomic Scientists Suspended, Many More Face Loyalty Board," "Oak Ridge Sunk in Gloom over Loyalty Inquiry," "Why Morale Sags at Oak Ridge," and "Senior Scientist Rolls Depleted at Oak Ridge."

22. While the Youth Council on Atomic Crisis in Oak Ridge had a special relationship to the emergence of the Atomic Age, it was not alone in youth organizations devoted to the peaceful uses of the atom; similar Youth Councils were formed in twenty-five states in the years immediately following the atomic bombings of Japan. See Sheibach, *Atomic Narratives and American Youth*, 34.

23. Ibid.

24. "Yak-Ac," 1.

25. There were several drafts of this petition written by the scientist Leó Szilárd. The Oak Ridge Petition was circulated in mid-July 1945 and was signed by sixty-seven scientists, including the physicist Alvin Weinberg, longtime director of the Oak Ridge National Laboratory. The letter was terse and to the point. Here is the full text:

To the President of the United States:

We, the undersigned scientific personnel of the Clinton Laboratories, believe that the world-wide social and political consequences of the power of the weapon now being developed on this Project impose a special moral obligation on the government and people of the United States in introducing the weapon in warfare.

It is further believed that the power of this weapon should be made known by demonstration to the peoples of the world, irrespective of the course of the present conflict, for in this way the body of world opinion may be made the determining factor in the absolute preservation of peace.

Therefore we recommend that before this weapon be used without restriction in the present conflict, its powers should be adequately described and demonstrated, and the Japanese nation should be given the opportunity to consider the consequences of further refusal to surrender. We feel that this course of action will heighten the effectiveness of the weapon in this war and will be of tremendous effect in the prevention of future wars.

The final version, the so-called Szilárd Petition, was signed by 155 scientists from those working in Oak Ridge and in the Chicago Metallurgical Laboratory. None of the drafts of the petition made it to President Truman in time even to be considered. The military director of the Manhattan Project, General Groves, thwarted its delivery and sought evidence against Szilárd, as a possible enemy of the United States. The complete record can be found in U.S. National Archives, Record Group 77, Records of the Chief of Engineers, Manhattan Engineer District, Harrison-Bundy File (Washington, D.C.), folder 76.

26. Quoted in Cartwright, "Where the Atom Bomb Was Born," 4.

27. Seyfert, "Atom's Children," 141.

28. "Yak-Ac," 1.

29. See Lilienthal, *Journals*, particularly vol. 2, *The Atomic Energy Years (1945–1950)*.

30. J. Robert Oppenheimer appeared on the cover of *Time* on November 8, 1948, and *Life* on October 10, 1949. He appeared once more on the cover of *Time* on June 14, 1954, after losing his security clearance. For more on *The Beginning or the End*, see Reingold's "MGM Meets the Atomic Bomb" and Yavenditti's "Atomic Scientists and Hollywood: The Beginning or the End?" 51–66. Reingold and Yavenditti utilize MGM's archives and other sources to reconstruct the back-and-forth between the studio and the Manhattan Project's military leaders and scientists in the making of the film.

31. Yavenditti, "Atomic Scientists and Hollywood," 54; Smith, *A Peril and a Hope*, 314; Tompkins to Enrico Fermi, January 16, 1947, J. Robert Oppenheimer Collection, Government File, box 171, Library of Congress (Washington, D.C.); Tompkins to Donna Reed Owens, October 23, 1945, as quoted in the MGM Announcement, "Facts about the Making of MGM's Remarkable Motion Picture, 'The Beginning or the End,'" 16, National Committee on Atomic Information (NCAI) Collection, box 32, Library of Congress.

32. Tompkins to Fermi, January 16, 1947, J. Robert Oppenheimer Collection, Government File, box 171 Library of Congress (Washington, D.C.); Yavenditti, "Atomic Scientists and Hollywood," 53.

33. Quoted in Paul Boyer, *By the Bomb's Early Light*, 61.

34. Einstein, "The Real Problem Is in the Hearts of Men."

35. Benjamin, "On the Concept of History," 392.

36. Present, *Dear Margaret*, 92.

37. Gailar, *Oak Ridge and Me*, 39.

38. Nan McLemore, interview with the author, Oak Ridge, Tennessee, January 3, 2011.

39. The use here of the phrase "atomic highway" is influenced by the "highway of the atom," a concept developed by Peter C. van Wyck, which describes the pathways of atomic materials and ideas. See *Highway of the Atom*.

40. Clarke, "Psychiatric Problems at Oak Ridge," 437.

41. Quoted in Bissell, "A Reminiscence of Oak Ridge," 71.

42. The term, first coined by E. L. Doctorow, was later taken up in Gusterson's *People of the Bomb*.

43. Gailar, *Oak Ridge and Me*, 41.

44. Alvin Weinberg, "History of ORNL."

45. Quoted in Lang, *Early Tales of the Atomic Age*, 57.

46. Oppenheimer quoted in Boyer, *By the Bomb's Early Light*, 8.

47. Helen Jernigan, interview by Jim Kolb, Center for Oak Ridge Oral History, Oak Ridge, Tennessee, March 27, 2002.

48. White, "Report on Oak Ridge Hearings," 194–97.

49. For more on the rhetoric of "nukespeak," see Hilgartner, Bell, and O'Connor, *Nukespeak*.

50. Eisenhower, "Atoms for Peace Speech."

51. On occasion, the poor conditions of the hutments are still downplayed, as a recent book of historic Manhattan Project photographs illustrates. Under a photograph of several hutments a caption reads, "There were few complaints among workers about living conditions at the facilities. Everyone understood the demands of the war effort and simply took everything in stride." See Joseph, *Historic Photographs of the Manhattan Project*, 135.

52. Thornton, "Cumberland Incongruity," 35.

53. Wallace, "Housing Desegregation," 1.

54. Ibid.

55. Ibid.

56. Hunner, *Inventing Los Alamos*, 185–87.

57. Jacobs, *The Death and Life of Great American Cities*, 49.

58. See, for example, Robinson, *Oak Ridge Story*, 130.

59. Jay Searcy in Director Keith McDaniel's *Secret City: The Oak Ridge Story*, DVD, 2009.

60. Simmel, "The Secret Society," 345.

61. Jay Searcy, interview with the author, Oak Ridge, Tennessee, January 3, 2011; also *Secret City: The Oak Ridge Story*, dir. McDaniel.

62. Rod Cameron was an actor in countless Hollywood westerns; his career spanned forty years, from 1930 to 1970. He also gained some infamy when he divorced his young wife and subsequently married her mother.

63. Lafitte Howard, interviewed by Thelma Present, in Present, *Dear Margaret*, 53.

64. Colleen Black, interviewed by Jim Kolb, Center for Oak Ridge Oral History, Oak Ridge, Tennessee, February 20, 2002.

65. Oak Ridge Heritage and Preservation Association, *Oak Ridge, Tennessee*, 69.

66. Gordon Browning served as governor of Tennessee from 1937 to 1939, and then again from 1949 to 1953. Quoted in Oak Ridge Heritage and Preservation Association, *Oak Ridge, Tennessee*, 71.

67. Rhodes, *Dark Sun*, 242–43; Hunner, *Inventing Los Alamos*, 153.

CHAPTER 6

1. Oak Ridge Heritage and Preservation Association, *Oak Ridge, Tennessee*, 75.

2. McCarthy, "My! How ORAU Has Grown," 379.

3. According to American Museum of Science and Energy exhibit manager Lenell Woods. See Tabler, "Irradiated Dimes: Tourist Items or Health Threat?"

4. The radioactive turtles at AMSE preceded their more famous brethren, the comic book Teenage Mutant Ninja Turtles, created by Kevin Eastman and Peter Laird, by decades. Eastman and Laird's first edition of the reptilian, pizza-obsessed New York City crime fighters, known by their catchphrase "Heroes in a half shell," was released by Mirage Studios in 1984.

5. See Eisenhower, "Atoms for Peace Speech," and also Chernis, *Eisenhower's Atoms for Peace*, 51.

6. Frank McLemore, phone interview with the author, May 12, 2013.

7. The quote is from Eisenhower. After a trip to Germany in 1945 that included the experience of driving on the autobahns, Eisenhower discovered the benefits of an interstate highway system. The Dwight D. Eisenhower National System of Interstate and Defense Highways was from the very beginning sold to Congress and by proxy to the American people as a benefit to both the military and civilian interests of the United States. See Farish, *Contours of America's Cold War*, 232–35; Gutfreund, *Twentieth- Century Sprawl*, 42; Lewis, *Divided Highways*, 107–8.

8. AMSE director Jim Comish, email correspondence with the author on November 20, 2006, regarding the museum's name change.

9. For more on the notion of nuclear renaissance, see Nuttall, *Nuclear Renaissance*.

10. Hunner, *Inventing Los Alamos*, 173.

11. See Engelhardt, *The End of Victory Culture*.

12. On American victory culture and the culture of innocence, see ibid., and Sturken, *Tourists of History*, 7.

13. Ronnell, *The Telephone Book*, xv.

14. Statement recorded by Linus Pauling in his notebook after chatting with Einstein at his home on November 16, 1954. See Oregon State University Libraries Special Collections, filed under E: Individual Correspondence, box#107.1, and Clark, *Einstein: The Life and Times*, 672. Pauling repeated this recollection in a July 28, 1969, letter to Clark.

15. For more on the role women played in Oak Ridge, see Howes and Herzenberg, *Their Day in the Sun*, and Kiernan, *Girls of Atomic City*.

16. The Tiller Girls were a dance troupe created by John Tiller in Manchester, England, in the early 1900s. They were characterized by their uniformity and uncanny ability to dance as a unit.

17. Kracauer, "The Mass Ornament," 75–76.

18. Halleck, "Perpetual Shadows," 75.

19. Barthes, *Camera Lucida*, 43; Halleck, "Perpetual Shadows," 75.

20. Taylor, "Radioactive History," 57.

21. The National Museum of Nuclear Science and History was originally known as the National Atomic Museum, yet another example of the historicizing of the once-imagined atomic future.

22. Wray, "A Blast from the Past," 483.

23. Smith, "κ-25: Authenticity Key Element of Heritage Tourism."

24. Landsberg, *Prosthetic Memories*, 74.

25. Smith, "κ-25: Authenticity Key Element of Heritage Tourism."

26. See also Freeman, "Plutonium Tourism Ode."

CHAPTER 7

1. On industrial tourism, see MacCannell, *The Tourist*, and Urry, *The Tourist Gaze*. On nuclear tourism, see, for example, Blackwell, *Visit Sunny Chernobyl*; Hodge and Weinberger, *Nuclear Family Vacation*; Vanderbilt, *Survival City*; and Veitch, "Dr. Strangelove's Cabinet of Wonder."

2. The title of world's fastest computer changes frequently as technology advances. In November 2012, Oak Ridge's supercomputer Titan was named the fastest in the world with a measured 17.59 sustained petaflops on Linpak's scale.

3. Bill Wilcox, interview with the author, January 10, 2011, Oak Ridge, Tennessee.

4. The post-tourist takes an ironic stance toward tourist sites; she notices their social constructedness and she understands that this artifice is an integral part of the enjoyment of such spaces. The post-tourist travels with a wink. See Feifer, *Going Places*; Urry, *The Tourist Gaze*, 90–92.

5. See, for example, Lennon and Foley, *Dark Tourism*; Seaton, "Guided by the Dark," 234–44; and Tarlow, "Dark Tourism."

6. M. Christine Boyer, "Cities for Sale," 201.

7. Boym, *Future of Nostalgia*.

8. MacCannell, *The Tourist*, 82.

9. Ibid.

10. Landsberg, *Prosthetic Memory*.

11. Augustine, *Confessions*, 319.

12. The festival is organized by the City of Oak Ridge, the Arts Council of Oak Ridge, and the Oak Ridge Convention and Visitors Bureau.

13. In 2010, Chubby Checker received top billing on the musical stage to celebrate fifty years of the Twist.

14. Le Goff, *History and Memory*, 95.

15. Mojtabai, *Blessed Assurance*, xi.

16. This catchphrase comes from the popular American science fiction television program *Star Trek*. The phrase was a command frequently uttered by Captain James T. Kirk to his chief engineer Montgomery Scott ("Scotty") when the captain needed to be transported back to the mothership, the Enterprise, from a planet the ship was orbiting.

17. *The Twilight Zone* was a popular, genre-crossing American television show that combined science fiction, suspense, horror, and psychological drama. The original series ran from 1959 to 1964.

18. Scheck, "Bunnies Are in Deep Doo-Doo When They 'Go Nuclear' at Hanford."

19. Smith, "Secret City Train Derails."

20. De Certeau, *Practice of Everyday Life*, 113.

21. Ibid.

22. The Atomic City's nostalgic train tours began in 1998 through the support of the Department of Energy, Community Reuse Organization of East Tennessee, Heritage Railroad, and a small group of rail enthusiasts who started the Southern Appalachia Railway Museum.

23. Superfund sites are highly contaminated locations that have been given special priority for cleanup by the federal government under the Comprehensive Environmental Response, Compensation, and Liability Act of 1980.

24. Huotari, "K-25 Demolition Begins."

25. "Secret City Excursion Train," http://www.techscribes.com/sarm/srm_scs.htm.

26. The vintage passenger cars are pulled by Alco diesel locomotives from the 1950s.

27. De Certeau, *Practice of Everyday Life*, 112.

28. For an excellent history of Pullman, see Buder, *Pullman*.

29. Lang, *Early Tales of the Atomic Age*, 18–19.

30. Adorno, "A Portrait of Walter Benjamin," 229.

31. "Murder Mystery Dinner Train," Southern Appalachia Railway Museum, http://www.techscribes.com/sarm/murder_mystery_2009.htm.

32. Le Goff, *History and Memory*, 51; Bergson, *Matter and Memory*.

33. Present, *Dear Margaret*, 192.

34. Quoted in Rhodes, *Making of the Atomic Bomb*, 294.

35. For more about Manzanar, see Daniell, "Making Visible."

36. If approved by Congress, the Department of the Interior and the Department of Energy will jointly manage the Manhattan Project National Park; this double stewardship would be another first for the National Park Service. The Department of the Interior, which typically manages the parks, has felt unable to assess the safety of the sites and needs the Department of Energy to determine levels of radiation and toxicity in order to move forward. At the time of this writing, the measure has passed the House of Representatives as part of the National Defense Authorization Act of 2014, but it has not yet passed the Senate to become law.

CHAPTER 8

1. This story was confirmed by Ed Westcott through correspondence with Emily Honeycutt, October 20, 2011.

2. Barthes, *Camera Lucida*, 34.

3. Fuller uses the phrase "the atomic bomb as their birthmark" in *Utopia or Oblivion*, 308.

4. See van Wyck, *Highway of the Atom*.

5. While Westcott was the only official photographer stationed in Oak Ridge, there was at least one reported incident where someone else took photographs of top-secret areas there. In order to check security, an intelligence agent snuck into the K-25 atomic plant carrying a camera, flashbulbs, and a tripod. He was horrified that he was able to photograph classified buildings and was never asked for his pass. See Johnson and Jackson, *City behind a Fence*, 148.

6. Westcott's western counterpart was Robely Johnson, the official Manhattan Project photographer at the Hanford site. See Sanger's interview with Johnson in *Working on the Bomb*, 110–12.

7. Mills, *The Sociological Imagination*, 225.

8. Barthes, *Camera Lucida*, 15.

9. Sontag, *Where the Stress Falls*, 223.

10. Benjamin, *Arcades Project*, 476.

11. This site became Camp Crossville, which housed 1,500 mostly German POWs from 1943 to 1945. For more, see "Barbed Wire in the Scrub Oaks."

12. Westcott, *Oak Ridge*, 8.

13. The "Atom Smasher" photograph was taken after 1945, when Oak Ridge's World War II secret was already widely known. See ibid., 69, 85.

14. Ibid., 96–99.

15. Barthes, *Camera Lucida*, 34.

16. Lee, "James Edward Westcott," 31.

17. See Wolkowitz, " 'Papa's Bomb,' " 104.

18. By many accounts of early Oak Ridgers, it was in fact an ideal community; see, for example, Gailar, *Oak Ridge and Me*; Robinson, *Oak Ridge Story*; and Hiestand, *Angela the Upside-Down Girl*.

19. Emily Honeycutt, correspondence with the author, October 20, 2011.

20. Hales, *Atomic Spaces*, 261.

21. Westcott, *Oak Ridge*, 103.

22. Frederick Schlegel quoted in Benjamin, "Paralipomena to 'On the Concept of History,' " 405.

23. Groves, *Now It Can Be Told*, 325.

24. Ibid.

25. Robinson, *Oak Ridge Story*, 102–5.

26. For more on the controversy, see Lifton and Mitchell, *Hiroshima in America*, and Goodman and Goodman, "The Hiroshima Cover Up."

27. Hales, "Atomic Sublime," 10.

28. Smith, "Ed Westcott," 3.

29. De Certeau, *Practice of Everyday Life*, 102.

30. Barthes, *Camera Lucida*, 28.

31. Benjamin, "Theses on the Philosophy of History," 254.

32. See, for example, Robinson, *Oak Ridge Story*.

33. Hirsch, "The Generation of Postmemory," 107; see also Hirsch, *The Generation of Postmemory*.

34. Hirsch, "The Generation of Postmemory," 103.

35. Spiotta, *Stone Arabia*, 1.

36. Hales, *Atomic Spaces*, 269, 264.

37. During the Apple II tests conducted in May 1955, the Federal Civilian Defense Administration employed mannequins to spectacular effect. They were dressed in J. C. Penney attire and posed in domestic situations. After the tests were conducted, the mannequins were filmed and even "interviewed" by television news reporters.

38. Hirsch, "The Generation of Postmemory," 116.

39. Lee, "James Edward Westcott"; Smith, "Ed Westcott," 3.

40. Smith, "Ed Westcott," 3.

41. Yates, "Acknowledgments," 13–14.

42. Smith, "Ed Westcott," 3.

43. Halbwachs, *The Collective Memory*, 82.

44. The concept "generation 1.5" first appears in the work of Susan Rubin Suleiman and refers to child survivors of the Holocaust. Suleiman's intervention marks an important midway point between the first generation who lived through the experience as adults and those who were born after. Generation 1.5, then, was alive at the time and experienced events firsthand but did so from a child's rather than an adult's perspective. See Suleiman, "The 1.5 Generation."

45. For examples of atomic nostalgia from generation 1.5, see Hiestand, *Angela the Upside-Down Girl*, 40; Searcy, "My Nuclear Childhood"; or ask my mother, Bobbie Freeman.

46. Kracauer, "Photography," 50.

47. Foucault, *The Archeology of Knowledge*, 129.

48. Rose, *States of Fantasy*.

49. Benjamin, "On the Concept of History, 392."

CHAPTER 9

1. The phrase *nostalgie de la boue*, as Krauss points out, "is not in fact idiomatic French; indeed, it is not a part of spoken French at all, being instead a purely Anglophonic invocation of the English notion of slumming transposed into the magically resonant frame of a supposedly French turn of phrase." See Krauss, "Nostalgie de la Boue," 112.

2. Others make this argument as well; see, for example, Hales, "Topographies of Power," 282.

3. Baudrillard, "Simulcra and Simulations," 166.

4. Borges, "On Exactitude in Science," 325.

5. De Certeau, *Practice of Everyday Life*, 129.

6. Thomas, "ABCs of Oak Ridge Housing," H1.

7. Ibid.

8. This nostalgic move coincided with the opening of a permanent exhibit of an original Cemesto Flattop on the grounds of the American Museum of Science and Energy. The exhibit opened on March 19, 2009, the sixtieth anniversary of the city's gate opening.

9. Here I owe a debt to Masco, who uses the similar turn of phrase "weapons gerontology" to describe the process of storing and processing aging nuclear weapons. See his *Nuclear Borderlands*.

10. See Zak, "Prophets of Oak Ridge."

11. Benjamin, "The Storyteller," 87.

References

INTERVIEWS

Ayers, R. L. Interviewed by Mitch Jerald. Center for Oak Ridge Oral History, Oak Ridge, Tennessee, September 21, 2005.

Banic, Earline. Telephone discussion with the author. May 10, 2013.

Black, Colleen. Interviewed by Jim Kolb. Center for Oak Ridge Oral History, Oak Ridge, Tennessee, February 20, 2002.

———. Interviewed by Stanley Goldberg. Video recording, Oak Ridge, Tennessee. Manhattan Project Session 5, Smithsonian Video History Program, Smithsonian Archive, Washington, D.C., March 3, 1987.

Brummitt, Naomi. Interviewed by D. Ray Smith, Y-12 Oral History Project, Oak Ridge, Tennessee, 2012.

Comish, Jim. Email interview with the author. November 20, 2006.

———. Email correspondence with the author. June 10, 2011.

Fairstein, Edward. Interviewed by Jim Kolb. Center for Oak Ridge Oral History, Oak Ridge, Tennessee, November 13, 2002.

Galloway, Marilyn. Interviewed by Keith McDaniel. Center for Oak Ridge Oral History, Oak Ridge, Tennessee June 21, 2001.

Harris, Kattie. Interviewed by Valerie Smith. Center for Oak Ridge Oral History, Oak Ridge, Tennessee, September 20, 2005.

Holmberg, Reba. Interviewed by Jim Kolb and Anne Garland. Center for Oak Ridge Oral History, Oak Ridge, Tennessee, April 30, 2002.

Honeycutt, Emily. Email interview with the author. October 20, 2011.

Jernigan, Helen. Interviewed by Jim Kolb. Center for Oak Ridge Oral History, Oak Ridge, Tennessee, May 27, 2002.

Lyon, Barbara. Interviewed by Jim Kolb. Center for Oak Ridge Oral History, Oak Ridge, Tennessee, July 22, 2004.

Lyon, Margene. Interviewed by Jim Kolb. Center for Oak Ridge Oral History, Oak Ridge, Tennessee, August 23, 2002.

McLemore, Frank. Telephone interview with the author. May 12, 2013.

McLemore, Nan. Interviewed by the author. Oak Ridge, Tennessee, March 15, 2005.

———. Interviewed by the author. Oak Ridge, Tennessee, January 3, 2011.

Moneymaker, Dorathy. Interviewed by Patricia Clark. Oak Ridge Institute for Continued Learning Panel, Part 2: "Wheat Community: The Way We Were: Pre-Oak Ridge and Early Oak Ridge." Transcribed by Jordan H. Reed. July 10, 2000. American Museum of Science and Energy, Oak Ridge, Tennessee.

Morgan, Karl Z. Interviewed by Michael Yuffee and Marissa Caputo. Indian Springs, Florida, January 7, 1995. Department of Energy Archives, DOE-EH-0475.

Rockwell, Theodore. Interviewed by D. Ray Smith. Center for Oak Ridge Oral History, Oak Ridge, Tennessee, April 29, 2011.

Schween, Helen. Interviewed by the author. Oak Ridge, Tennessee, March 15, 2005.

Searcy, Jay. Interviewed by the author. Oak Ridge, Tennessee, January 3, 2011.

Smith, D. Ray. Interviewed by the author. Oak Ridge, Tennessee, January 9, 2011.

Snyder, Herb. Interviewed by the author. Oak Ridge, Tennessee, March 15, 2005.

Van Wie, Lois. Conversation with the author. Oak Ridge, Tennessee, June 22, 2013.

White, Leroy. Interviewed by Bart Callan. Center for Oak Ridge Oral History, Oak Ridge, Tennessee, April 16, 2005.

Whitman, Graydon. Interviewed by Jim Kolb. Center for Oak Ridge Oral History, Oak Ridge, Tennessee, November 12, 2001.

Wilcox, Bill. Interviewed by the author. Oak Ridge, Tennessee, January 10, 2011.

———. Email correspondence with the author. August 9, 2012.

Woods, Shirley. Interviewed by Joan Craig. Oral Histories of World War II, Morse Institute Library, Natick, Massachusetts, October 30, 2007.

FILMS

John Hendrix. Directed and produced by Keith McDaniel. Oak Ridge: Secret City Studios, 2010. DVD.

October Sky. Directed by Joe Johnston. Hollywood: Universal Studios, 1999. DVD.

Operation Open Sesame: Opening the Gates of the Secret City. Directed by Keith McDaniel. Produced by Keith McDaniel and Oak Ridge Heritage and Preservation Association. Oak Ridge: Secret City Studios, 2009. DVD.

Secret City: The Oak Ridge Story, "The War Years." Directed and produced by Keith McDaniel. Oak Ridge: Secret City Studios, 2009. DVD.

OTHER PUBLISHED AND UNPUBLISHED WORKS

Abbot, Carl. "Building the Atomic Cities: Richland, Los Alamos, and American Planning Language." In *The Atomic West*, edited by Bruce Hevly and John M. Findlay, 90–118. Seattle: University of Washington Press, 1998.

Adamson, June. *From Bulletin to Broadside: A History of Early Journalism in Oak Ridge, Tennessee*. Knoxville: University of Tennessee Press, 1969.

———. "Woman with a Big Stick." In *These Are Our Voices: The Story of Oak Ridge, 1942–1970*, edited by James Overholt, 346–56. Oak Ridge: Children's Museum of Oak Ridge, 1987.

Adorno, Theodor. "A Portrait of Walter Benjamin." In *Prisms*, 227–41. Cambridge, Mass.: MIT Press, 1967.

———. *Minima Moralia*. New York: Verso, 1974.

Agee, James. *A Death in the Family*. St. Albans: Panther Books, 1973.

Agee, James, and Walker Evans. *Let Us Now Praise Famous Men*. New York: Mariner Books, 2001.

Anderson, Benedict. *Imagined Communities*. New York: Verso, 1991.

"Atom Town." *Architectural Forum*, September 1945, 7–9.

Augustine. *Confessions*. Boston: Gould & Lincoln, 1860.

Awiakta, Marilou. "Pine Ridge: Pilgrimage to the Prophet." In *Abiding Appalachia: Where Mountain and Atom Meet*, 43–45. Blacksburg, Va: Pocahontas Press, 2006.

Bacon, Francis. "New Atlantis." In *Ideal Commonwealths*, 70–213. New York: E. P. Dutton & Co., 1919.

"Barbed Wire in the Scrub Oaks." *Tennessee Magazine*, April 14, 1968, 6.

Barthes, Roland. *Camera Lucida*. New York: Hill & Wang, 1980.

———. *Mythologies*. New York: Hill & Wang, 1972.

Bascom, William. "The Forms of Folklore: Prose Narrative." *Journal of American Folklore* 78 (1965): 3–20.

Bass, Jefferson. *Bones of Betrayal*. New York: William Morrow, 2009.

Bataille, Georges. *The Absence of Myth: Writings on Surrealism*. New York: Verso, 1994.

Baudrillard, Jean. "Simulcra and Simulations." In *Jean Baudrillard: Selected Writings*, edited by Mark Poster, 166–84. Stanford, Calif.: Stanford University Press, 1984.

Baxter, Samuel S. "A Letter from the Town Manager." *Oak Ridge Journal*, September 11, 1944, 1.

Berger, Peter. *Invitation to Sociology*. New York: Anchor Books, 1963.

Bergson, Henri. *Matter and Memory*. New York: Zone Books, 1991.

Benjamin, Walter. *The Arcades Project*. Cambridge, Mass.: Belknap Press of Harvard University Press, 1999.

———. "Excavation and Memory." In *Selected Writings*, vol. 2, pt. 2, *1931–1934*, 576. Cambridge, Mass.: Belknap Press of Harvard University Press, 1999.

———. "On the Concept of History." In *Selected Writings*, vol. 4, *1938–1940*, 389–400. Cambridge, Mass.: Belknap Press of Harvard University Press, 2003.

———. "Paralipomena to 'On the Concept of History.'" In *Selected Writings*, vol. 4, *1938–1940*, 401–11. Cambridge, Mass.: Belknap Press of Harvard University Press, 2003.

———. "The Storyteller." In *Illuminations*, 83–110. New York: Schocken Books, 1968.

Best, Edna. "I Worked at Oak Ridge: An Early Narrative of Life in the Secret City." *Journal of East Tennessee History* 78 (2006): 73–83.

Bird, Kai, and Martin J. Sherwin. *American Prometheus: The Triumph and Tragedy of J. Robert Oppenheimer*. New York: Vintage, 2005.

Bissell, A. K. "A Reminiscence of Oak Ridge." *East Tennessee Historical Society Publications* 39 (Fall 1967): 71–86.

Blackwell, Andrew. *Visit Sunny Chernobyl: And Other Adventures in the World's Most Polluted Places*. New York: Rodale, 2012.

Blondin, George. *When the World Was New: Stories of the Sahtú Dene*. Yellowknife, Northwest Territories: Outcrop, 1990.

Bloom, Justin L., and Asano Shinsuke. "Tsukuba Science City: Japan Tries Planned Innovation." *Science*, June 1981, 1239–46.

Bollings, Connie. "Work at Y-12, 1944." In *These Are Our Voices: The Story of Oak Ridge, 1942–1970*, edited by James Overholt, 76–85. Oak Ridge: Children's Museum of Oak Ridge, Tennessee, 1987.

Borges, Jorge Luis. "On Exactitude in Science." In *Collected Fictions*, 325. New York: Penguin, 1999.

Boyer, M. Christine. "Cities for Sale: Merchandising History at South Street Seaport." In *Variations on a Theme Park*, edited by Michael Sorkin, 181–204. New York: Hill & Wang, 1992.

Boyer, Paul. *By the Bomb's Early Light: American Thought and Culture at the Dawn of the Atomic Age*. Chapel Hill: University of North Carolina Press, 1994.

Boym, Svetlana. *The Future of Nostalgia*. New York: Basic Books, 2001.

Brokaw, Tom. *The Greatest Generation*. New York: Random House, 1998.

Buck-Morss, Susan. "The City as Dreamworld and Catastrophe." *October* 73 (Summer 1995): 3–26.

———. *Dreamworld and Catastrophe*. Cambridge, Mass.: MIT Press, 2002.

Buder, Stanley. *Pullman: An Experiment in Industrial Order and Community Planning, 1880–1930*. New York: Oxford University Press, 1967.

Burgess, Gelett. *The Romance of the Commonplace*. San Francisco: Ayloh, 1902.

Bush, Vannevar. *Science: The Endless Frontier*. Washington, D.C.: U.S. Government Printing Office, 1945.

Calvino, Italo. *Invisible Cities*. New York: Harcourt, Brace, & Jovanovich, 1978.

Cartwright, Sally. "Where the Atom Bomb Was Born." *Progressive Education* 24 (October 1946): 4–6, 43–44.

Céline, Louis-Ferdinand. *Journey to the End of the Night*. New York: New Directions, 2006.

Chernis, Ira. *Dr. Strangegod: On the Symbolic Meaning of Nuclear Weapons*. Columbia: University of South Carolina Press, 1986.

———. *Eisenhower's Atoms for Peace*. College Station: Texas A&M Press, 2002.

Clark, Ronald W. *Einstein: The Life and Times*. New York: HarperCollins, 1984.

Clarke, Eric Kent. "Psychiatric Problems at Oak Ridge." *American Journal of Psychiatry* 102 (January 1946): 437–44.

———. "Psychiatry on a Shoestring." In *These Are Our Voices: The Story of Oak Ridge, 1942–1970*, 178–90. Chapter edited by Amy K. Wolfe; volume edited by James Overholt. Oak Ridge: Children's Museum of Oak Ridge, Tennessee, 1987.

Compton, Arthur. *Atomic Quest*. New York: Oxford University Press, 1956.

Confino Alon, and Peter Fritzsche. *The Work of Memory: New Directions in the Study of German Society and Culture*. Champaign: University of Illinois Press, 2002.

Connerton, Paul. *How Societies Remember*. Cambridge: Cambridge University Press, 1989.

"Construction Progress Reports." Presented monthly by the architectural firm Skidmore, Owings, and Merrill to the Manhattan Project managers. National Archives and Records Administration regional center, East Point, Ga., RG 4nn-326-8505, box 49.

Cousins, Norman. *Modern Man Is Obsolete*. New York: Viking Press, 1945.

Crawford, Grace Raby. "Back of Oak Ridge." In *John Hendrix Story*, edited by D. Ray Smith, 25–50. Self-published, 2009.

Creese, Walter L. *TVA's Public Planning: The Vision, the Reality*. Knoxville: University of Tennessee Press, 1990.

Daniell, Rachel. "Making Visible: Reflexive Narratives at the U.S. Manzanar 'War Relocation Center' National Historic Site." In *Silence, Screen, and Spectacle: Rethinking Social Memory in the Age of Information*, edited by Lindsey A. Freeman, Benjamin Nienass, and Rachel Daniell, 38–58. New York: Berghahn Books, 2014.

Davis, Fred. *Yearning for Yesterday: A Sociology of Nostalgia*. New York: Free Press, 1979.

Davis, Lee. "Evacuation Area Residents All Ready to Leave 'If It Will Help to Win This War.'" *Knoxville News-Sentinel*, October 18, 1942, A1–3, 9–11.

Dearing, James W. *Growing a Japanese Science City: Communication in Scientific Research*. London: Routledge, 1995.

Debord, Guy, and Asger Jorn. *Mémoires*. Copenhagen: Editions Situation International, 1959.

De Certeau, Michel. *The Practice of Everyday Life*. Berkeley: University of California Press, 1984.

———. *The Writing of History*. New York: Columbia University Press, 1988.

DeLillo, Don. *Underworld*. New York: Simon & Schuster, 1997.

DeLyser, Dydia. "Authenticity on the Ground: Engaging the Past in a California Ghost Town." *Annals of the Association of American Geographers* 89, no. 4 (December 1999): 602–32.

Didion, Joan. *Slouching towards Bethlehem*. New York: Farrar, Straus & Giroux, 1961.

———. *Where I Was From*. New York: Vintage, 2004.

Dillon, Millicent. "In the Atomic City." *The Believer*, June 2011. http://www.believermag .com/issues/201106/?read=article_dillon. Accessed August 10, 2013.

Dings, Bonnie Lee. "A Teenage Remembrance of 'Monumental Maggie.'" In *These Are Our Voices: The Story of Oak Ridge, 1942–1970*, edited by James Overholt, 341–45. Oak Ridge: Children's Museum of Oak Ridge, 1987.

Douglas, Mary. *How Institutions Think*. Syracuse: Syracuse University Press, 1986.

Dubin, Steven C. "Battle Royal: The Final Mission of the Enola Gay." In *Displays of Power*, 186–226. New York: New York University Press, 1999.

Edwards, Elizabeth. "Notes for Bookworms." *Oak Ridge Journal*, August 3, 1944, n.p.

Einstein, Albert. "'The Real Problem Is in the Hearts of Men'; Professor Einstein Says a New Type of Thinking Is Needed to Meet the Challenge of the Atomic Bomb." Interview with Michael Amrine. *New York Times Sunday Magazine*, June 23, 1946, SM4.

Eisenhower, Dwight. "Atoms for Peace Speech." DDE's Papers As President, Speech Series, box 5, United Nations Speech, December 8, 1953. Eisenhower Presidential Library Museum and Boyhood Home, Abilene, Kansas.

Engelhardt, Tom. *The End of Victory Culture: Cold War America and the Disillusioning of a Generation*. Amherst: University of Massachusetts Press, 1998.

Evans, Walker. "James Agee in 1936." In *Let Us Now Praise Famous Men*, v–vii. New York: Mariner, 2001.

Farish, Matthew. *Contours of America's Cold War*. Minneapolis: University of Minnesota Press, 2009.

Feifer, Maxine. *Going Places*. London: Macmillan, 1985.

Fermi, Laura. *Atoms in the Family: My Life with Enrico Fermi*. Chicago: University of Chicago Press, 1995.

Ficken, Robert E. "Grand Coulee and Hanford: The Atomic Bomb and the Development of the Columbia River." In *The Atomic West*, edited by Bruce Hevly and John M. Findlay, 21–38. Seattle: University of Washington Press, 1998.

Findlay John M., and Bruce Hevly. *Atomic Frontier Days: Hanford and the American West*. Seattle: University of Washington Press, 2011.

Fine, Lenore, and Jesse Remington. *The Corps of Engineers: Construction in the United States.* Washington, D.C.: Center of Military History, 1972.

Foucault, Michel. *The Archeology of Knowledge.* New York: Pantheon, 1972.

———. *Discipline and Punish: The Birth of the Prison.* New York: Vintage, 1979.

———. *The History of Sexuality.* New York: Vintage, 1990.

Freeman, Lindsey A. "Happy Memories under the Mushroom Cloud: Utopia and Memory in Oak Ridge, Tennessee." In *Memory and the Future: Transnational Politics, Ethics, and Society,* edited by Yifat Gutman, Adam D. Brown, and Amy Sodaro, 158–78. London: Palgrave Macmillan, 2010.

———. "A Plutonium Tourism Ode: The Rocky Flats Cold War Museum." In *Moral Encounters of Tourism,* edited by Mary Mostafanezhad and Kevin Hannam, 155–66. Honolulu: Ashgate, 2014.

Freud, Sigmund. "Mystic Writing Pad *der Wunderblock.*" 1925. In *General Psychological Theory: Papers on Metapsychology,* 211–16. New York: Simon & Schuster, 1963.

Frye, Northrop. *The Great Code: The Bible and Literature.* New York: Mariner Books, 2002.

Fuller, Buckminster. *Utopia or Oblivion: The Prospects for Humanity.* Baden: Lars Müller Publishers, 2008.

Gailar, Joanne Stern. *Oak Ridge and Me: From Youth to Maturity.* Oak Ridge: Children's Museum of Oak Ridge, 1991.

Garner, John. *The Company Town: Architecture and Society in the Early Industrial Age.* New York: Oxford University Press, 1992.

Gates, Francis Smith. "Silence Means Security." *Oak Ridge Journal,* August 3, 1944.

Gehman, Richard. "Oak Ridge Witch Hunt." *New Republic,* July 5, 1948, 12–13.

Germanuska, Pál. "Between Theory and Practice: Planning Socialist Cities in Hungary." In *Urban Machinery,* edited by Mikael Hard and Thomas J. Misa, 233–56. Cambridge, Mass.: MIT Press, 2008.

Goldberg, Stanley. "General Groves and the Atomic West." In *The Atomic West,* edited by Bruce Hevly and John M. Findlay, 39–89. Seattle: University of Washington Press, 1998.

———. "Groves and the Scientists: Compartmentalization and the Struggle to Build the Bomb." *Physics Today* 48 (August 1995): 38–43.

Goodchild, Peter. *Edward Teller: The Real Dr. Strangelove.* Cambridge, Mass.: Harvard University Press, 2004.

Goodman, Amy, and David Goodman. "The Hiroshima Cover Up." *Baltimore Sun,* August 5, 2005.

Gosling, F. G. *The Manhattan Project: Making the Atomic Bomb.* National Security History Series. Washington, D.C.: United States Department of Energy, 2005.

Graburn, Nelson H. H. "The Anthropology of Tourism." *Annals of Tourism Research* 10 (1983): 9–33.

Grandin, Greg. *Fordlandia: The Rise and Fall of Henry Ford's Forgotten Jungle City.* New York: Henry Holt, 2009.

Green, Hardy. *Company Town: The Industrial Edens and Satanic Mills That Shaped the American Economy.* New York: Basic Books, 2010.

Groueff, Stephane. *Manhattan Project: The Untold Story of the Making of the Atomic Bomb.* Boston: Little, Brown, 1967.

Groves, Leslie. *Now It Can Be Told: The Story of the Manhattan Project*. New York: Da Capo, 1983.

Gusterson, Hugh. *Nuclear Rites: A Weapons Laboratory at the End of the Cold War.* Berkeley: University of California Press, 1998.

———. "Nuclear Tourism." *Journal for Cultural Research* 8, no. 1 (January 2004): 23–31.

———. *People of the Bomb: Portraits of America's Nuclear Complex*. Minneapolis: University of Minnesota Press, 2006.

Gutfreund, Owen. *Twentieth-Century Sprawl: Highways and the Reshaping of the American Landscape*. Oxford: Oxford University Press, 2004.

Gutman, Yifat, Adam D. Brown, and Amy Sodaro, eds. "Introduction: Memory and the Future: Why a Change of Focus Is Necessary." In *Memory and the Future: Transnational Politics, Ethics and Society*. London: Palgrave Macmillan, 2010.

Halbwachs, Maurice. *The Collective Memory*. New York: Harper Colophon Books, 1980.

———. *Social Frameworks of Memory*. Chicago: University of Chicago Press, 1992.

Hales, Peter Bacon. *Atomic Spaces: Living on the Manhattan Project*. Champaign: University of Illinois Press, 1997.

———. "Levittown: Documents of an Ideal Suburb." 2009. http://tigger.uic .edu/~pbhales/Levittown.html. Accessed July 12, 2011.

———. "Topographies of Power: The Forced Spaces of the Manhattan Project." In *Mapping American Culture*, edited by Wayne Franklin and Michael Steiner, 251–90. Iowa City: University of Iowa Press, 1992:

Halleck, DeeDee. "Perpetual Shadows: Representing the Atomic Age." *Wide Angle* 20, no. 2 (1998): 70–76.

Hannigan, John. *Fantasy City: Pleasure and Prophet in the Postmodern Metropolis*. New York: Routledge, 1998.

Haraway, Donna. "A Cyborg Manifesto: Science, Technology, and Socialist Feminism in the Late Twentieth Century." In *Simians, Cyborgs, and Women: The Reinvention of Nature*, 149–81. New York: Routledge, 1991.

Henderson, Jim. "Community at Oak Ridge Remains an Isolated Culture." *Tulsa Sunday World*, November 5, 1967, section 1, pt. 2.

Herken, Gregg. *Brotherhood of the Bomb: The Tangled Lives and Loyalties of Robert Oppenheimer, Ernest Lawrence, and Edward Teller*. New York: Henry Holt, 2003.

Hewlett, Richard G., and Oscar E. Anderson. *The New World, 1939–1946: A History of the United States Atomic Energy Commission*. University Park: Pennsylvania State University Press, 1962.

Hiestand, Emily. *Angela the Upside-Down Girl*. Boston: Beacon Press, 1999.

Hilgartner, Stephen, Richard C. Bell, and Rory O'Connor. *Nukespeak: Nuclear Language, Visions, and Mindset*. San Francisco: Sierra Club Books, 1982.

Hilton, James. *Lost Horizon*. New York: World Publishing Company, 1947.

Hirsch, Marianne. "The Generation of Postmemory." *Poetics Today* 29, no. 1 (Spring 2008): 103–28.

———. *The Generation of Postmemory: Writing and Visual Culture after the Holocaust*. New York: Columbia University Press, 2012.

Hodge, Nathan, and Sharon Weinberger. *A Nuclear Family Vacation: Travels in the World of Atomic Weaponry*. New York: Bloomsbury, 2008.

Hofer, Johannes. "Medical Dissertation on Nostalgia." 1688. Translated by Carolyn K. Anspach. *Bulletin of the History of Medicine* 2 (1934): 276–391.

Howes, Ruth, and Caroline Herzenberg. *Their Day in the Sun*. Philadelphia: Temple University Press, 2003.

Hunner, Jon. *Inventing Los Alamos: The Growth of an Atomic Community*. Norman: University of Oklahoma Press, 2004.

Huotari, John. "K-25 Demolition Begins." *Oak Ridger*, December 16, 2008. http://www .oakridger.com/localnews/x1009172630/K-25-demolition-begins. Accessed January 14, 2009.

———. "Oak Ridge Council OKs Home Near Grave of 'Prophet.'" *Oak Ridger*, April 14, 2011. http://www.oakridger.com/highlight/x1798429125/Oak-Ridge-Council-OKs-home-near-grave-of-prophet. Accessed June 6, 2011.

Irwin, John Rice. "New Places, Strange People." In *These Are Our Voices: The Story of Oak Ridge, 1942–1970*, edited by James Overholt, 20–25. Oak Ridge: Oak Ridge Children's Museum, 1987.

Jackson, Charles O., and Charles W. Johnson. *City behind a Fence: Oak Ridge, Tennessee, 1942–1946*. Knoxville: University of Tennessee Press, 1981.

———. "The Urbane Frontier: The Army and the Community of Oak Ridge, Tennessee, 1942–1947." *Military Affairs* 41, no. 4 (February 1977): 8–15.

Jacobs, Jane. *The Death and Life of Great American Cities*. New York: Vintage, 1992.

Jameson, Fredric. "Walter Benjamin, or Nostalgia." *Salmagundi* 10/11 (Fall–Winter 1969–1970): 52–68.

Johnson, Leland, and Daniel Schaffer. *Oak Ridge National Laboratory: The First Fifty Years*. Knoxville: University of Tennessee Press, 1994.

Joseph, Timothy. *Historic Photographs of the Manhattan Project*. Nashville: Turner Publishing Company, 2009.

Josephson, Paul R. *New Atlantis Revisited: Akademogorodok, the Siberian City of Science*. Princeton, N.J.: Princeton University Press, 1997.

Kanon, Joseph. *Los Alamos*. New York: Island Books, 1997.

Kargon, Robert, and Arthur Molella. *Invented Edens: Techno-Cites of the Twentieth Century*. Cambridge, Mass.: MIT Press, 2008.

Kaufman, Lois M. "A House Stronger Than Time." In *These Are Our Voices: The Story of Oak Ridge, 1942–1970*, edited by James Overholt, 38–44. Oak Ridge: Oak Ridge Children's Museum, 1987.

Kean, Sam. *The Disappearing Spoon*. New York: Little, Brown, 2010.

Keely, Susan Bowman. "You Rose above the Ugliness." Unpublished manuscript.

Keim, Chris. "A Scientist and His Secrets." In *These Are Our Voices: The Story of Oak Ridge, 1942–1970*, edited by James Overholt, 66–75. Oak Ridge: Children's Museum of Oak Ridge, 1987.

Kennedy, Philip E. "Oak Ridge's Youth Council on the Atomic Crisis." *Clearing House* 21, no. 9 (1945): 540–44.

Kersten, Andrew. *Race, Jobs, and the War*. Champaign: University of Illinois Press, 2007.

Kevles, Daniel. *The Physicists: The History of a Scientific Community in Modern America*. Cambridge, Mass.: Harvard University Press, 1995.

Kiernan, Denise. *The Girls of Atomic City: The Untold Story of the Women Who Helped Win World War II*. New York: Touchstone, 2013.

Kracauer, Siegfried. *The Mass Ornament: Weimar Essays*. Cambridge, Mass.: Harvard University Press, 1995.

———. "Photography." *Critical Inquiry* 19, no. 3 (Spring 1993): 421–36.

Krauss, Rosalind. "Nostalgie de la Boue." *October* 56 (Spring 1991): 111–20.

Kuletz, Valerie L. *The Tainted Desert*. New York: Routledge, 1998.

Landsberg, Alison. "America, the Holocaust, and the Mass Culture of Memory: Toward a Radical Politics of Empathy." *New German Critique* 71 (1997): 63–86.

———. *Prosthetic Memory: The Transformation of American Remembrance in the Age of Mass Culture*. New York: Columbia University Press, 2004.

Lang, Daniel. *Early Tales of the Atomic Age*. New York: Doubleday, 1948.

Larson, Jane Warren. "Women Also Served." In *These Are Our Voices: The Story of Oak Ridge, 1942–1970*, edited by James Overholt, 194. Oak Ridge: Children's Museum of Oak Ridge, 1987.

Lee, Baldwin. "James Edward Westcott: Photographer." In *Through the Lens of Ed Westcott*, edited by Sam Yates, 15–32. Knoxville: University of Tennessee Press, 2005.

Le Goff, Jacques. *History and Memory*. New York: Columbia University Press, 1996.

Lennon, John, and Malcolm Foley. *Dark Tourism*. London: Continuum, 2000.

Lewis, Thomas. *Divided Highways: Building the Interstate Highways, Transforming American Life*. New York: Viking, 1997.

Lifton, Robert Jay, and Greg Mitchell. *Hiroshima in America: Fifty Years of Denial*. New York: Grosset/Putnam, 1995.

Lilienthal, David E. *The Journals of David E. Lilienthal*. Vols. 1–3. New York: Harper & Row, 1964.

Lippard, Lucy. *On the Beaten Track: Tourism, Art, and Place*. New York: New Press, 1999.

Loeb, Paul. *Nuclear Culture: Living and Working in the World's Largest Atomic Complex*. Philadelphia: New Society Publishers, 1986.

Luce, Henry. "The American Century." *Life*, February 17, 1941, 61–65.

MacCannell, Dean. *The Tourist: A New Theory of the Leisure Class*. Berkeley: University of California Press, 1999.

Margalit, Avishai. *The Ethics of Memory*. Cambridge, Mass.: Harvard University Press, 2002.

Marx, Karl. *The Eighteenth Brumaire of Louis Bonaparte*. 1852. New York: International Publishers, 1998.

Marx, Leo. *The Machine in the Garden: Technology and the Pastoral Ideal in America*. New York: Oxford University Press, 2000.

Masco, Joseph. *The Nuclear Borderlands: The Manhattan Project in Post–Cold War New Mexico*. Princeton, N.J.: Princeton University Press, 2006.

———. "'Sensitive but Unclassified': Secrecy and the Counterterrorist State." *Public Culture* 22, no. 3 (2010): 433–63.

Masters, Dexter, and Katharine Way, eds. *One World or None*. New York: New Press, 2007.

McCarthy, Thomas F. X. "My! How ORAU Has Grown." In *These Are Our Voices: The Story of Oak Ridge, 1942–1970*, edited by James Overholt, 374–84. Oak Ridge: Children's Museum of Oak Ridge, 1987.

Mead, Margaret. "The Crucial Role of the Small City in Meeting the Urban Crisis." In *Margaret Mead and the World Ahead: An Anthropologist Anticipates the Future*, 185–208. New York: Berghahn Books, 2005.

Miller, James. "The Frontier Experience." In *These Are Our Voices: The Story of Oak Ridge, 1942 –1970*, edited by James Overholt, 1–10. Oak Ridge: Children's Museum of Oak Ridge, 1987.

Mills, C. Wright. *The Sociological Imagination*. New York: Oxford University Press, 2000.

Mojtabai, A. G. *Blessed Assurance: At Home with the Bomb in Amarillo, Texas*. Syracuse: Syracuse University Press, 1986.

Moneymaker, Dorathy. *We'll Call It Wheat*. Oak Ridge: Adroit Printing, 1979.

Monk, Ray. *Oppenheimer, His Life and Mind (A Life inside the Center)*. New York: Random House, 2013.

Moore, Patrick Kerry. "Federal Enclaves: The Community Culture of Department of Energy Cities: Livermore, Los Alamos, Oak Ridge." PhD diss., Arizona State University, 1997.

Morse, Libby. "A Need for Me to Stay." *Oak Ridger*, February 14, 1977, 1.

Munger, Frank. "Oak Ridge Reveals World's Fastest Supercomputer, Titan." *Knoxville News Sentinel*, November 11, 2012, 1.

———. "Sain: Looks Like K-25's Pad Can Be Saved." In *Frank Munger's Atomic City Underground, Knoxville News Sentinel*, May 31, 2013. http://blogs.knoxnews.com/munger/2013/05/sain-looks-like-k-25s-pad-can.html. Accessed June 2, 2013.

"Mystery Town Cradled Bomb." *Time Life*, August 20, 1945, 94.

Nadkarni, Maya, and Olga Shevcheko. "The Politics of Nostalgia: A Case for Comparative Analysis of Post-Socialist Practices." *Ab Imperio: Theory and History of Nationalities and Nationalism in the Post-Soviet Realm* 2 (2004): 485–519.

Nash, William J., and O. L. Persechini. "The First Thousand Days." *Monsanto Magazine*, February 1946, 4–11.

Nichols, Colonel Kenneth. *Oak Ridge Journal*, August 9, 1945, 1.

Nora, Pierre. "Between Memory and History: Les Lieux de Mémoire." *Representations* 26, Special Issue: Memory and Counter-Memory (Spring 1989): 7–24.

Norris, Robert S. *Racing for the Bomb: General Leslie R. Groves, The Manhattan Project's Indispensable Man*. New York: Steerforth, 2003.

Nuttall, William J. *Nuclear Renaissance: Technologies and Policies for the Future of Nuclear Power*. New York: Taylor & Francis, 2004.

Oakes, Joe. "John Hendrix, Prophet of Oak Ridge, Predicted Project and Railroad More than 40 Years Ago!" *Oak Ridge Journal*, November 2, 1944, 3.

Oak Ridge Heritage and Preservation Association. *Oak Ridge, Tennessee, the Secret City: Celebrating the Sixtieth Anniversary of the Gates Opening*. Oak Ridge: Oak Ridge Heritage & Preservation Association, 2009.

Olwell, Russell. *At Work in the Atomic City: A Labor and Social History of Oak Ridge, Tennessee*. Knoxville: University of Tennessee Press, 2004.

———. "Help Wanted for Secret City: Recruiting Workers for the Manhattan Project at Oak Ridge, TN, 1942–1946." *Tennessee Historical Quarterly* 58 (1999): 52–69.

Orwell, George. *Animal Farm: A Fairy Story*. London: Secker & Warburg, 1945.

Overholt, James, ed. *These Are Our Voices: The Story of Oak Ridge, 1942–1970*. Oak Ridge: Children's Museum of Oak Ridge, 1987.

Park, Robert. *The City*. Chicago: University of Chicago Press, 1967.

Parnell, Thomas, J. "Reds in Our Atom-Bomb Plants." *Liberty*, June 21, 1947, 15, 90–93.

Peelle, Elizabeth. "A History of Segregation in Oak Ridge, 1943–1960." Unpublished manuscript prepared for the Oak Ridge Community Relations Council, August 1960.

Phillips, Cabel. "Oak Ridge Ponders Its Clouded Future." *New York Times Magazine*, November 13, 1947, 12–13, 42.

Porteous, J. D. "The Nature of the Company Town." *Transactions of the Institute of British Geographers* 51 (November 1970): 127–42.

Present, Thelma. *Dear Margaret: Letters from Oak Ridge to Margaret Mead*. Knoxville: East Tennessee Historical Society, 1985.

Radstone, Susannah. "Nostalgia: Home-comings and Departures." *Memory Studies* 3 (2010): 187–91.

Reingold, Nathan. "MGM Meets the Atomic Bomb." *Wilson Quarterly* 8, no. 4 (Autumn 1984): 154–63.

Rhodes, Richard. *Arsenals of Folly: The Making of the Nuclear Arms Race*. New York: Vintage, 2008.

———. *Dark Sun: The Making of the Hydrogen Bomb*. New York: Simon & Schuster, 1995.

———. *The Making of the Atomic Bomb*. New York: Simon & Schuster, 1986.

———. *Twilight of the Bombs: Recent Challenges, New Dangers, and the Prospect for a World without Nuclear Weapons*. New York: Vintage, 2011.

Robinson, George O., Jr. *The Oak Ridge Story: The Saga of a People Who Share in History*. Kingsport, Tenn.: Southern Publishers, 1950.

Rockwell, Theodore. *Creating the New World: Stories and Images from the Dawn of the Atomic Age*. Bloomington, Ind.: 1st Books.

———. "Frontier Life among the Atom Splitters." *Saturday Evening Post*, December 1, 1945, 28–48.

Ronnell, Avital. *The Telephone Book: Technology, Schizophrenia, Electric Speech*. Lincoln: University of Nebraska Press, 1989.

Roosevelt, Theodore. *The Winning of the West*. 1894. Reprint, New York: New York Public Library, 2011.

Rose, Jacqueline. *States of Fantasy*. New York: Oxford University Press, 1998.

Rose, Kenneth D. *One Nation Underground: The Fallout Shelter in American Culture*. New York: New York University Press, 2004.

Rush, J. H. "Prometheus in Tennessee." *Saturday Review*, July 2, 1960, 10–11, 50.

Sanderson, George A. "America's No. 1. Defense Community." *Progressive Architecture* 6 (June 1951): 63–84.

Sanger, S. L. "Robely L. Johnson." In *Working on the Bomb*, 110–12. Portland: Portland State University Press, 1995.

Scheck, Justin. "Bunnies Are in Deep Doo-Doo When They 'Go Nuclear' at Hanford." *Wall Street Journal*, December 23, 2010.

Searcy, Jay. *The Last Reunion*. Evans, Ga: Graphix Network, 2010.

———. "My Nuclear Childhood." *Philadelphia Inquirer Magazine*, August 6, 1992. Republished with permission of The Manhattan Project Heritage Association. http://www.mphpa.org/classic/OR/OR_Story_1.htm. May 20, 2008.

Seaton, A. V. "Guided by the Dark: From Thanatopsis to Thanatourism." *International Journal of Heritage Studies* 2, no. 4 (1996): 234–44.

Seeber, Clifford. "From Acorns to Atoms." *Antioch Review* 12, no. 3 (Autumn 1952): 263–80.

Sennett, Richard. *The Craftsman*. New Haven, Conn.: Yale University Press, 2008.

Seyfert, W. C. "Atom's Children." *American Magazine*, September 1946, 141.

Sheibach, Michael. *Atomic Narratives and American Youth: Coming of Age with the Atom, 1945–1955*. Jefferson, N.C.: McFarland, 2003.

Simmel, Georg. "The Metropolis and Mental Life." In *On Individuality and Social Forms*, 324–39. Chicago: University of Chicago Press, 1971.

———. "Secrecy." In *The Sociology of Georg Simmel*, translated and edited by Kurt H. Wolff, 330–44. New York: Free Press, 1950.

———. "The Secret Society." In *The Sociology of Georg Simmel*, translated and edited by Kurt H. Wolff, 345–76. New York: Free Press, 1950.

Skidmore, Owings, and Merrill. "Oak Ridge Report." Unpublished manuscript, 1948.

Smith, Alice Kimball. *A Peril and a Hope: The Scientists Movement in America, 1945–1947*. Cambridge, Mass.: MIT Press, 1971.

Smith, Anthony. *The Ethnic Origins of Nations*. Oxford: Wiley-Blackwell, 1999.

Smith, Donna. "Secret City Train Derails." *Oak Ridger*, June 19, 2010. http://www.oakridger.com/breaking/x1501907775/Secret-City-Fest-train-derails. Accessed June 21, 2010.

Smith, D. Ray. "Ed Westcott—Oak Ridge Photographer Extraordinaire." *Oak Ridger*, February 21, 2006, 3. http://www.oakridger.com/article/20131202/NEWS/131209990/1001/NEWS?template=printart. Accessed August 25, 2014.

———. "Historically Speaking: Fred Heddleson—Artist, Aeronautical Engineer and Friend." *Oak Ridger*, December 2, 2013.

———. *John Hendrix Story*. Self-published, 2009.

———. "K-25: Authenticity Key Element of Heritage Tourism." *Oak Ridger*, March 3, 2009. http://www.oakridger.com/columnists/x844651591/K-25-Authenticity-key-element-of-heritage-tourism. Accessed March 5, 2009.

Smyser, Dick. "City's Most Unique Neighborhood." *Oak Ridger*, December 10, 1977, 1.

Sontag, Susan. *Where the Stress Falls*. New York: Farrar, Straus & Giroux, 2001.

Sparrow, Martha Cardwell. "The Oak Ridgers." M.A. thesis, Mississippi State University, 1980.

Speier, Hans. "Freedom and Social Planning." *American Journal of Sociology* 42 (1937): 463.

———. "Magic Geography." *Social Research* 8 (1941): 310–30.

Spiotta, Dana. *Stone Arabia*. New York: Scribner, 2011.

"Spreading the Know-How." *Time*, October 28, 1946, 65.

Stauth, Georg, and Brian S. Turner. "Nostalgia, Postmodernism, and the Critique of Mass Culture." *Theory, Culture and Society* 5, no. 2 (1988): 509–26.

Steele, Valerie D. "Black History in the Ridge." Unpublished manuscript, 1981.

————. "A New Hope." Presented to the Altrusa Club, Oak Ridge, Tennessee, February 28, 2001.

Stewart, Kathleen. "Nostalgia—A Polemic." *Cultural Anthropology* 3, no. 3 (1998): 227–41.

————. *A Space on the Side of the Road: Cultural Poetics in an "Other" America.* Princeton, N.J.: Princeton University Press, 1996.

Stewart, Susan. *On Longing: Narratives of the Miniature, the Gigantic, the Souvenir, the Collection.* Durham, N.C.: Duke University Press, 1993.

Stites, Richard. *Revolutionary Dreams: Utopian Vision and Experimental Life in the Russian Revolution.* New York: Oxford University Press, 1991.

Sturken, Marita. *Tangled Memories: The Vietnam War, the AIDS Epidemic, and the Politics of Remembering.* Berkeley: University of California Press, 1997.

————. *Tourists of History: Memory, Kitsch, and Consumerism from Oklahoma City to Ground Zero.* Durham, N.C.: Duke University Press, 2007.

Suleiman, Susan Rubin. "The 1.5 Generation: Thinking about Child Survivors and the Holocaust." *American Imago* 59, no. 3 (Fall 2002): 227–95.

Tabler, Dave. "Irradiated Dimes: Tourist Items or Health Threat?" *Appalachian History,* September 13, 2012. http://www.appalachianhistory.net/2012/09/irradiated-dimes-tourist-item-or-health.html. Accessed May 10, 2013.

Tarlow, Peter T. "Dark Tourism: The Appealing 'Dark' Side of Tourism & More." In *Niche Tourism: Contemporary Issues, Trends, and Cases,* edited by Marina Noveilli, 47–58. Amsterdam: Elsevier, 2005.

Taylor, Bryan C. "Radioactive History: Rhetoric, Memory, and Place in the Post–Cold War Nuclear Museum." In *Places of Public Memory: The Rhetoric of Museums and Memorials,* edited by Greg Dickinson, 57–87. Tuscaloosa: University of Alabama Press, 2010.

————. "Revis(it)ing Nuclear History: Narrative Conflict at the Bradbury Science Museum." *Studies in Cultures, Organizations, and Societies* 3 (1997): 119–45.

Taylor, Jessica. "G2: Let's Build a Bomb: The Nuclear Deterrent Is on the Agenda Again, but 63 Years Ago, the Atom Bomb Was Still on the Drawing Board and the Women Employed at Oak Ridge, Tennessee, Had No Idea of the Significance of Their Top Secret Work." *Guardian,* July 5, 2006, 14.

Thelan, David. "History after the Enola Gay Controversy: An Introduction." *Journal of American History* 82 (December 1995): 1029–35.

Thomas, Lois Reagan. "ABCs of Oak Ridge Housing." *Knoxville News-Sentinel,* May 5, 1985, H1.

Thorpe, Charles. *Oppenheimer: The Tragic Intellectual.* Chicago: University of Chicago Press, 2008.

Thornton, C. "A Cumberland Incongruity." *Commercial Appeal Mid-South Magazine,* April 17, 1969, 35.

Turner, Fredrick Jackson. "The Significance of the Frontier in American History." *Annual Report of the American Historical Association for the Year 1893.* Washington, D.C.: Government Printing Office, 1894.

Turner, Victor, and Elizabeth Turner. *Image and Pilgrimage in Christian Culture.* Oxford: Basil Blackwell, 1978.

Urry, John. *The Tourist Gaze.* 2nd ed. London: Sage, 2002.

Vanderbilt, Tom. *Survival City: Adventures among the Ruins of Atomic America.* Princeton, N.J.: Princeton Architectural Press, 2002.

Van Wyck, Peter C. *The Highway of the Atom.* Montreal: McGill-Queen's University Press, 2010.

————. *Signs of Danger: Waste, Trauma, and Nuclear Threat.* Minneapolis: University of Minnesota Press, 2004.

Veitch, Jonathan. "Dr. Strangelove's Cabinet of Wonder: Sifting through the Atomic Ruins at the Nevada Test Site." In *Ruins of Modernity*, edited by Julia Hell and Andreas Schönle, 321–38. Durham, N.C.: Duke University Press, 2010.

Virilio, Paul. *Speed and Politics: An Essay on Dromology.* Translated by Mark Polizzotti. Los Angeles: Semiotext(e), 1977.

Wagner-Pacifici, Robin, and Barry Schwartz. "The Vietnam Veterans Memorial: Commemorating a Difficult Past." *American Journal of Sociology* 97, no. 2 (September 1991): 376–420.

Wallace, Joan. "Housing Desegregation: How Well since First Step in '62?" *Oak Ridger*, December 11, 1985, 1

Wang, Jessica. *American Science in an Age of Anxiety: Scientists, Anticommunism, and the Cold War.* Chapel Hill: University of North Carolina Press, 1999.

Washington, Jerry. Unpublished manuscript.

Waters, Enoc. "Atomic City Birthplace of Paradoxes: Negro Kids Can't Go to School at Biggest Brain Center." *Chicago Defender*, December 29, 1945, 1.

————. "Negroes Live in Modern 'Hoovervilles' at Atom City." *Chicago Defender*, January 5, 1946, 1.

Watson, Peggy. "Nowa Huta: The Politics of Post-Communism and the Past." In *Generational Consciousness, Narrative, and Politics*, edited by June Edmunds and Bryan Turner, 165–78. New York: Rowman & Littlefield, 2003.

We the People. Script of a radio broadcast sponsored by Gulf Oil Corporation, February 9, 1947. Records of the Atomic Energy Commission, 1923–1978. National Archives and Records Administration Southeast Region. ARC identifier 281583.

Weinberg, Alvin. "History of ORNL." *ORNL Review* 25, nos. 3 and 4 (2002). http://www.ornl.gov/info/ornlreview/rev25-34/foreword.shtml. Accessed October 13, 2012.

Welsome, Eileen. *The Plutonium Files.* New York: Delta Books, 1999.

Welty, Eudora. "Place in Fiction." In *Stories, Essays and Memoir*, 781–96. New York: Library of America, 1998.

Wende, Ernest A. "Building a City from Scratch." *Engineering News Record*, December 13, 1945, 815–18.

Westcott, Ed. *Oak Ridge.* Charleston, S.C.: Arcadia, 2005.

————. *Through the Lens of Ed Westcott: A Photographic History of World War II's Secret City.* Edited by Sam Yates. Knoxville: University of Tennessee Press, 2005.

White, E. B. "Sootfall and Fallout." In *Essays of E. B. White*, 112–24. New York: Harper & Row, 1977.

White, Stephen. "2 Atomic Scientists Suspended, Many More Face Loyalty Board." *New York Herald Tribune*, May 19, 1948, 1, 35.

————. "Oak Ridge Sunk in Gloom over Loyalty Inquiry." *New York Herald Tribune*, May 20, 1948, 1, 35.

———. "Report on Oak Ridge Hearings." *New York Herald Tribune*. Reprinted in the *Bulletin of Atomic Scientists* 4, no. 7 (July 1948): 194–97.

———. "Senior Scientist Rolls Depleted at Oak Ridge." *New York Herald Tribune*, May 28, 1948, 11.

———. "Why Morale Sags at Oak Ridge." *New York Herald Tribune*, May 24, 1948, 18.

Wickware, Francis Sill. "The Manhattan Project." *Time & Life*. Reprinted for the Employees of Union Carbide and Carbon Corporation, 1945, 94.

Wilcox, Bill. "Oak Ridge's Dormitories." Unpublished manuscript.

Williams, Raymond. *The Country and the City*. Oxford: Oxford University Press, 1973.

Witherup, Bill. "Mother Witherup's Top-Secret Cherry Pie." In *Men at Work*, 54–57. Boise: Ahsahta Press / Boise State University, 1989.

Wolkowitz, Carol. *Bodies at Work*. New York: Sage, 2006.

———. " 'Papa's Bomb': The Local and the Global in Women's Manhattan Project Personal Narratives." In *Lines of Narrative: Psychosocial Perspectives*, 235–49. New York: Routledge, 2000.

Wray, Matt. "A Blast from the Past: Preserving and Interpreting the Atomic Age." *American Quarterly* 58 (2006): 467–83.

"Yak-Ac." *Time*, April 18, 1946, 1.

Yates, Sam. "Acknowledgments." In *Through the Lens of Ed Westcott*, edited by Sam Yates, 13–15. Knoxville: University of Tennessee Press, 2005.

Yavenditti, Michael J. "Atomic Scientists and Hollywood: The Beginning or the End?" *Film & History* 8, no. 4 (December 1978): 51–66.

Zak, Dan. "The Prophets of Oak Ridge." *Washington Post*, April 29, 2013. http://www.washingtonpost.com/sf/style/2013/04/29/the-prophets-of-oak-ridge/. April 30, 2013.

Zerubavel, Eviatar. *Time Maps: Collective Memory and the Social Shape of the Past*. Chicago: University of Chicago Press, 2003.

Zerubavel, Yael. *Recovered Roots: Collective Memory and the Making of Israeli National Tradition*. Chicago: University of Chicago Press, 1995.

Zolberg, Vera. "Contested Remembrance: The Hiroshima Exhibit Controversy." *Theory and Society* 27 (August 1998): 565–90.

Zukin, Sharon. *Landscapes of Power: From Detroit to Disney World*. Berkeley: University of California Press, 1991.

Index

Cade, Ebb, 76–77
Cafeterias, 47, 49, 58, 122
California, gangland tours in, 145–46
Calutron Girls, 71–75; origin of name, 3; Westcott's photos of, 131, *132*, 167; after World War II, 105
Calutrons, 66, 71
Calvino, Italo, *Invisible Cities*, 13, 35
Camera Lucida (Barthes), 160
Cameras: film shortage for, 163; of Westcott, 161
Cameron, Rod, 115, *123*, 193 (n. 62)
Camp Crossville, 161, 197 (n. 11)
Camp David, 184 (n. 17)
Capp, Al, 181 (n. 19)
Carbide and Carbon Corporation, 68
Carbide Courier (newspaper), 109
Cars: inspection of, 89; motto of Oak Ridge on, 106; Westcott's photos of, 161, 197 (n. 13)
Cartography. *See* Maps
Céline, Louis-Ferdinand, 67; *Journey to the End of the Night*, 75
Cemestos, 46–47, 51, 173–74, 185 (n. 32), 198 (n. 8)
Censorship: of historical information, 11, 160; of letters, 81; of media, 27, 182 (n. 49)
CEW. *See* Clinton Engineer Works
Chapel-on-the-Hill, 54, 186 (n. 65)
Chaplin, Charlie, 60
Chauffeurettes, 73–74
Checker, Chubby, 195 (n. 13)
Chernobyl, atomic tourism at, 140
Cherokee people, 17, 39
Chicago (Ill.): Fermi's plutonium experiment in, 18, 65, 136; relocation of pre-atomic communities to, 182 (n. 21); in selection of plutonium production site, 18
Chicago Defender (newspaper), 56, 111
Children: black, 57; as generation 1.5, 169–70; museum exhibits aimed at, 124; postwar views on atomic industry among, 100–101; reactions to use of bomb, 94, 100–101; regulation of naming of, 86

Church services, 54
Circle Line, 146
Circular narratives, 38–39
City behind the Fence, The (Johnson and Jackson), 4, 190 (n. 28)
City design of Oak Ridge: black workers in, 58; frontier in, 37–41; planning for, 45–46; as preview of postnuclear landscape, 5, 110–11; utopia in, 37, 44–46. *See also* Housing in Oak Ridge
Civilian control, of nuclear industry, 97–98, 101
Clarke, Eric, 91, 107, 190 (n. 30)
Class. *See* Social class
Clinton Engineer Works (CEW): as code name, xiii, 62; compartmentalization of work at, 61–64. *See also* Factories of Oak Ridge
Clothing: color coding of uniforms, 84; women's, 92, 117, 118
Clubs, social, 54
Code names: for atomic factories, 62–63; Clinton Engineer Works as, xiii, 62; for Manhattan Project sites, 1
Cohn, Waldo, 55, 186 (n. 67)
Cold War: Apple II tests in, 167, 197 (n. 37); Mutual Assured Destruction in, 110; "Neutron Dance" song in, 189 (n. 50); nuclear propaganda in, 125; plutonium demand in, 96; role of Oak Ridge in, 107–9; scientists' views on nuclear industry in, 97–99; social cohesion among workers in, 107–8; Soviet nuclear weapons in, 119; spies in, 109, 119. *See also* Postnuclear landscape; Postwar Oak Ridge
Collective memory. *See* Memory, collective
Collective nostalgia, 5–7, 9
Columbia University, 44, 61
Commercialization, of memory and nostalgia, 145
Committee for Nuclear Responsibility, 107
Communist sympathizers, suspected, 99. *See also* Red Scare
Company towns, segregation in, 59

Fuller, Buckminster, 184 (n. 19), 196 (n. 3)
Future, nostalgia for, 35–36
Future of Nostalgia, The (Boym), 7

Gailar, Joanne, 68, 108; *Oak Ridge and Me*, 50, 89
Gallaher, William, 26–27
Gamble Valley, 56, 111
Gangland tours, 145–46
Garden City Movement, 45
Gaseous diffusion, 68–69
Gates of Oak Ridge: removal of, 109, 112–15, *115*, 154; security at, 87–90, *88*
Gehman, Richard, 28, 99
Geiger counter, 65, 124
Gender: division of labor by, 74–75; segregation by, 56–57; and social status, 51. *See also* Men; Women
Gender normalization, 118
Generation 1.5, 169–70, 198 (n. 44)
Geography, magic, 1, 42, 43, 166, 173, 179 (n. 1)
George Jones Memorial Baptist Church (Wheat), 23, 34
Germany, Nazi: in atomic race, 16, 65, 130; Benjamin's flight from, 151–52; spies from, 82–83
Gerontology, atomic, 175, 198 (n. 9)
Ghost stories, 34–35; about ghost of Wheat, 8, 34–35, 149; and nostalgia, 8
Gilliam, Joan, 104
Girls of Atomic City, The (Kiernan), 186 (n. 71)
Glasglow, Richard, 100
Gore, Albert, Sr., 118
Government informants, 60
Grand Coulee Dam, 18
Great Smoky Mountains National Park, 17
Greenbelt, 45–46
Greenglass, David, 119
Groves, Leslie: in *The Beginning or the End* (movie), 101, 102; on compartmentalization of work, 63; and end of control of nuclear energy, 101; in establishment of Hanford, 18; in establishment

of Oak Ridge, 16, 20, 21; on forced labor by prisoners of war, 71; on frontier, 38; and media censorship, 182 (n. 49); *Now It Can Be Told*, 63; public interest in, 4; and Szilárd Petition, 192 (n. 25); Westcott's photo of, 164; on women workers, 72, 74
Gusterson, Hugh: *Nuclear Rites*, 189 (n. 6); *People of the Bomb*, 193 (n. 42)
Gyllenhaal, Jake, 150

Halbwachs, Maurice, 169
Hales, Peter Bacon, 165, 167, 181 (n. 21), 183 (n. 1); *Atomic Spaces*, 4, 163
Halleck, DeeDee, 55, 131–32
Hanford (Wash.): atomic nostalgia in, 174; code name for, 1; establishment of, 1–2, 18; forced removal of pre-atomic residents from, 18–19; as National Historical Park, 154; official photographer of, 197 (n. 6); vs. other Project sites, 2; plutonium at, 18, 66, 95; role in Manhattan Project, 1; security measures in, 85–86; selection of site, 18; after World War II, 96
Hannigan, John, *Fantasy City*, 44
Happy Valley trailer community, 49, 56, 106
Haraway, Donna, 73
Harris, Kattie, 77
Haynes, Dick, 100
Health care, universal, 44
Health risks, secrecy about, 65, 69, 172
Heistand, Emily, 170
Hendrix, Curtis Allen, 25, 182 (n. 38)
Hendrix, Ethel, 14
Hendrix, John, 14–36; accuracy of prophecies of, 15; in American Museum of Science and Energy, 30–33; and atomic tourism, 149; contents of prophecies of, 14–15, 180 (n. 2); family of, 14; grave of, 27, 28, 36; institutionalization of, 15, 180 (n. 2); as legend vs. myth, 22–23; media coverage of story of, 27–28; and

Nature, in utopian vision of Oak Ridge, 44
Nazi Germany. *See* Germany, Nazi
Neal, Patricia, 122
"Negro Village" (proposed), 58
Neighborhoods of Oak Ridge: design of, 48–50; segregation in, 50, 56–59, 111–12
Neurotics, atomic, 90
"Neutron Dance" (song), 79, 189 (n. 50)
New Hope (Tenn.), forced removal of pre-atomic residents from, 17
New Mexico. *See* Los Alamos
New Orleans (La.), Hurricane Katrina tours of, 146
New Republic (magazine), 99
Newspapers: on black workers' experience, 56; censorship of, 27, 182 (n. 49); on dropping of atomic bomb, 94–95; Hendrix myth in, 27–28; on removal of pre-atomic communities, 26. *See also specific publications*
New Yorker (magazine), 52
New York Herald Tribune (newspaper), 99–100
New York Times (newspaper), 164, 169
New York Times Magazine, 52
Nichols, Kenneth D., 95, 96
Nixon, Richard, 186 (n. 54)
Nora, Pierre, 6
Normalization, of postwar Oak Ridge, 109–19
Norris Dam, 17, 62
Nostalgia, 5–11; in atomic tourism, 140–43; and aura, 136; bridging, 35–36, 183 (n. 71); celebratory vs. critical, 5–6, 9, 142, 169–70; collective, 5–7, 9; commercialization of, 145; dangers of, 9, 141; definition of, 7–8, 141; experience of time in, 38; for frontier, 38–39, 59–60; as individual vs. social phenomenon, 9, 141; vs. memory, 141; origins of term, 7–8; symptoms of, 8. *See also* Atomic nostalgia
Nostalgic bridging, 35–36, 183 (n. 71)
Nostalgic tourism, atomic tourism as, 140–43
Nostalgie de la boue, 171, 198 (n. 1)

Now It Can Be Told (Groves), 63
Noyes, John Humphrey, 184 (n. 19)
Nuclear, vs. atomic, use of terms, 110
Nuclear Borderlands (Masco), 4
Nuclear Culture (Loeb), 4, 183 (n. 63)
Nuclear disasters, 126, 153–54
Nuclear Energy for the Propulsion of Aircraft, 98
Nuclear industry, Soviet, 119
Nuclear industry, U.S.: aging of arsenal in, 175–76; contradictory roles of, 110; current role of Oak Ridge in, 7, 138–39, 143, 175; current status of, 126; disasters in, 126; as monopoly, 104, 119; normalization of, 109–10; peace as goal of, 95, 108, 125; postwar battle for control over, 96–104; scientists' views and activism on, 96–104, 107, 129, 191 (n. 25); Westcott's photos in public relations for, 163–66
Nuclear memory, Oak Ridge in, 3–4
Nuclear optimism, 43
Nuclear reactors, at X-10 site, 65–66, 108, 147–48
Nuclear renaissance, 126
Nuclear Rites (Gusterson), 189 (n. 6)
Nuclear Security Administration, 175
Nuclear Security Enterprise, 7
Nuclear tests: Soviet, 119; U.S., 18, 35, 65
Nuclear tourism. *See* Atomic tourism
Nuclear waste, 10, 152, 172–73
Nuclear weapons. *See* Atomic bomb, development of; Atomic bomb, dropping of; Nuclear industry, Soviet; Nuclear industry, U.S.

Oak Ridge (Tenn.): as Atomic City, branding of, 121; author's connection to, xiii–xv, 12, 92; design of (*see* City design of Oak Ridge); end of federal control in, 22, 109; future of, 176–77; as incorporated municipality, 109; names for, xiii, 1, 43; in national memory, 3–4, 169; vs. other Project sites, 2; people of (*see* Residents of Oak Ridge; Workers at

103; of black workers, 162; of Calutron Girls, 131, *132*, 167; cameras used for, 161; declassification of, 168; functions of, 162–63; gaps in, 170; of Groves, 164; for Hendrix stories, 27, 28–30; of high school science class, 156–58, *158*; as "insider" art, 168–70; of McLemore (Frank), 158–59, *159*; myths in, 166–67; number of, 160; as only authorized photos, 28–30, 131, 144–45, 159; of opening ceremony in 1949, 114, *115*, *116*, *123*; of Oppenheimer, 145, 156, *157*; of pre-atomic communities, 28–30; propaganda in, 145, 163; in public relations, 163–66; recognizability of people in, 167; of Santa at gate, 87, *88*, 190 (n. 17); of security measures, *81*, *82*, *88*; start of career, 161; subject matter of, 160, 161–63; in "Through the Lens of Ed Westcott" exhibition and book, 162, 168; ubiquity of, 159–60

We the People (radio show), 26–27

Wheat (Tenn.): in atomic tourism, 149; erasure of structures and culture of, 23–24; forced removal of pre-atomic residents from, 17, 25–26; Ghost of, 8, 34–35, 149; mythic history of, 24

White, Leroy, 77

White, passing as, 78

White, Stephen, 99–100

White Bluffs (Wash.), forced removal of pre-atomic residents from, 18

White workers: unskilled, housing for, 47, 49, 56; wages for, 58. *See also specific types of workers*

Wigner, Eugene, 51, 99, 130

Wilcox, Bill, 47, 139

Wildlife habitat, 155

Williams, Hal, 75

Willis, Allee, 189 (n. 50)

Witherup, Bill, 85–86

Wolkowitz, Carol, 162, 190 (n. 28)

Women: black vs. white, experience of, 56–57; clothing of, 92, 117, *118*; housing for, 56–57; vs. men, in population, 48; as wives, social status of, 51

Women workers, 71–75; Chauffeurettes, 73–74; children of, 57; Computers, 74–75, 79, 189 (n. 38); housing for, 56–57; at laundry, 64–65; occupations open to, 51, 71–75; recruitment of, 70, 72; scientists and engineers, 74. *See also* Calutron Girls

Woods, Shirley, 74, 93

Workers at Oak Ridge, 61–79; absenteeism among, 70–71; on city as utopia, 44–46; compartmentalization of, 61–64; departure of, after war, 105–6; diversity of, 2; firing and eviction of, during war, 86; geographical origins of, 69–70, 75, 188 (n. 25); health risks to, 65, 69, 172; hours worked, 53; housing for, 46–52; identification badges of, 84; lack of knowledge about Project among, 3, 90–91, 172; number of, 3, 46, 70; physical dangers faced by, 67; postwar, 105–9; reactions to use of bomb, 93–96, 97, 106–7; recreation opportunities for, 52–55; recruitment of, 69–70, 72, 75, 163; secrecy required of, 3, 71–72, 81–83; security tests given to, 60, 81, *81*; social class of, 50–52; in success of Manhattan Project, 107. *See also* Black workers; Women workers; *and specific types of workers*

World War I, experience of soldiers in, xiii

World War II: atomic bomb dropped on Japan in, 1, 35, 93–96; experience of soldiers in, xiii; Hanford after, 96; Los Alamos after, 96; Oak Ridge after (*see* Postwar Oak Ridge); Oak Ridge as battlefield in, 67–68; Secret City Festival reenactments of, 144; surrender of Japan in, 95–96

Wray, Matt, 135

Wright, Frank Lloyd, 46

Writing of History, The (de Certeau), 14

Wunderblock, 19, 181 (n. 18)

X-10 site, 65–66; atomic tourism at, 147–48; laundry at, 64–65; nuclear reactor at, 65–66, 108, 147–48; production techniques used in, 62; security gaps on rooftop of, 80; after World War II, 108. *See also* Oak Ridge National Laboratory

Y-12 site (National Security Complex), 66–68; atomic tourism at, 146, 147; break-in at (2012), 175–76; Calutron Girls at, 71–75, 131; construction of, 66, 185 (n. 24); current status of, 7, 139; design of, 66; electricity usage by, 66–67; as electromagnetic separation plant, 66–68; and Hendrix myth, 32–33; modernization of aging arsenal at, 175; number of workers at, 105; production techniques used in, 62; after World War II, 105–6, 108

Yavenditti, Michael J., 192 (n. 30)

Yellow pantsuit, 92

Yogi and the Commissar, The (Koestler), 109

Youth Council on the Atomic Crisis (Yak-Ac), 98, 100–101, 185 (n. 21), 191 (n. 22)

Zerubavel, Eviatar, 183 (n. 71)